MEMOIRS
OF A
SERGEANT

MEMOIRS
OF A
SERGEANT

NONSUCH

First published 1835
Copyright © in this edition 2005
Nonsuch Publishing Ltd

Nonsuch Publishing Limited
The Mill, Brimscombe Port, Stroud, Gloucestershire, GL5 2QG
www.nonsuch-publishing.com

British Library Cataloguing in Publication Data.
A catalogue record for this book is available from the British Library.

ISBN 1-84588-034-X

Typesetting and origination by Nonsuch Publishing Limited
Printed in Great Britain by Oaklands Book Services Limited

CONTENTS

INTRODUCTION TO THE MODERN EDITION

Being born in a stable does not make one a horse
Arthur Wellesley, Duke of Wellington.

Despite his aversion to being reminded of his Anglo-Irish background, and his clear distaste at the thought of being labelled Irish, the Duke of Wellington would have found it difficult to win the Peninsular War without the Irish soldiers who made up as much as 60% of his army at that time. The war had brought about the necessity of expanding the British army in order to meet Napoleon's challenge and a number of Irish regiments were raised including the 83rd, 87th and 89th. While all these regiments played a major role in the campaign, the 87th in particular distinguished itself. On 5 March 1811, a Sergeant Patrick Masterson of the 87th took the first French eagle to be captured in battle, and as a result the regiment was renamed The Prince of Wales' Own Irish Regiment, with the eagle as its badge of honour.

However, it was not with an Irish Regiment that the Irish author of *Memoirs of a Sergeant* served, but with the 43rd Regiment of Light Infantry. This regiment was raised in 1741 as the 54th Regiment of Infantry, but with reductions in the army in 1748 it was renumbered as the 43rd. The concept of light infantry had been developed during the North American Wars of the 1750s, where the close formation fighting used by the British army proved to be no match for the more mobile Indian and French colonist opposition. A new corps of 'light' troops was developed who were trained to scout, skirmish and disperse with stealth and speed. These troops were so successful that it became common practice for regiments to have their own 'light companies' and by the end of the eighteenth century commanders often grouped these companies together for specific tasks. In 1803, along with the 52nd, the 43rd was chosen to form the first Corps of Light Infantry and joined with the 95th to form the Light Brigade under the command of Sir John Moore, 'the best trainer of troops that England has ever possessed'.

The 43rd played an active part in the Napoleonic Wars, starting with the campaign against Denmark, caused by British fears that the French would attempt to use the Danish fleet for its own purposes. It went on to serve in the Peninsular War in Portugal and Spain, playing a crucial role at Vimiera and also distinguishing itself in the rearguard when the army was forced to retreat in midwinter to Vigo and Corunna. During the Penisular War the company received battle honours, a token of the Sovereign's recognition of a particularly gallant and distinguished action, for its actions at Vimiera, Corunna, Talavera, Busaco, Barrosa, Fuentes d'Onoro, Albuhera, Ciudad Rodrigo, Badajoz, Salamanca and Vittoria.

During the Peninsular campaign just over 35,000 officers and men are believed to have died: almost 7,000 were killed outright, just under 4,000 died of their wounds and a staggering 24,000 succumbed to disease. The total strength of the Duke of Wellington's army in the Iberian Peninsula in 1813 was 70,000. From these figures it is immediately obvious just how lucky the author was to survive the conflict: even if a soldier was not killed by the enemy (and the Sergeant was indeed hit by enemy fire, although not fatally), there was a good chance that his life would be claimed by typhus, dysentry or another of the diseases which were prevalent in an early nineteenth-century army on campaign.

It was at Badajoz that the author of *Memoirs of a Sergeant* received the wound that was to invalid him home and finish his involvement in the Peninsular campaign. He remained in the army until 1823, but on a reduction in numbers, chose to retire. On his retirement the author turned his thoughts to the question of faith. Having faced his own mortality on the battlefield this was a particularly pertinent subject for him. Despite having been brought up in a devout Irish Catholic family, he turned from this faith as being 'at variance with the revealed will of God, and subversive of sound morality', turning instead to the new faith of Methodism.

The Methodist faith had been founded by John Wesley, a Church of England minister. The name 'Methodists' was awarded to Wesley and a group of his friends at Oxford because of their methodical approach to religion, but the name stuck and Wesley himself later used the term to mean the methodical pursuit of biblical holiness. Although Wesley hoped that the movement would remain part of the Church of England, its impact made a separation inevitable and in 1795 the Methodists were granted the legal right to perform the sacraments and conduct marriages, thereby becoming an independent church body.

Memoirs of a Sergeant is a fascinating description of the life of an ordinary soldier during the horrors of the Peninsular War and how his soldiering experiences challenged his faith and made him look to the church to explain his survival through a conflict in which so many others died. Written from the personal perspective of a man who had faced enemy fire and lived to tell the tale, it is an involving narrative of what life was really like to serve under two of the greatest commanders in British military history, Sir John Moore and the Duke of Wellington, in the elite of the early nineteenth-century army, the Light Brigade. Of interest to the both general readers and scholars of military history, *Memoirs of a Sergeant* is an important account of the Peninsular War and how it affected those who particpated in it.

CHAPTER I

I HAVE the advantage of being an Irishman. My parents had also the felicity of first seeing the light of day as it shone upon the soil of the land which for ages has seemed to possess such passing interest in the eyes of Britain. Their family consisted of six children: four boys, and two girls. I was the youngest of the whole, and, for reasons I do not profess to comprehend, was a special favourite. I was named Thomas; which, interpreted by parental love, was converted into Benjamin, with a double portion of all that substance so scanty as theirs could supply. I was born in the small townsland of Enneham, King's County, in the province of Leinster, about the year 1790, be the same a little earlier or later. The exact period I cannot specify; as at that time and place, and in consequence of the culpable negligence generally prevalent in parochial registration, very little thought or care was shown in recording such events. Those were the days of intestine broil and vengeance. The seeds of rebellion, which had been sown with an unsparing and remorseless hand, were just ready to produce their baneful first-fruit. Such was the jeopardy in which Protestants especially were placed, that no one who beheld the morning sun arise, could safely calculate upon seeing it go down. "Domestic fury, and fierce civil strife," kindled and mainly maintained by Papal cupidity and violence, raged through the fairest portions of the country. No one had courage to trust his neighbours; for no one could tell who was worthy of trust. Mutual confidence, based upon moral principle, which alone can cement society, was blotted from the list of social virtues. Not many dared depend even upon former fiends. The ties of relationship, and those arising from nearness of kin, were frequently forgotten. Natural affection, usually invincible, was unheeded; and under cover of night, or even in open day, the unwary traveller became frequently a prey to instantaneous death from the bullet of some skulking assassin, concealed behind the road-side bush or brake.

My parents, I regret to state, were Roman Catholics. They knew no better; for no other teaching had reached their minds. Their membership with that fallen community was their misfortune rather than their fault. I believe the profession they made was sincere; and that, though mingled with the dross of Popish superstition, they were possessors of at least some few grains of sterling piety. My mother, in particular, was remarkably constant and fervid in her devotions; and the earnest manner in which her beads were counted, though I could never detect the meritorious points of calculation, is to be numbered among the earliest and most powerful impressions I ever received. My father had for several years acted as steward to Archibald Nevens, Esq., a gentleman who, at that time, was the owner of considerable estates in the vicinity of Portarlington. Ours was a happy family. My father, though a plain man, was excelled by few in attachment to his wife and children. "Hope springs eternal in the human breast;" and we flattered ourselves that futurity offered to our notice lengthened years of comfort. But we soon found that our hold on earthly happiness was fragile as the spider's thread. My father was taken ill and died. Even now the procession of his funeral is pictured on my memory. The gentleman already named as my father's employer had fallen upon evil days. His property passed into other hands; and as the purchaser knew nothing of our family, no one cared for the widow and her orphan charge. A house with every needful convenience had been built for us by the original proprietor. This we were abruptly ordered to quit. Another king had arisen, who knew not Joseph or his father's house. We went away, weeping at every step. I saw my mother's tears, and to this day her low wailing strikes my ear. But though destitute, we were not forsaken; though in straits, we did not perish; and by the blessing of Almighty Providence upon the well-directed industry of my mother and my elder brothers, we were sustained with food convenient.

The desolate condition of the moneyless and unprotected widow was aggravated in no common degree by the political commotion already adverted to. Persons unacquainted with the approaching terrors of that era may imagine that an obscure and uninfluential family, like ours, had little to apprehend; that our poverty was protection enough; and that those who had nothing to lose had nothing to fear. Not so. The conflict then impending arose from the dark designs of men "cursed with a heart unknowing how to yield," and who were bent on havoc and rapine. Personal robbery might not be planned, but many were ready for that and a great deal more. Heresy and sedition were closely in league; the emissaries of each were in ceaseless motion; and the ultimate design was, to burst forth from the unsuspected places of mischief, suddenly, and wide wasting as the simoom of the desert, and sweep with indiscriminating ire, from the abodes of their peaceful countrymen, every vestige of existing government, and every temple devoted to the Reformed religion, as by law and right reason established. Perfect secrecy on the part of the rebels was happily unattainable. Every now and then circumstances and facts transpired, the tendency of which could not be mistaken. Hair-brained but hot-headed men became the self-elected orators of secluded nocturnal assemblies. Liberty and equality, and reason versus religion, neat as imported from the French Directory at Paris, was the order of the day. Uproarious vociferation took the place of argument; and though the majority of these Hibernian gentry were as ignorant of jurisprudence as the more modern destructionist, nothing less than the dismemberment of the British empire, and the establishment of a republic, formed probably on the model of citizen Robespierre, would suit their purpose. All this was designed, and most of it was divulged. Experience has shown, that where numerous and unequally gifted agencies are employed, let the pursuit be good or evil, entire privacy is next to impossible. The parties may promise to be silent, or may bind themselves to be so by oath; but concealed know ledge is a treasure, of which the custody is to some communicative souls impracticable. They find them selves in the possession of a secret; it struggles to break away; but they remember their vow, and in order to hold it fast, they get a friend or two to help them. The sons of Irish misrule assumed several names: there were white-boys, and steel-boys; oak-boys, and right-boys. Distinctions are, however, needless,—they were all bad boys; and at length the entire series were drawn into the wild and powerful vortex of United Irishmen; it being understood that this body consisted chiefly of persons professing the Roman Catholic religion.

The storm at length came down, and the consequences were awful. Although not quite nine years of age when our neighbourhood rang with war's alarms, the scenes I was then compelled to witness cannot be forgotten. I distinctly remember the transactions of an eventful day which took place in a small town near my mother's residence. The rebels had taken possession of the place, and had murdered a magistrate who attempted to oppose them. At that crisis a squadron of dragoons, stationed at Tullamore, received orders to march and endeavour to dislodge them. The cavalry rode into the main street with great gallantry, but were received by a tremendous fire of musketry from the windows of the houses on each side; so that, after sustaining a considerable loss, they were compelled to retreat. Several of the soldiers were killed; and a number of wounded men were afterwards conveyed on cars from the place of action to the military hospital. My poor mother was in the midst of these dangers; and I well remember that she experienced great rudeness from the ruffian rabble. But the Almighty preserved her from serious injury. He can restrain at pleasure the wrath of man, as well as divert it into a new and unintended channel. That night we were afraid of entering into any house, lest we should attract the notice of the rebels, who were now flushed into insolence and inebriety by their recent victory: we therefore crept behind the foliage of some low trees, and passed the night in the open air. Our next precaution was to protect the little remaining household furniture from pillage. To effect this, we buried the most valuable articles in the earth, as nothing above ground appeared to offer the least protection. The property thus secreted was saved; but on raising it subsequently, almost every thing was spoiled by the dampness of the soil in which it had been embedded.

One of my neighbours, John Tinkler, was singled out by these barbarians as a victim. He was a man of singular benevolence, and held in general esteem by the surrounding inhabitants but he was a Protestant, and that had long been placed at the head of the list of unpardonable crimes. The house of this worthy man, whom I well knew, was beset by a horde of armed ruffians, who commenced an immediate attack. Tinkler, in the midst of his family, consisting of a wife and seven or eight children, though surprised, determined to defend himself to the last extremity. He fought desperately, though oppressed by numbers, until one of the villains posted outside the house, and guided by the sound of his voice, deliberately levelled his piece and fired. The bullet passed through the door, and struck Tinkler, who fell dead just within the threshold, valiantly defending his home and property; and I regret to add, that the widow and her helpless charge, ejected by some means from the farm and land, were obliged to seek shelter elsewhere.

These were but the beginning of sorrows. The spirit of ruinous anarchy spread far and wide. It was particularly observed, that the Roman Catholics were very much devoted to their chapels. Mass was celebrated every day throughout most parts of the country; whereas, formerly, it was chiefly observed only on the Sabbath-day. The chapel of Ballycanoe was attended by a very numerous congregation at both morning and evening prayers. Michael Murphy was officiating Priest of that parish; a young man, strongly made, and of a dark complexion, who had been a few years resident in the place, and not long in holy orders. This person was master of profound dissimulation, and contrived to throw around himself the garb of saintly innocence at the very moment in which he was preparing to smite with the sword. This military saint actually took the oath of allegiance, in which he expressly declared himself ready to "be true and faithful to His Majesty, King George the Third, and to the succession of his family to the throne; and that he would prevent tumult and disorder by every means within his reach, and give up all sorts of arms in his possession." "All the above," quoth Michael, "I swear, so help me God, and my Redeemer!" Meantime, in the immediate vicinity and all around the residence of his Reverence, timber was missing out of the gentlemen's nurseries. It was observed that the woods and shrubberies were gleaned of such materials as would suit for the construction of offensive weapons.

In fact, this genuine sample of Popish fidelity, who, had he lived, ought to have been rewarded with at least a Cardinal's hat,—this pretended pattern of all that is good and praiseworthy; went his way from the altar, put down the Testament on which, after the perpetration of his delusive affidavit, his lips had been pressed, and straightway began to exemplify the inviolability of his oath to existing government, by the manufacture of pike-handles, and granting absolution to those who helped him.

Without going into the history of the Irish Rebellion, which is foreign from my present purpose, the fact is sufficiently evident, that the whole of that sanguinary struggle from first to last may be ascribed to the crafty domination of the Roman Catholic Clergy. It is not a little singular, that three of the most daring military leaders, those I mean who were principally signalized in the wholesale butchery of their Protestant fellow-subjects, were Priests in that persecuting Church. One of these, named Roche, assumed the power of working miracles. Indeed, each of them, as occasion required, did a little business in that line. Roche declared, that in battle his person was invulnerable; that no shot could hit or hurt him; and having picked up several bullets after an engagement at Ross, he assured his dupes that he caught them in his hand during the fight. The wily Ecclesiastic, true worshipper as he was at the shrine of Mammon, conceived the idea of turning the thing to good account, by the alternate practice of hypocrisy and theft, for either of which his hand was ready. He succeeded; and I hardly know which to admire most, the consummate impudence of the holy father, or the folly of his disciples. Roche procured slips of paper, each of which he termed a "Protection, or Gospel." In the centre was a figure of the Cross, with an inscription underneath, stating, "In the name of God and of the blessed Virgin, no gun, pistol, sword, or any other offensive weapon can hurt or otherwise injure the person who has this paper in his possession; and it is earnestly recommended to all women to carry it, as it will be found an infallible preservation against the fatality of child-bed." Anxious to secure customers in every rank, the price of these tickets to the better sort of people was half-a-crown. As the poor might haggle at parting with a coin so large, the vender discreetly condescended to open a retail trade at six-pence each. The circulation of this trumpery, the value of which was equal to every other product of the Catholic Church, was immense; customers were to be computed by thousands.

Friar Murphy has already been noticed. His career, as has been related, commenced with daring perjury; and as the progress and end of such a man may be instructive, he shall have a parting glance. Like his iniquitous associate, he was disposed to do the wonderful. His campaign, however, with those of many other villains, was soon over. Bloody and deceitful men do not live out half their days. It was at the battle of Arklow, in 1798, that Commander Murphy determined by a decisive movement to blast the hopes of the Protestant cause. On the morning of the 9th of June, the rebel army was observed, amounting to 34,000 men, with three pieces of artillery, advancing on the town. Had this formidable force arrived only two days earlier, it would in all probability have captured the place; but, providentially, reinforcements bad been procured from Dublin, so that the garrison amounted in the whole to 1500 men, under the command of Major General Needham. Arklow, considered as a military position, presented no points susceptible of advantageous defence, and was altogether open and unprotected. About two o'clock PM. advice was received that the enemy was approaching: this was so little credited that the garrison, which had been ordered under arms, was just going to be dismissed, when a dragoon came galloping into the town with intelligence that the rebels were at hand. The drums instantly beat to arms, the troops flew to their respective stations, and preparations were made to give the enemy a proper reception. Having advanced to the suburbs of the town, the rebels set fire to several buildings, in hope that the smoke would annoy the garrison, and confuse their operations. Just then the wind shifted to the opposite quarter, so that the scheme not only failed, but served to confound their own devices. The action commenced between a column of the rebels, and a detachment of the Dunbarton fencibles, who were ordered out to line the ditches on each side of the road. When they had exchanged about a dozen rounds, the fencibles received orders to retreat, which was performed, but with a little confusion. On perceiving this movement, the rebels pursued with loud huzzas, and one of their officers, waving his hat, called out, "Come on, my boys! the town is our own." That was an error. He was suddenly surrounded by the troops, his horse was shot, and himself wounded; on which he fell as though slain. In a little time curiosity constrained him to lift up his head and look about; when he was perceived, and shot dead. The rebels pressed on with obstinacy worthy of a better cause; but on receiving a close fire of musketry and grape-shot, they fell back to some distance. They then endeavoured to extend their line in order to turn the left flank, but the fire of the Cavan battalion was so severe, that the attempt was abortive. Another column of the rebels tried to gain the lower end of the town by the beach; but here they were repulsed by a desperate charge of cavalry, headed by Colonel Sir Watkin Wynne. They then proceeded in great force to a passage that led to the centre of the town, which was defended only by a Sergeant and twelve privates: this handful of men, however, made good their position, and, as the pass they held was narrow, rendered every effort to dislodge them from it ineffectual. At this critical juncture Priest Murphy appeared, animating his men to renewed acts of outrage: many of these, terror-stricken by the clamour of this clerical warrior, were driven before him to the thickest of the fray. As no new deception presented itself, he had recourse to the worn-out pretension of working miracles, He declared, like brother Roche, that he could catch the bullets, or ward them off at pleasure; in proof of which, he advanced at the head of a strong party in order to take a cannon stationed near a barrack. In that moment his bowels were torn out with canister-shot. The rebels, on observing him fall, fled with precipitation, swearing, the Priest himself was down. On that day a thousand rebels fell. Their retreat, as might be expected, was marked by dreadful excesses: they broke the windows of churches and other places consecrated to divine service. They had an intolerable hatred to Protestant Prayer-books, and tore to pieces all that came within their reach. They carried the leaves of the church Bible on their pikes, shouting, "Behold the French colours!" and, to complete their impiety, they put two Protestants to death in the aisle of a church. In other parts they made saddles of the Bibles, and rode about upon them.

The retrospect of these vengeful days, while it serves to fix my faith in true religion, as contrasted with that which is false, calls forth unfeigned gratitude to God for his protecting mercy. Exposed as my mother and family were to the pelting of the pitiless hurricane, none of us sustained material personal injury. I have before stated that my mother was conscientiously attached to the tenets, such as they are, of the Church of Rome. I never observed anything reprehensible in her conduct, though no one was more constant than she at the confessional; neither know I to which of the saints she was disposed, on emergency, to turn. That she loved the Saviour, and was willing to wash the feet of the servants of her Lord, I can safely affirm. I can vouch for the constancy and zeal of her private prayers and intercessions: I know that the practices of her life agreed with the engagements of her lips: and I cannot help thinking that she was a noble proof that God is no respecter of persons; that holiness of heart may subsist in the most defective dispensation; and that whoever seeks the face of God, through the merits of his Son, in the path of penitence and faith, even though cumbered with mistaken doctrinal views, shall not be cast away. The time, the extent, and the unwitting nature of her ignorance God winked at: he saw that she erred through ignorance. The eye of his omniscience pierced through the veil of her mental delusion to the uprightness of intention that dwelt within; and I believe, through divine mercy, she went down to her grave justified by grace, "hallowed, and made meet for heaven." Agreeably with the religious views which my mother had entertained, she endeavoured to teach me the principles of Papacy. I was more over frequently taken to mass: but, being young and heedless, one system of religion was to me as good as another; in other words, I was careless respecting them all. Indeed, I have reason to believe that my indifference in this respect was to my mother a source of great grief. Meantime I had arrived at the fourteenth year of my age; a period, generally speaking, of no small vanity and self-complacency, and in which many *men* think themselves qualified, by the dignity of their teens, to shake off the trammels of parental guidance. Among others, I determined to walk alone; but unfortunately I cannot, on reflection, boast of my first step.

Among the youths with whom I contracted some acquaintance, was a dissolute lad about my own age; by whose enticement, when only just turned fifteen, I enlisted in the Queen's County militia. Not that my conduct, like his, had been openly immoral; yet he had gained over me an ascendancy I could not resist. Evil communications corrupt good manners; and perhaps the apparent freedom, the frankness and gaiety of an open-hearted soldier's holiday life, had an influence which, though not acknowledged, was really felt. But, O, my mother! for when I became a soldier she was still living. I had in this deed of hardihood well-nigh forgotten her.

But she remembered me; and when I thought thereon, I wept. Never shall I forget her last, her parting look! My elder brother had settled at some distance; and on the eve of my departure to share in unknown danger, had unexpectedly arrived. If bereaved of her children, she was bereaved; and I know she said in her heart, "All these things are against me." Her farewell was accompanied with a prayer for my future prosperity; and I impute my preservation, under Providence, through life, to the pious lessons and examples of my excellent mother. On leaving her presence on this eventful occasion, I was taken before Captain Fitzmaurice, the officer in command at the recruiting station, and was kindly received. He expressed himself pleased with my look and healthy appearance; made several minute inquiries relative to my family, and at once engaged me as his servant. After serving in the corps about twelve months, I received, principally, I believe, on account of my youth, an honourable discharge, while the regiment was stationed at the Castle-barrack in Limerick, and returned to the quietude of home.

Habits of dissipation may be contracted at pleasure; but when once confirmed by repetition, they are not so easily dismissed. This is especially true in youth; and I soon found that though I had retired beneath the roof of an excellent parent, my disposition to wander wide was still the same. Contentedness of mind I found was a state, not a place. The roll of the spirit-stirring drum, the glittering file of bayonets, with the pomp and circumstance of military parade, not unmingled perhaps with undefined thoughts of ultimate promotion, passed in review before my imagination, in colours vividly charming: resistance was vain. To this alluring panorama was added the consideration that, though only seventeen, I had reached the height of persons required by regimental rule. In fact, on the 6th of April, 1806, I enlisted in the 43d regiment of the line, and in company with several other recruits proceeded to Cork, where we embarked for Bristol, at which place, after a rough passage, we safely landed; and in a few days reached the town of Ashford, in Kent, where the regiment was quartered.

Events and shifting scenes had crowded one after another, with such rapidity since I left home, that reflection was drowned; but the first night in which I lay down in the barracks, memory began to be busy. I could not help thinking of the peaceful fire-side I had left; and in despite of my most vigorous effort to shake off the intrusion, conscience would not be denied, and the image of my mother, deserted at her utmost need, and pinched perhaps by want, was a source of great uneasiness. But having passed the rubicon, retreat I knew was out of the question. Independently of the conflict within, my situation in the barrack was not adapted to afford much present consolation. The sleeping-room of which I was an inmate was an oblong building of unusually large dimensions, and was occupied by three companies, of an hundred men each. They were chiefly volunteers, and of course young soldiers. Many were Irish, many more were English, several Welshmen were intermingled, and a few Scotchmen came in to complete the whole. Most of these, and that was the only point of general resemblance, had indulged in excessive drinking. Some were uproariously merry; on others the effect was directly the reverse; and nothing less than a fight, it mattered not with whom, would satisfy. Meantime as they were unable to abuse each other in language mutually intelligible, exclamations profanely jocular, or absurdly rancorous, rang through the building; altogether the coalition of discordant verbiage was such as to beggar all description, and can be likened to nothing of which I ever heard or read, except the confusion on the plains of Babel. Never will the occurrence of that night be effaced from my mind. Surely, thought I, hell from beneath is moved to engulf us all. These disorderly proceedings, thank God, were of short continuance. In a few weeks we marched to more convenient quarters, a few miles distant. The salutary restraints of discreetly managed discipline spake chaos into order, and my situation became comparatively comfortable.

How it has happened I know not, but through all the changes of my life, and they have been neither few or trifling, I never lacked a friend. One of the first of these has been alluded to; and another belonged to the battalion to which I found myself attached, and, though no relative of mine, was of the same name. He was exceedingly kind on numerous occasions; and it will be readily believed, that the smallest act of civility in favour of a mere novice, at the commencement of his military life, was valuable. The drill of the regiment was severe; but I passed muster without difficulty, and had, in addition, the good fortune, to attract the notice of our Colonel, a fine old Scotchman; and the first time I mounted guard I was selected by the Adjutant as his Orderly. This preference, as I had never seen actual service, was perhaps to be imputed to neatness of dress, and, the condition of my arms and accoutrements, in which, though only a private, I saw it my duty to be particular; added to this, I was remarkable for flexibility of limb and muscular power, thoroughly understood the use of my weapons, and, unless flattered, had the advantage of a good figure. That was a period of uncommon vigilance throughout the British army, especially with regard to the corps stationed along the shores of Kent. On the opposite side, and almost within sight, numerous and well-disciplined masses of troops had for some time been encamped under the personal inspection, it was said, of Napoleon, who entertained the vain-glorious project of conquering Britain. The harbour of Boulogne contained a numerous and well-appointed flotilla, in which were to embark the long-expected invading force. In the opinion of the best judges, the attempt, even with favouring wind and tide, would have failed. Had the navigation of the high seas by the medium of steam been understood and applied at that time, a naval engagement, in the view of perhaps both countries, might have recalled the fury of the ancient Armada, and would probably have been fought upon principles of destructive tendency, till then untried. Not that the result need be doubted. Had it been possible for a few gun-boats or flat-bottomed craft to elude the vigilance of an English fleet, and shoot a little rubbish upon our borders, no material injury could have arisen. Not a foreigner would have survived to tell the tale of his rashness. I know the spirit of the British army both at home and abroad, and can safely aver, that they would have given an excellent account of the intruders, or perished in repelling them. The experiment was not to be made: Providence ordered that these aggressive movements should begin and end in gasconade. Some good man has said, that the Almighty places the hedge of his providence around the abode of his people, and the hedge of his grace around their souls. My opinion is, that these are the defences within which we are en trenched; and that while we keep within the guarded circle, every foe, whether secret or open, will be kept at bay.

In June, 1807, our regiment, which numbered a thousand effective men, was called into actual service; and I soon had an opportunity of observing the difference between the good-humoured rencontres of a holiday review, and the tug and strife of desperate conflict. This country, as is well remembered by thousands, stood, at the beginning of the present century, nearly, if not quite, alone against the colossal influence of continental despotism. The Emperor of the French, then at the zenith of power and ambition, seemed determined to compass the globe in exertions to ruin the commerce and prosperity of England. Its welfare was an intolerable worm at the root of all his enjoyment; and among other plans in which it gratified his soul to revel, was that of forming a confederacy among the northern powers of Europe, for the purpose of excluding the vessels of this country from the navigation of the Germanic waters, and bringing against it the concentrated strength of hostile navies. In this alliance it was supposed that Denmark had largely shared; and as Lord Nelson had already shown that the passage of the Sound was not so impregnable as had been thought, the British Ministry resolved to send an expedition, consisting both of land and sea forces, for the purpose of capturing Copenhagen, together with the fleet in that harbour. This singular determination was defended in Parliament, not by charging the Danes with hostile intentions, but by urging their inability to resist the increasing power of France. In the opinion, however, of several creditable writers on jurisprudence and the laws of nations, the measure is to be deplored, not only because it is dishonourable in itself, but calculated to render our name odious in a country where we should otherwise have found cordial allies. There are some, observes an Apostle, that say, "Let us do evil, that good may come." Such was the case apparently here, and the abettors of the act place themselves within the malediction that followed. The argument of the British Cabinet was,—It is possible that our antagonists, who want valuable ships, may seize the Danish navy: this is the more likely because effectual resistance cannot be offered: to remedy this awful breach of justice, in respect of a harmless neutral power, we will save all farther trouble, by taking possession of the property ourselves. An illustration of three lines exhibits the unfairness of the transaction:—A well-armed freebooter pounces upon his peaceable neighbour, ransacks his habitation, breaks open his coffers, abstracts the property, seriously wounds the sufferer in the scuffle, and marches off with the spoil: the burglar then justifies the act, because he has heard, that unless he make haste, an acquaintance of his, as great a thief as himself, but a far inferior pirate, with whom he has quarrelled, has thought of doing the very same thing. The Government of this country supported itself on the occasion by several reasons. They urged that the Danish fleet and stores, but for the proposed interposition, must fall into the hands of Buonaparte, who wanted exactly that kind of force to act against his formidable foe; that Denmark was totally unable to prevent the seizure of her ships; that there was ground to believe that in order to conciliate the esteem of the French ruler, she would willingly yield to his desire; that in either case, the result would be equally unfavourable to this country, inasmuch as the well-appointed fleet of our northern neighbours would supply our inveterate enemy with the means of annoyance in which his greatest deficiency was apparent; and that the rigid inexorable law of necessity and self-preservation not only permitted, but demanded, the previous seizure of the instruments of intended war. But the causes of hostility between nations involve considerations concerning which a soldier is seldom called upon to trouble himself. Generally speaking, he has little right to meddle or make concerning them. While others reason, he is to obey orders, to fight and fear not; the questions he asks for conscience sake being few and far between.

It was on the morning of a delightful day, that we broke up our quarters at Hythe, on our route to the place of embarkation. The scene was novel, and to myself, who witnessed it for the first time, highly impressive. We breakfasted on the heights of Dover, and in the course of the day marched to Deal. On the following morning, we proceeded to Ramsgate. Boats for our conveyance to the transports then at anchor in the Downs were moored off the pier-head, and in a short time I found myself on board the Sally, formerly of Shields, which had been engaged by Government, and fitted up for the reception of troops. The embarkation was effected in August, 1807; and I know not that any event, either before or since, connected with the casualties and privations of military life, ever struck my mind with greater force than that to which I now refer. I allude principally to the strength of affection evinced by the soldiers' wives and children, many of whom resolutely followed in the line of our march, and whom it was impossible to shake off, though permitted to follow to the edge of the water. Indeed many were not con tent with that: several women insisted on going with their husbands into the boats, and actually did so. "Father," I heard a little child say, "shall I never see you again!" The grief of separation at last was inevitable; and on nearing the ship's side, I saw many an embrace, destined by the fitful chances of war to be the last indulged on earth.

Having had some experience in the army, and a tolerably extensive acquaintance with the men who compose it, I cannot permit this occasion to pass, without pointing out the necessity for, and the advantage arising, in a national sense, from the asylum for the children of deceased soldiers in the British army, instituted at Chelsea, by the late Duke of York. No person ever understood and maintained the rights and reasonable solaces of a soldier better than the then Commander-in-chief. Nothing on earth can exceed the coolness and intrepidity with which a British column enters into action. Their firm and steady step has often been the theme of foreign admiration; and in the clash and hurra of crossing bayonets they are known to be unequalled. Yet, every one acquainted with the finer workings of human nature must suppose, (for the reflection is inevitable,) that on entering within the range of a shower of bullets, the bravest heart may be troubled by thoughts of an absent family, especially if left in an unprotected and unprovided condition. But if the man have the consolation of knowing, that in the event of any personal fatality, the shield of his country's honour and beneficence will be exhibited for the protection of his orphan family, the tendency of the recollection at such a crisis is to arm his mind with triple fortitude, and, if possible, give greater ardour to his moral courage. The mind of a man thus circumstanced is at once believed from a load of domestic anxiety; and having nothing on earth for which to care, but the maintenance of the national weal, he casts himself upon the protection of the God of armies, and cheerfully advances to the assigned position, on the grim and serried ridge of war. It has been objected that these are times of public economy and retrenchment; and that no portion, however small, of national property should be frittered needlessly, away. Granted. But terms of that class, if I mistake not, are thrown away, if applied to the case now considered. Support granted to the children of a slain soldier is at once an act of justice and of mercy. It presents itself to the mind, commended quite as much by the laws of sound policy, as by those of genuine philanthropy. In fact, an institution like that for which I contend may be fairly considered as part of the soldier's compensation, and the last reward for toil and service rendered to his country. This arrear of pay, though not immediately made, is nevertheless certain; and is to be viewed by the faint and dying warrior as a kind of life-insurance, granted by the generosity of his friends at home, secured by public faith, and payable whenever his children are deprived of their best earthly benefactor. Besides, I apprehend that economy, which deserves the name, if of any service, must be practised with judgment. When ever general expenditure is to be reduced, items of outlay of the least possible consequence should be selected for excision, while such as are essentially right remain untouched. If superfluities be detected, or abuses abound, be their magnitude great or small, let them be swept. away with the besom of impartial honesty, and consigned to the Lethean lake. But surely, the little pittance needful for the support of a modest but valuable charity, in behalf of a soldier's orphan progeny is not to be proscribed. To a great nation like this, which has for ages taken the lead in acts of general beneficence, such a step would present a solecism utterly irreconcilable either to right reason or good feeling. Were an hypothesis so eccentric and deceptive to prevail, every act of charity and alms-giving might be superseded. Hospitals might be closed; gratuitous education might cease; the stream of benevolence through its countless ramifications might no longer flow; pity itself, that gentle though honoured inmate of the human breast, might be known no more: but to call this economy would be a sad abuse of terms. Instances often arise, in which judicious expenditure is the way to effect the greatest saving; while, on the other hand, money hoarded up on parsimonious and short-sighted motives is sure to melt away. Does he save who rots the roof of his house for want of a tile? Can the ruralist talk of management, who reaps just half an average crop, for want of sufficient manure? Is it not better to preserve health, than first lose and then try to regain it? These questions scarcely wait for reply. The affirmation is written either on the mind or heart of all; and upon principles exactly similar, the work of juvenile education, combined as it is in the Military Asylum with the sustenance of the children, and through that with the moral improvement of one of the finest armies in the world, amounts to an expression of English liberality and discrimination, the suppression of which would be a common calamity. The extinction of an asylum so valuable is the more to be deprecated on account of the excellence of the system adopted in its internal management, and the exactness with which the original design is carried into effect through every department. It has been affirmed, and is frequently the subject of sore com plaint, that in some charitable foundations now in existence, for the gratuitous guardianship and instruction of youth, admissions are procured by favouritism and a species of implied purchase; so that while the gate of reception is closed upon the hapless orphan, who cannot find an advocate, the entrance is invitingly open to those whose influence is sufficiently powerful to command the omnipotent "vote and interest." By this means the pious intent, nourished during the life of many a noble benefactor, is defeated; and, while he sleeps in the dust, the benefits of his endowment are diverted into channels altogether at variance with those in which the wealth bequeathed was intended to flow. Not so in the Military Asylum. It was built in order to promote the prosperity of the children of English soldiers; none but such are received, nor can admission be procured in any other form, than that projected by the impartial and even-handed rules of the institution. It is the widow and the father less whose cause is heard, and whose pleadings win the day. Another proof of the superiority of the institution arises from the order observed within doors: this has for years excited the admiration of visitors, numbers of whom have inspected the school at various periods. Great and persevering efforts are also made to improve and elevate the morals of the children: they are taught to fear God, and honour the King; to be grateful to their benefactors, and kind to all. The services of religion are, in fact, so interwoven with the daily practices of the school, that serious impressions, unless in instances of peculiar depravity, can scarcely fail of being made. For this essential and all important advantage, the institution is indebted chiefly to the uncommon zeal and exertions of the Chaplain, the excellence of whose ministerial and private reputation stands in no need of this feeble tribute. One of the most interesting sights imaginable is, to see the whole body of children assemble at the dinner hour. The perfect order and silence produced by the application of something like military system,—the clean and healthy condition of the lads, on whose countenances no shadow of care is cast,—the neatness of their simple but comfortable uniform,—together with the judicious general arrangement, contribute to form one of the most pleasing spectacles that the world can afford. Not a word is spoken, nor is there the slightest irregularity, while in the act of assembling. The dining-tables having been previously arranged, and plates of food for each man being placed upon them, the youths march, in single file, and cap in hand, along the floor of the spacious apartment. They step out together with as much trueness as a veteran regiment: indeed, the steadiness of their advance, and simultaneous tread, have a beautiful effect. In this animated procession of health and vigour, imagination almost calls up their fathers' forms, though slain and buried in the battle-field. When the head of each column arrives at the farther end of the tables, which are placed three abreast, and of great length, the word "halt" is given. In that instant every foot is still. Each boy then places his cap upon the floor, when, on a given signal, the entire corps face about to their respective seats. Having clasped their hands in a devotional form, which is also done together, one of the larger lads, placed at the end, pronounces, in a distinct and audible voice, the "grace before meat:" at the conclusion the whole of the boys respond a loud Amen. The effect is beautiful, and has often been witnessed by the moistened eye of many a delighted observer. A roll of, or rather a single touch upon, the drum is then heard, when the children take their seats and commence their meal; and, it is needless to add, enjoy the bounty of their benefactors. A similar ceremony is practised at the close. The accuracy of these arrangements; the efficiency of the institution, by a close and vigilant adherence to the principles and purposes for which it was founded; and the admirable provision made for the present and future welfare of the children, are to be imputed to the unintermitted care and effort of the Commandant, who acts like the adopted father of an orphan family; who, to great firmness of mind, unites true benevolence of heart, has the art of securing obedience, and at the same time of making himself beloved, thus fitting him in no ordinary degree for his onerous and responsible situation.

CHAPTER II

THE fleet destined for the north bore away from the Downs with a fine leading breeze. It consisted of forty-two ships of war, twenty-two of which were of the line, several frigates, and a forest of transports, on board of which the forces destined to act on shore were embarked: these amounted to twenty thousand effective men, and were under the command of Lord Cathcart, while Admiral Gambier directed the naval operations. After a rough passage, we came in sight of the Danish coast about the middle of August; and early on the morning of the 16th of that month, the debarkation of the troops, under cover of several gun-brigs, commenced. We landed at Wisbeck, a small place in the island of Zealand, about eight miles from Copenhagen. Just before leaving the vessel in which I had sailed, I had a narrow escape. The weather being warm and fine, several of the soldiers and sailors took the advantage of bathing, and I made one of the number. One morning, after having enjoyed this luxury, and just as I was half-dressed, a cry of distress was heard, and on looking over the ship's side, a sailor, evidently unable to swim, was observed, endeavouring to float on the surface of the water by grasping an oar that happened to be within his reach: unfortunately he was unable to retain his hold, and immediately disappeared. The sea was calm, and so remarkably clear, that the spot in which he sank was easily recognised. Not a moment was to be lost; and, being an expert swimmer, I divested myself of the clothing I had put on, and dived after him. On looking about, I saw the poor fellow faintly struggling near the bottom, among some long sedgy weeds: his head being still uppermost, I seized him with one hand by the hair, and with the other was so far able to swim, as to raise both the man and myself to the surface, when on a sudden he fastened on me with a grasp so deadly, that I was incapable of

moving hand or foot; and had I not been able to disengage myself,
I must inevitably have perished. The struggle between us was
terrific, being myself at that time scarcely seventeen years of age,
and he a powerful full-grown man. At length, by a desperate effort;
I escaped from his grasp. Deprived of my buoyancy, he sank like a
stone. On account of the length of time I had been under water,
my preservation was little less than miraculous; indeed, one of the
officers, and several of the crew, who witnessed the transaction,
had given me up for lost; when to their surprise, I again emerged,
and was safely taken on board. Thus was I given back to light and
life: but was the deliverance wrought by the prowess of my own
arm? So I once thought; but the film is taken from my eyes. It was
the Lord who preserved my life, by the agency of his overruling
providence. The sea confessed his mighty power and my days
declining like a shadow were graciously renewed. Diligent search
was made for the body of the poor man, but without effect: it had,
no doubt, drifted with the current far from the place in which the
accident occurred, to be found probably no more till the sea shall
give up her dead.

After the army had made good its landing, which was effected
without opposition, one of the first acts of our commander was to
issue a proclamation, in which he announced the object of the
expedition, lamented the necessity of the cause of it, and expressed
a hope that the Danish fleet, then at anchor in the roads, would be
surrendered without bloodshed; at the same time declaring, that if
it were not given up, force would be used to secure it; in which
event, he argued, the innocent blood unavoidably shed would be
chargeable on those who advised resistance to a measure dictated
by imperious necessity. To this specimen of military logic, rendered
so conclusive by the force of arms, the Danes deigned no reply. The
Government resolved to defend the capital, and thus convince the
world, that the country intended to maintain its honour and
property against the assailants, whether they came from the Thames
or the Seine, and show the fallacy of the reasoning upon which the
British Ministry founded the expediency of their present
extraordinary measure. Paper contentions and the rivalry of
manifestoes were therefore relinquished; and as neither party chose

to recede, negotiation was succeeded by the rude appeal to arms. On the side of the invaders, the best understanding subsisted between the army and navy, and suitable arrangements were promptly made by the respective commanders for mutual co-operation. Several frigates and gun-boats took advantage of a favourable wind to place themselves in front of the harbour, taking care to secure a position which enabled them to throw shells into the city, while the troops advanced by land: the operations on both elements were conducted with equal vigour and success. The plan of defence adopted by the Danes was similar to that projected some years previously, in the memorable engagement with Nelson. Strong lines of gun-boats and praams were securely moored for the defence of the harbour flanked at each extremity by the crown Battery, and a Block-House, in which upwards of an hundred pieces of cannon were mounted: this force, which was judiciously planned, offered formidable resistance to the British squadron. The Danes fired red hot balls, and soon after the commencement of the action several of our ships in advanced positions were compelled to haul off: they, however, shortly resumed their places, and poured an incessant fire on the rafts and armed craft. As it was deemed imperatively needful to put an end to all resistance on the harbour side of the city, batteries were erected on shore by the English forces, who opened a well-directed fire on every vessel in which Danish colours were visible. Congreve rockets flared through the lurid sky without intermission. One of the Danish vessels blew up with tremendous explosion: the fire of the others gradually abated, and in a few hours all opposition from the flotilla ceased. Meantime the main body of the besieging army pushed on its advanced posts with great vigour: they carried their approaches to within four hundred yards of the ramparts, and forced one of the strongest redoubts, which was turned against the enemy. Having heard that a considerable body of troops had assembled in order to surprise us, a detachment, consisting of four regiments of British infantry, with a squadron of Hussars, under the command of Sir Arthur Wellesley, was ordered to march against it. We found the Danes fourteen thousand strong, advantageously posted in front of the small town of Kioge. The attack began on our part with the usual spirit. Some little impression having been made on the enemy's line, the 92d were ordered to charge: the movement was executed with astonishing celerity; the shock was irresistible, and the Danes, unused perhaps to such personality, fled in all directions: numbers, however, remained lifeless on the battle-field, and many more were taken prisoners, and consigned to the British fleet. As this was the first action of any importance in which I had been closely engaged, it put my firmness to the test. The regiment in which I served was placed on the right of the British line. The first thing that startled me, was the forceful rebound of a cannon ball that struck the ground within a few paces of the place where I stood: it scattered the earth with violence, but fortunately did no injury; and the impression of danger was soon erased by the heavy and rapid trampling of a cavalry charge made in our favour, and which laid many a brave fellow low. Of those who escaped from the destructive sweep, several sought refuge in a church-yard, where a large body were overtaken and captured. I recollect meeting with an exhausted Dane, concealed in the side of a ditch: the interview seemed particularly disagreeable to him, and was quite unexpected by myself. I soon put an end to all explanations, by conducting him to head-quarters. But after the battle had ceased, and my spirits became composed, I was subdued beyond all I ever felt before. This emotion was produced by leisurely traversing the scene of action on the following day. There lay the dead, just as they had fallen. They were said to be enemies, but I felt that they and myself were partakers of one common nature. I saw several Danish women, moving with terror among the slain, anxious to discover, and yet afraid to ascertain, who pressed the field. The day before I was among the foremost of those fearless spirits who dealt out wounds and carnage, careless of danger, and destitute of fear. But when the soul is allowed quietly to look within; when the hurricane of wrath has spent its fierceness, and nothing remains, save the desolation it has produced, views and sensations are strangely transposed. My compassionate musings were, however, exceedingly brief. A soldier's moral meditations seldom take place; and if nature will occasionally assert her right, the hasty tear is brushed away for sterner thoughts and deeds. There is to be perceived among the

Danes an amiable simplicity of manners, coupled with remarkable firmness and bravery in action: this was conspicuous in every conflict. Private emolument, or the protection of property was never suffered to compete with the measures necessary for public defence. Life itself seemed of value only so far as it could contribute to national honour. Gardens, smiling with the choicest fruits, all but ripe, were cheerfully resigned as the site for erecting batteries. Masses of soldiery were quartered in the corn-fields. The furniture of several mansions belonging to the nobility was hastily removed, and the buildings offered to the service of Government, as the exigency of affairs required. The palace of the Crown Prince resembled a barrack more than the residence of royalty. The entire people, of whatever age or rank, emulous only to be distinguished in the defence of home, came simultaneously forward, with the suffrage of their best services. This unflinching devotedness, estimable, whether in friend or foe, was met by corresponding energy on the part of the besiegers, who were persons not to be trifled with. Before I report further progress, a few brief notices of the city of Copenhagen may not be uninteresting. It is universally acknowledged to be the best-built capital in the north. Petersburg excels it in superb edifices, but is disfigured by multitudinous wooden houses, and exhibits therefore a striking contrast of pomp and penury. Copenhagen presents a more equable and uniform appearance. The town is surrounded toward the land with regular ramparts and bastions, a broad ditch full of water, and several outworks. Its circumference is about five miles. The streets are well paved, with a foot-way on each side, but are inconveniently narrow. The greater part of the buildings are of brick, and a few of freestone brought from Germany. The houses of the nobility are in general splendid, and constructed in the Italian style of architecture: the palace, which was erected by Christian VI., is a large pile of building, the front of which is stone, and the wings of brick stuccoed. Maritime affairs, and the facilities of trade, have also received proper attention. The haven is commonly crowded with merchant ships, and the streets are intersected with broad canals, by which merchandise is brought close to the warehouses that line the quays. The city owes its principal beauty, and healthiness, to a cause similar to that to which the renovation and improvement of London are to be ascribed. A dreadful fire broke out in Copenhagen, in 1728. Five churches and sixty-seven streets were destroyed; the whole of which, and many others, have since been rebuilt in modern style. The new part of the town, raised by the late King, Frederick V., is extremely beautiful, scarcely inferior to Bath. It consists of an octagon, containing four uniform and elegant buildings of hewn stone, and of four broad streets leading to it in opposite directions. Part of Copenhagen, which is called Christianshafen, is built upon the isle of Amak.

The British Commander, unwilling to injure the city, had hitherto confined his offensive operations to the adjacent suburbs. It was, however, notified to the Danes in occupation as a garrison, that unless the terms proposed for the surrender of the fleet were immediately accepted, an attack might be expected. On the 31st of August the platform was raised, and the mortar batteries were ready for action. General Pieman, the Governor, having refused to listen to the proposals forwarded, a vigorous fire was opened from the batteries and bomb-vessels, and in a few hours it was observed that the city was on fire in several places: the bombardment continued with little intermission till the evening of the 7th of September. By that time, extensive injury had ensued, and it became evident that if the bombardment continued much longer, the city would be reduced to ashes. A flag of truce was in this extremity despatched, requesting a suspension of hostilities for twenty-four hours, to afford time for proposing terms of capitulation. The reply of Lord Cathcart was, that nothing of the kind could be entertained, unless grounded on the entire and unconditional surrender of the Danish fleet. This was a bitter pill; but necessity, which has often laid the mighty in the dust, compelled the besieged to take it; and in the night of the 7th of September, the articles of capitulation were settled, to be ratified the following morning. According to these, the British were put into possession of the citadel and dockyards; all the ships of war and naval stores were to be delivered up; a mutual restoration of prisoners was to take place, private property to be respected, and in the space of six weeks the citadel to be restored to the King of Denmark, and the whole island of Zealand to be evacuated by the

British army. In consequence of this capitulation, we were put into possession of sixteen sail of the line, fifteen frigates, six brigs, and twenty-five gun-boats, all of which were nearly ready for sea. A vast abundance of stores of all kinds necessary to equip or build a fleet were found in the arsenals. It was therefore necessary to load all the ships of the line and frigates which were delivered up, with masts, spars, and timber; so that ninety-two transports were employed to bring the property to England. Whatever may be the opinion respecting the justice or policy of the expedition to Copenhagen, there can be but one relative to the mode in which Lord Cathcart conducted it. While he did all that his duty as an officer required, he was throughout the whole of the operations attentive to the suffering Danes: he levied no contributions; not the slightest military excess was committed; and had it not been that the British army was engaged in bombarding their capital, the Danes might have taken them for friends and allies, instead of hostile troops. Even after the surrender of Copenhagen, we were not quartered in it for some days; the Danish troops remaining in possession of all the gates but that which was connected with the citadel. No interference took place with respect to the police, or any other internal regulation of the city, and every thing was done to tranquillize the public mind: but all was in vain to reconcile the Danish Government or people to the bombardment of the capital, and the seizure of their fleet in time of peace. As might have been foreseen, the outrage was deemed intolerable: it is true they were plundered with comparative politeness,—nobody hurt them when their treasures were given up; still that did not alter the character of the transaction: it conferred honour upon the agencies employed, who might, without any special departure from the laws of war, have added fierceness to bravery, and wasted what they did not want. But the national spirit of the Danes was roused to unquenchable indignation; they considered themselves the victims of lawless freebooters, superior to themselves only in brute force, and infinitely inferior in every thing else. Under feelings excited by these galling considerations war was proclaimed between Denmark and Great Britain.

Every one will readily believe, that, notwithstanding the good behaviour of their visitors, the Danes were by no means enamoured

with our company, and not a little pleased when preparations were
made for departure. We had caused great injury to several of the
finest erections in the city; had thrown down the steeple of one of
the best churches; had created an entire suspension of commerce
for a wearisome season; and having collected as much naval
property as we could grasp, and more than we could carry, were
getting it on board the captured vessels with as much deliberation
and order as if nothing more were in hand than a regular shipment
of purchased merchandise. The design of the expedition having
been fully executed, the troops were re-embarked towards the end
of October. On observing the signal for sailing, the whole of the
fleet prepared to weigh, and stand out to sea; and when under sail,
the almost interminable line of shipping presented an extensive
and magnificent spectacle. The first part of the homeward voyage
was performed under favourable circumstances; but on nearing
the English coast, the weather, which had been fine, became rough
and boisterous. Soon after we came in sight of land, the regiment
to which I belonged, for reasons with which I am unacquainted,
was shifted from the vessel we had occupied, to the Sirion, of
seventy-four guns, one of the Danish prizes; and though so near
our destined port, we were exposed to danger, greater perhaps than
any we had hitherto experienced. There were on board, beside the
crew, seven companies of the 43d, amounting to nearly as many
hundred men. Just at midnight, during a gale of wind, when all
were wrapt in security, and the greater part in slumber, the ship
struck on a sand-bank. The shock was excessively violent. Alarmed
by the concussion, which was attended by an ominous straining of
the timbers, an immediate rush was made by the soldiers below to
gain the main deck. To prevent this dangerous intrusion, the hatches
were secured, and a strong guard appointed to keep them from
being forced. The confusion and contention that prevailed among
such a body of resolute men, cooped up in their berths between
decks, and with the consciousness of danger, which they were not
even permitted to view, may be conceived, but not easily described.
To increase our alarm, the foremast went over with several men
in the top, one of whom fell on the shank of an anchor, and was
killed. By the mercy of God we were after all preserved. Several of

the most active soldiers, among whom I was one, were eventually ordered to assist the crew, whose exertions were beyond all praise. The damaged rigging and running tackle were all repaired; we contrived, under the direction of the ship's officer, to elevate a jury mast, and exhibit canvass that answered the purpose of a foresail; and though in a shattered condition, we had the happiness, assisted by a favourable breeze, to feel the ship glide over the shoal, and swing into deep water. On the following day, the sailor who lost his life by falling from the fore-top was committed to the deep. The body was carefully enclosed in a blanket, and placed on an oblong grating, to each end of which two round shot were lashed. The sea-service for the burial of the dead was then performed with great solemnity; immediately after which, the grating was lowered from the ship's side, and, being heavily weighted, sunk with the velocity of a stone. We landed in safety at Yarmouth, on the first day of December, and marched without loss of time into the barracks, where all traces of our recent perils and exposure to sudden mortality were soon forgotten, or remembered only for amusement.

Having saved a little money, I was soon able to furnish myself with such extra articles of necessity and convenience as appeared desirable to a young man just returned to his native shore, and aiming to appear respectable. But, alas! I regret to state, that my ambition was not limited to things altogether needful. Surrounded by evil examples, I became an easy prey to vicious men and their sinful practices. Prodigal of cash, while it lasted, the earnings of many a watchful, hard-fought day were speedily dispersed; and among other considerations which now occur to my mind, I am amazed that at the season of life now described, although just escaped almost miraculously from the jaws of death, not the smallest sense of gratitude to the Almighty seemed to enter the minds either of my comrades or myself. That this acknowledgment is discreditable to myself, I am sensible; but since such was the fact,—and I am determined to represent things as they really were,—it must not be suppressed merely for the purpose of putting a gloss upon conduct essentially wrong. I shall not stoop even to concealment: the advice of old Herbert is homely, but sound,—

Dare to be true; nothing can need a lie:
The fault that needs it most, grows two thereby.

Subsequent reflection upon the debased condition of my mind at
that time has shown me, and my experience has borne out the fact,
that man by nature is spiritually insensible, and in a condition that
exactly verifies the declaration of holy writ. His soul is touched
with an iceberg. The faculties are chained down by invincible
ignorance. There is a moral chaos within; through every power
darkness and confusion reign with total absence of form and
order. In the more emphatic language of inspiration, he is "dead in
trespasses and sins," nor can an archangel's voice awaken or revive
him. But when the Spirit of truth shall descend, the frozen heart
shall melt, and flow down before the Lord in streams of contrition
and obedience. Equally sure am I, that no power less than divine
can effect the change alluded to. Reason can do many things; it
may distinguish right from wrong, and can prove the truths on
which the distinction rests. But the knowledge of good and evil
is one thing power to choose the former and reject the latter is
another; and without pretending to unusual research, I fearlessly
affirm, and challenge refutation, that spiritual influence, and that
alone, is sufficient to overcome the spiritual malady of the human
race. Man does not want his heart to be merely mended,—it must
be renewed. To attempt the repair of bad principles is wide of the
mark: that would be like decorating the outside of a building, the
rottenness of whose timbers betokens the nearness of its fall. All
such trash and lumber must be cleared away: they seldom pay even
for stowage, and the safer way is to carry them out of sight. A new
foundation must be laid, based on firmer ground, and constructed
with better materials. Old things must pass away, and all things
become new. Principles are to be engrafted which had no previous
existence; and this decisive and comprehensive reformation, which
is not to he viewed as an accessory or appendage to religion, but
as its leading feature, constitutions the chief difference between
refinement in morals, and actual conversion to God. Some apology
is perhaps due for thus breaking out into meditations instead of
pursuing my narrative: all I have to offer is, that, reflecting on the

goodness of God, I cannot refrain from exulting in the change I have myself experienced, grounded on the sacred verities just described. Feeling myself invigorated by the review, perhaps others may share in the privilege, and rejoice in possession of the same hope. Travelling through the great and terrible wilderness of this world, I gather solace from such recollections, and go forward. The retrospect is like an oasis in the desert; a beautiful green spot, amid the aridity of desolating barrenness, verdant as the garden of the Lord, and refreshing as the dew of Hermon.

CHAPTER III

WHEN war's alarms are heard, the soldier reckons only upon short repose; and after remaining a few weeks on the coast, the regiment to which I belonged was ordered into winter quarters. While stationed there, we bad the misfortune to lose two of our officers, both of whom sank into an untimely grave. One of them fell a victim to the pernicious practice of duelling, and the other was drowned by incautiously venturing beyond his depth while bathing. During the time we remained in the neighbourhood the unceasing kindness of the inhabitants was remarked by us all. In the spring of the ensuing year we were ordered to Colchester, in the vicinity of which several regiments were quartered ready for active service, and expecting daily orders to embark for the Continent. The anticipated directions from London, so impatiently desired, arrived in the autumn of 1808: we were ordered instantly to prepare for foreign service; and never, I verily believe, was an invitation to a feast more readily obeyed. The regiment mustered in full strength, the men were in excellent condition; a brief and hearty farewell was all we could spare for friends at home, and in an incredibly short period we were afloat at Harwich, from whence we sailed to Falmouth to await the arrival of other transports. In the course of a few days, the squadron had assembled, and immediately made sail.

We soon found that our destination was Corunna, in the north of Spain. The discovery led to a variety of conjecture, and speculation was busy in marking out the nature of our future service. The general opinion was, that we should not suffer from idleness: eager for the fray, nothing was coveted save a clear stage and no favour; victory was reckoned on as a matter of course, and as to the hardships and disasters of a hostile or contested land, every inch of which was to be fought for, the idea had no existence, or was dismissed as a trifle. Happy ignorance of the future! where prescience itself, unless true wisdom had been added, could only have depressed the mind. I am happy on reflecting that during the whole of our march not a man was missing; no one slinked, and in the future conduct of the 43d, no one, that I ever heard of, deserted his colours or disgraced his country: but out of the many hundred of gallant fellows that then composed our honourable corps, how few were destined to see their native land again! Our voyage was remarkably pleasant, and we landed at the desired haven without danger or loss. The harbour of Corunna is spacious and safe, and the town is defended by batteries and guns mounted at all points. The citadel is also strongly fortified, but both are commanded by heights within a short distance. Within the houses of the inhabitants there is little to suit the taste of an Englishman the weather when I was there, though cold and chilly, seldom produced the sociable sight of a cheerful fire within doors; indeed, I never observed so much as a hearth or stove in which to kindle one. The superstitious contrarieties and absurdities of Papacy have here an unmolested reign. While holidays were observed with punctilious scruples, for which no sound reason could be urged, the Sabbath, though guarded by scriptural injunction, was violated with impunity. The churches are well built, but the altar-pieces are disfigured by a profusion of tinsel and ornament. The Virgin Mary is frequently exhibited in a figure some three feet high, dressed in laced clothing; the saints also keep her company, some being placed in niches of the building, and others enclosed in cases of glass with care proportioned, perhaps to the merit assigned to each by their capricious and fanciful worshippers.

Without in the least entering into political detail connected with the causes and result of the memorable Peninsular campaign, which is not within my present design, it may be enough to state, that the expedition in which I had sailed was planned by the British Government to act in concert with several simultaneous movements in favour of the Spanish Constitutionalists then contending with their French invaders. Our arrival in October, 1808, proved to be a momentous crisis: a few weeks previously, Buonaparte had entered Spain, and taken the command of the hostile army, with the avowed purpose of driving the English into the sea. He advanced as usual by marches prodigiously rapid, on Madrid, so that at the end of November his advanced guard reached the important pass of Somosierra: this pass was defended by 13,000 Spaniards, with sixteen pieces of cannon. They were attacked by the French under the Duke of Belluna, and after a vigorous resistance entirely defeated. On the 2d of December Buonaparte arrived in the vicinity of Madrid, and in three days from that period was master of that capital. Dispirited and overwhelmed as the Spanish generally were by the presence of the hero of Jena and Austerlitz, it was evident they were unable, unless assisted by foreign allies, to resist the advances of such masses of troops as those now within their dominions. British co-operation was therefore sought and obtained. Its value, and the fidelity of the army it employed, had already been proved in Portugal, where, with a force decidedly inferior, the invaders were repulsed at Vimiera, with unusual loss.

As a temporary residence at Corunna, we had been placed in a long uncomfortable building, formerly used as a factory or rope-walk. On the following day marching orders were received, when the entire division was put into motion; and leaving the coast, our route lay through Lugo, Villa Franca, and Bonevente. After halting for a short time, we crossed the Esla, and arrived at Sahagan, where we were ordered to remain. The light corps occupied an extensive convent built on each side of a square, in whose immense galleries several thousand infantry were accommodated: a numerous body of Monks, with other persons of similar sanctity, notwithstanding our heretical exterior, had also taken refuge under the same roof. On leaving the convent, we advanced in close order for several miles; when from the superior force of the enemy, it was judged advisable to retreat. A counter-march by sections was ordered, and just be fore midnight we had fallen back upon the line of our former route. Here we were directed to lighten our knapsacks as much as possible, and divest ourselves of every needless incumbrance. Meantime the advanced guard of Buonvente's army had broken up from Tordesillas, and strong detachments of cavalry had been pushed forward to Majorga. On the 26th Lord Paget fell in with one of these parties at the latter place; his Lordship directly ordered

Colonel Leigh, with two squadrons of the 10th Hussars, to attack this corps, which had halted on the summit of a steep hill. On approaching the top, where the ground was rugged, the Colonel judiciously reined in to refresh the horses, though exposed to a severe fire. When he had nearly gained the summit and the horses had recovered their breath, he charged boldly, and overthrow the enemy; many of whom were killed and wounded, and above a hundred made prisoners. The brigade of which our regiment formed part, was under the command of General Crawford. Just before, or nearly at the moment of, our arrival on the banks of the river Esla, the principal part of the British forces, under Sir John Moore, were rapidly passing; the stores were conveyed by Spanish mules. We were in the rear, and the enemy pressed forward with such impetuosity that the chasseurs of the Imperial Guard were frequently in sight, and, unable perhaps to do more, captured some women and baggage. Exposed as we were to the assault of a vigilant and superior foe, not a moment's repose could be obtained; and it has seldom happened that personal courage has been put to a severer test. Permit me to recite an instance:—John Walton, an Irishman, and Richard Jackson, an Englishman, were posted in a hollow road on the plain beyond the bridge, and at a distance from their piquet. If the enemy approached, one was to fire, run back to the brow of the hill, and give notice if there were many or few; the other was to maintain his ground. A party of cavalry, following a hay-cart, stole up close to these men, and suddenly galloped in, with a view to kill them and surprise the fort. Jackson fired, but was overtaken, and received twelve or fourteen severe wounds in an instant; he came staggering on, notwithstanding his mangled state, and gave the signal. Walton, with equal resolution and more success, defended himself with his bayonet, and wounded several of the assailants, who retreated, leaving him unhurt; but his cap, his knapsack, his belt, and his musket were cut in above twenty places, and his bayonet was bent nearly double, his musket covered with blood, and notched like a saw from the muzzle to the lock. Jackson escaped death in his retreat, and finally recovered of his wounds. On the 27th, the cavalry being all over the river, preparations were made to destroy the bridge: torrents of rain and snow were descending. The cavalry scouts of the enemy were abroad, and a large party, following the store-waggon, endeavoured to pass the piquet, and gallop down to the bridge. The design was perceived and defeated. Smart skirmishing was kept up all the day; but the masonry of the bridge was so solid, that midnight had arrived before the arches could be materially injured. We then descended the heights on the left bank, and passing with the greatest silence by single files over planks laid across the broken arches, gained the other side without loss,—an instance of singular preservation, as the night was dark and tempestuous, and the enemy almost within hearing. The mine was almost immediately after sprung with good effect,—I mean the bridge was ruined; while we marched forward to Benevente, where the cavalry and the reserve still remained. Here we re-entered the convent which had given us protection on a former occasion. During the brief stay made here, we experienced a remarkable escape from imminent danger. The lower corridors of the building were filled with the horses of the cavalry and artillery, so thickly stowed that it was scarcely possible for a single man to pass them, and there was but one entrance. Two officers returning from the bridge, being desirous to find shelter for their men, entered the convent, and with terror perceived that a large window-shutter was on fire. The flame was spreading to the rafter above; in a few moments the straw under the horses would ignite, and six thousand men and animals be involved in inevitable ruin. One of the officers, (Captain Lloyd, of the 43d,) a man of great activity, strength, and presence of mind, made a sign to his companions to keep silence, and springing upon the nearest horse, ran along the backs of the others until he reached the flaming shutter, which he tore off its hinges, and threw out of the window; then returning quickly, he awakened some of the soldiers, and cleared the passage without creating any alarm, which in such a case would have been as destructive as the flames. I scarcely need add, that Captain Lloyd was a man of more than ordinary talent.

The town of Benevente, a rich open place, is remarkable for a small but curious Moorish palace or castle, containing a fine collection of ancient armour, and is situated on an extensive plain, that, extending from the Gallician mountains to the neighbourhood of Burgos, appeared to be boundless. Here the army rested two days; but as little could be done to remove the stores, the greater part was destroyed, of which I was a reluctant eye-witness. I am sorry to say, that during this sojourn, the fine discipline of our corps, thus far maintained without a flaw, was sadly broken down. Some circumstances may be urged in mitigation of the fault, though, looking at that eventful crisis, nothing can altogether extenuate the excesses into which numbers of the troops descended. Exhausted as they were with privation and fatigue, it is no wonder that they were eager in search of repose and refreshment. Unfortunately one of the first objects of attention was an extensive range of vaults, in which pipes of wine were deposited. In such haste were the half-famished men to quench their thirst, that shots were fired at the heads of the casks, which sent them in altogether, so that the choice and heady liquor ran in all directions, and was ankle-deep on the pavement; beside which, and this was the most serious part of the calamity at such a moment, the men, regardless of the potent and intoxicating beverage, drank it like water. The result need not be told; and I have often thought it was a special mercy that at such a juncture the services of the men were not required. Had the enemy approached, no one could have averted the fate of the aggressors. Unable either to fight or fly, they must have fallen into hostile hands, in all the disgrace of impotent inebriety. It has often been to myself a source of satisfaction, that on the occasion referred to I was preserved from the excesses described. Not that I can take credit for possessing at the time any extraordinary measure either of virtuous principle or religious light; yet I was not without a strong sense of duty. The good advices of my mother were frequently uppermost; and many a time, when hard pressed by hunger and perilous service, my mind was supported by a persuasion that my mother was praying for my preservation.

From the temporary mischief alluded to we soon recovered. Sobriety marshalled our ranks as heretofore, and on the 29th the brigade quitted Benevente, but the cavalry remained in the town, leaving parties to watch the fords of the Esla. Soon after day-break, General Lefebre Desnouettes, seeing only a few cavalry-posts on the great plain, rather hastily concluded that there was nothing to support them, and crossing the river at a ford a little way above the bridge, with six hundred horsemen of the Imperial Guards, he advanced into the plain. The piquets at first retired fighting; but being joined by a part of the 3d German Hussars, they charged the leading French squadron with some effect. General C. Stewart then took the command, and the ground was obstinately disputed. At this moment the plain was covered with stragglers, and baggage-mules, and followers of the army; the town was filled with tumult; the distant piquets and videttes were seen galloping in from the right and left; the French were pressing forward boldly, and every appearance indicated that the enemy's whole army was come up, and passing the river. Lord Paget ordered the 10th Hussars to mount and form under the cover of some houses at the edge of the town: he desired to draw the enemy, whose real situation he saw at once, well into the plain before he attacked. In half an hour, every thing being ready, he gave the signal: the 10th Hussars galloped forward, the piquets that were already engaged, closed together, and the whole charged. In an instant the scene changed, the enemy were seen flying at dill speed towards the river, and the British close at their heels. The French squadron, without breaking their ranks, plunged into the stream, and gained the opposite heights, where, like experienced soldiers, they wheeled instantly, and seemed inclined to come forward a second time; but a battery of six guns being opened upon them, after a few rounds, they retired. During the pursuit in the plain, an officer was observed separating from the main body, and making towards another part of the river: being followed, and refusing to stop when overtaken, he was cut across the head, and brought in a prisoner. He proved to be General Lefebre. In this spirited action the French left fifty-five killed and wounded on the field, and seventy prisoners, besides the General, and other officers. The British loss was also severe.

Rencontres of this sort had their value, as they served to curb the audacity of the enemy, and furnished a seasonable sample of what might be expected in the event of a general battle. Meantime the tide of superior force, against whose overpowering number it was physically impossible to present an effective check, came rolling on in waves of gathering might. Napoleon had arrived at

Valderas, Ney at Villator, and Lapisse at Touro. The French troops were worn down with fatigue, yet the Emperor still urged them forward. He flattered himself, and wished to persuade others, that he should intercept the retreat of the English at Astorga; but the destruction of the bridge of Castro Gonzalo had been so complete, that twenty-four hours were required to repair it, and the fords were now impassable. After all, the Emperor, with whom it was never safe to trifle, was near the accomplishment of his design; for scarcely had the rear of the British army quitted Astorga, when advanced parties of French soldiery appeared in view.

Upon the 1st of January, 1809, the Emperor Napoleon took possession of Astorga. On that day seventy thousand French infantry, ten thousand cavalry, and two hundred pieces of artillery, after many days of incessant marching, were thus united. The assemblage of this mighty force, while it evinced the energy of the French Monarch, attested also the genius of the English General, who, with a handful of men, had found means to arrest the course of the conqueror, and to draw him, with the flower of his army, to this remote and unimportant part of the Peninsula, at the moment when Portugal, and the fairest provinces of Spain, were prostrate before him. That Sir John Moore intercepted the blow which was then descending on Spain, no man of honesty can deny; for what troops were there in the south to have resisted even for an instant the progress of a man, who in ten days, and in the depth of winter, crossing the snowy ridge of the Carpentinos, had traversed two hundred miles of hostile country, and transported fifty thousand men from Madrid to Astorga in a shorter time than a Spanish diligence would have taken to travel the same distance? This stupendous march was rendered fruitless by the quickness of the adversary; but Napoleon, though he had failed to destroy the English army, resolved nevertheless to drive it from the Peninsula; and being himself recalled to France by tidings that the Austrian storm was ready to burst, he fixed upon the Duke of Dalmatia to continue the pursuit, adding, for this purpose, three divisions of cavalry, and three of infantry, to his command. This formidable pursuing force was separated into three divisions, and entrusted to the command of Laborde, Heudelet, and Loison; so that after leaving a considerable corps in reserve in the Montagna de St. Andre, nearly sixty thousand men, and ninety-one guns, were put on the track of the English army.

About this period of the retreat an affair took place in the rear which excited the admiration of all who heard of it, and has seldom been exceeded for cool and determined valour under circumstances the most disadvantageous. So rapid were the advances of the British troops on their route to Corunna, that none but men of athletic mould and vigorous health could keep in column. As an unavoidable result, many of the weaker men, and some that had been overtaken by sickness, were at some distance behind. The number of stragglers thus compelled to fall out was nearly five hundred. They were placed under the direction of Sergeant William Newman, no other officer being present. In addition to the personal ailments of these poor fellows, they were little more than half clothed, and many of them barefooted, so that but for their muskets, which they knew how to handle, they exhibited an appearance altogether pitiable and defenceless. Shortly after the army had quitted the village of Betanzos, an alarm was given that the French cavalry was approaching, when the men were instantly thrown into confusion by an eager but fruitless endeavour to overtake the British forces. In this exigence, Sergeant Newman pushed on a little way to a narrow part of the road. He there managed to hasten on the most feeble of the detachment, and detained about a hundred of the best men, whom he ordered to face about and contest the passage. This was promptly done, and with complete success. The little corps of invalids, consisting of soldiers from different regiments, withstood and repelled repeated attacks of the French horsemen. The Sergeant then gave orders to retire, and when again pressed, reformed as before, and again repulsed the enemy. In this spirited manner they covered the retreat .of their helpless comrades for four miles, when they were relieved from their perilous situation by the rear-guard of the British cavalry. It is pleasing to add, that the intrepid Sergeant who led this spirited movement, was promoted to an ensigncy in the 1st West India regiment; besides which, by way of putting him in gentlemanly trim, a gift was added of fifty pounds sterling.

Thus Sir John Moore was pressed in his retreat with fury that seemed to increase every moment. The separation of the light brigade already alluded to, a measure which he adopted by advice of the Quarter-Master General, weakened the army by three thousand men. Fifteen days only had elapsed since Sir John Moore had left Salamanca; and already the torrent of war, diverted from the south, was foaming among the rocks of Gallicia. Nineteen thousand British troops, if posted on strong ground, might have offered battle to very superior numbers; but where was the use of merely fighting an enemy who had three hundred thousand men in Spain? Sir John Moore felt the impolicy and rashness of such an attempt; his resolution therefore was, to fall down to the coast, and embark with as little loss and delay as might be. Vigo, Corunna, and Ferrol were the principal harbours, and their relative advantage could be determined only by the reports of the engineers, none of which had yet been received, so rapidly did the crisis of affairs come on.

It will be imagined by every person, civil or military, that the mind of a Commander, though of the firmest texture, in the situation of Sir John Moore, must have been severely exercised; and during this stage of the retreat the unavoidable difficulties of the army were inflamed by the unhappy intemperance of several who ought to have known and acted better. On arriving at Bembibre, the immense wine-vaults established there exhibited such temptations, that hundreds of the men, unable to exert themselves, or even to stand, were unavoidably left behind. That refreshment was needed, no one can doubt; but it is more difficult to be temperate than abstemious; the first healthful draught led to many an inordinate one. Confusion worse confounded was the necessary result. There was an heterogeneous mass of marauders, drunkards, muleteers, women, and children: the weather was dreadful; and notwithstanding the utmost exertions of the superior officers, when the reserve marched next morning, the number of these unfortunate persons was not diminished. Leaving a small guard to protect this bacchanalian craw, Sir John Moore proceeded to Calcabellos; and scarcely had the reserve marched out of the village, when some French cavalry appeared. In a moment the road was filled with the miserable stragglers, who came crowding after the troops, some with loud shrieks of distress, others with brutal exclamations. Many, overcome with fear, threw away their arms. Many more who preserved theirs, were so stupidly intoxicated that they were unable to fire; and kept reeling to and fro, insensible both to their danger and disgrace. The enemy's horse men, perceiving this confusion, bore down at a gallop, broke through the disorderly mob, cutting to the right and left as they passed, and riding so close to the columns, that the infantry were forced to halt in order to check their forwardness. Nothing, in the nature of things, can be more mischievous, though it endure only for a day, or even half that time, than such a violation of discipline as that recorded. It not only tends to produce discouragement in the ranks of well-ordered troops, whose resolution, founded on mutual support, is by such means sadly assailed, but so far as it is observed, and it can seldom be concealed, it gives proportionate confidence to the enemy, of which, on this very occasion, there was almost instantaneous proof. On the 3d of January, 1809, just after mid-day, the French General, Colbert, approached with six or eight squadrons; but observing the ground behind Calcabellos strongly occupied, he demanded reinforcements. Marshal Soult, believing the English did not mean to make a stand, sent orders to Colbert to charge without delay. The latter, stung by the message, which he thought conveyed an imputation on his courage, obeyed with precipitate fury. The Riflemen had withdrawn when the French first came in sight, and were just passing the bridge when a crowd of staff officers, the cavalry, and the enemy, came in upon them in one mass. In the confusion, thirty or forty men were taken; and Colbert, crossing the river, charged on the spur up the road. The remainder of the Riflemen threw themselves into the vineyards, and permitting the enemy to approach within a few yards, suddenly opened such a deadly fire, that the greater number of the French horsemen were killed on the spot, and among the rest Colbert himself. His fine martial figure, his voice, his gestures, and, above all, his daring valour, had excited the admiration of the British, and a general feeling of sorrow prevailed when he fell, The French Voltigeurs then crossed the river, and a smart skirmish was maintained, in which two or three hundred men on both sides were killed or wounded. Night put an end to the combat.

The reserve at length reached Nogales, having by a forced march of thirty-six miles gained twelve hours' start of the enemy; but at this period of retreat the road was crowded with stragglers and baggage; the peasantry, although armed, did not molest the French; but fearing both sides alike, drove their cattle and carried away their effects into the mountains on each side of the line of march. Under the most favourable circumstances, the drooping portion of a retreating force indicates sensible distress; and on the road near Nogales the followers of the army were dying fast from cold and hunger. The soldiers, barefooted, harassed, and weakened by their excesses at Bembibre and Villa Franca, were dropping to the rear by hundreds. Broken carts, dead animals, and the piteous appearance of women with children, struggling or falling in the snow, completed the picture of war and its desolating results. On the evening of the 4th the French recovered their lost ground, and passed Nogales, galling the rear-guard with a continual skirmish. Here it was that dollars to the amount of twenty-five thousand pounds were abandoned. This small sum was kept near head-quarters, to answer sudden emergencies; and the bullocks that drew it being tired, the General, who could not save the money without risking an ill-timed action, had it rolled down the side of a mountain. Part of it was gathered by the enemy, and part by the Gallician peasantry.

After exchanging several shots with the enemy, wherever appearances called for resistance, the army retired to Lugo, in front of which the entire force was assembled; and on the 7th of January Sir John Moore announced his intention to offer battle. Scarcely was the order issued, when the line of battle, hitherto so peeled and spread abroad, was filled with vigorous men, full of confidence and courage. At day-break on the 8th the two armies were still embattled. On the French side seventeen thousand infantry, four thousand cavalry, and fifty pieces of artillery were in line; but Soult deferred the attack till the 9th. On the English side sixteen thousand infantry, eighteen hundred cavalry, and forty pieces of artillery, awaited the assault. No advance was, however, made;

darkness fell without a shot being fired; and with it the English General's hope of engaging his enemy on equal terms.

This was a season of singular and almost unexampled peril. The French were posted on the declivity of a precipitous range of mountains with a numerous body of cavalry to protect their infantry, wherever necessary. Besides this, twenty thousand fresh troops were at the distance of two short marches in the rear. Then it should be considered that the British army was not in a condition to fight more than one battle. It was unprovided with draught cattle, had no means of transporting reserve ammunition, no magazines, no hospitals, no second line, no provisions. In the opinion of competent judges a defeat would have been irretrievably ruinous, and a victory of no real use. Some have suggested that Sir John Moore might have remained longer in expectation of a battle. That was not only inexpedient, but impossible. The state of the magazine; decided the matter; for there was not bread for another day's consumption in the stores at Lugo. It is true the soldiers ware at the moment in fighting mood; but want of necessary food would have deprived them of physical energy; so that to expose an army of gallant but starving men to the uncertain issue of an obstinate and probably prolonged engagement, would not only have been absurd in policy, but have amounted to a wanton and unmeaning waste of human life. An effort, therefore, to gain a march as quietly as possible, and get on board without molestation, or at least so to establish the army as to cover the embarkation, was the most, if not the only, reasonable proposition to which prudence ought to listen. The General adopted this third plan and prepared to decamp in the night. He ordered the fires to be kept bright, and exhorted the troops to make a great effort, which he trusted would be the last required of them. The face of the country immediately in the rear of the position was intersected by stone walls, and a number of intricate lanes. Precautions were taken to mark the right track by placing bundles of straw at certain distances, and officers were appointed to guide the columns. At ten o'clock the troops silently quitted their ground, and retired in excellent order; but at this critical juncture a terrible storm of wind and rain arose, so that the marks were destroyed, and the guides lost the true direction.

Only one of the divisions gained the main road; the other two were bewildered; and when day-light broke, the rear columns were still near Lugo. The fatigue and depression of mind occasioned by this misfortune, and the want of shoes especially, contributed to break the order of the march, and the stragglers were becoming numerous, when, unhappily, one of the Generals commanding a leading division, thinking to relieve the men during a nightly halt, desired them to take refuge from the weather in some houses a little way off the road. Complete disorder followed this untimely indulgence: from that moment it became impossible to make the soldiers of the division keep their ranks; and in this disastrous condition the main body of the army, which had bivouacked for six hours in the rain, arrived at Betanzb on the evening of the 9th. During the two following days Sir John Moore was indefatigable in restoring the needful order and discipline. He assembled the army in one solid mss. The loss of men in the march from Lugo to Betanzos had been greater than in all the former part of the retreat; so that the infantry then in column did not much exceed fourteen thousand men.

As the troops approached Corunna, many an anxious look was directed towards the harbour. *Nothing was to be discovered but the wide waste of water.* The painful truth became evident, that contrary winds had detained at Vigo the fleet on board of whose ships the forces sought to embark; so that after one of the severest and most prolonged tests to which human endurance could be submitted, and the consuming exertions, pushed on through storm and tempest, of many wearisome days, the whole was rendered nugatory by an event over which human foresight or power had no control; and the point to which they had fought their way, instead of presenting the means of effectual retreat, became a *cul de sac*, or place leading no where. The men were immediately put into quarters, and their leader awaited the progress of events. Three divisions occupied the town and suburbs: the reserve was posted with its left at the village of El Burgo, and its right on the road of St. Jago de Compostella. For twelve days these hardy soldiers had covered the retreat, during which time they had traversed eighty miles of road in two marches, passed several nights under arms in the snow of the mountains, were seven times engaged with the enemy; and they now assembled at the outposts, having fewer men missing from the ranks than any other division of the army. The bridge of El Bingo was immediately destroyed, and an engineer was sent to blow up that of Combria, situated a few miles up the Mero river. This officer was mortified at the former failures, and so anxious to perform his duty in an effectual manner, that he remained too near the mine, and was killed by the explosion. This was followed by the destruction of an immense quantity of combustible material. Three miles from the town four thousand barrels of powder were piled in a magazine built on a hill; a smaller quantity collected in another storehouse was at some distance from the first: to prevent these magazines from falling into the hands of the enemy, they were both fired on the 13th. The inferior one blew up with a terrible noise, and shook the houses in the town; but when the train reached the great store, there ensued a crash like the bursting forth of a volcano; the earth trembled for miles; the rocks were torn from their bases, and the agitated waters rolled the vessels as in a storm. A vast column of smoke and dust, shooting out fiery sparks from its sides, arose perpendicularly and slowly to a great height, and then a shower of stones and fragments of all kinds bursting out of it with a roaring sound, killed several persons who remained too near the spot. A stillness, interrupted only by the lashing of the waves on the shore, succeeded, and the business of the war went on.

The plot now rapidly thickened. Hemmed in by the gathering forces of the numerous French corps, whose advance had been hastened by prodigious sacrifices, both of men and means, the handful of British troops, thinned by recent losses, and worn down by the length of a harassed and contested march, were now cooped within the surface of a few square miles. Negotiation with the enemy, having for its object the permissive embarkation of the army, had been intimated to the Commander by some of the officers as a prudent step, under the continued and increasing difficulties of the army, but was properly rejected, with that high spirit and clear judgment which was safely founded on an intimate knowledge of the army he commanded, and the resistance it could offer, even in its dangerous and unfavourable position. The enemy having collected in force on the Mero, it became necessary to choose a position of battle. A chain of rocky elevations, commencing on the sea-coast, and ending on the Mero, just behind the village of El Burgo, offered an advantageous line of defence; but this ridge was too extensive for the British army, and, if not wholly occupied, the French might have turned it by the right, and moved along a succession of eminences to the gates of Corunna. There was no alternative but to take post on an inferior range, enclosed, as it were, within the other, and completely commanded by it within cannon shot. The French army had been so exhausted by toil, that it was not completely assembled on the Mero before the 12th. The same evening the expected transports from Vigo hove in sight, and soon after entered the harbour of Corunna; and the dismounted cavalry, the sick, all the best of the horses, and fifty-two pieces of artillery, were embarked during the night: eight British and four Spanish guns were, however, retained on shore, ready for action. Towards evening on the 15th, the English piquets opposite the right of the French got engaged, and being galled by the fire of two guns, Colonel M'Kenzie, of the 5th, at the head of some companies, endeavoured to seize the battery, when a line of infantry, hitherto concealed by some stone walls, arose, and poured in such a fire of musketry, that the Colonel was killed, and his men forced back with loss.

The morning of the 16th at length arose. All the incumbrances of the army had been shipped on the preceding night, and every measure that prudence could suggest was adopted for the safe and expeditious embarkation of the men, whenever the darkness would permit them to move without being perceived; but about two o'clock in the afternoon every one saw that these preparations, though skilfully arranged, would not then be required. A general movement along the French line gave notice of immediate action, and nothing remained on our side but to give them a proper reception. The British infantry, fourteen thousand five hundred strong, occupied the inferior range of hills already named. The French force could not be less than twenty thousand men; and the Duke of Dalmatia, having made his disposition, lost little time in idle evolutions. His lighter guns being distributed along the front of his line, a heavy fire was opened from the battery on his left, when three solid masses of infantry led to the assault. A cloud of skirmishers led the way, and the British piquets being driven back in disorder, the village of Elvina was carried by the first column, which afterwards dividing, one half pushed on against Baird's front, the other turned his right by the valley. The second column made for the centre. The third engaged the left by the village of Palavia Abaxo. The weight of the French guns overmatched the English six-pounders, and their shot swept the position to the centre. The ground about the village of Elvina was intersected by stone walls and hollow roads: a severe scrambling fight ensued, but in half an hour the French were borne back with great loss. The 50th regiment entered the village with them, and after a second struggle, drove them to some distance beyond it. Meanwhile the General, bringing up a battalion of the brigade of Guards to fill the space in the line left vacant by those two regiments, the 42d mistook his intentions, and at that moment the enemy, being reinforced, renewed the fight beyond the village; the officer commanding the 50th was wounded and taken prisoner, and Elvina became the scene of another struggle. This being observed by the Commander-in-Chief, he addressed a few animating words to the 42d, and caused it to return to the attack. General Paget, with the reserve, now descended into the valley, and the line of skirmishers, being thus supported, vigorously checked the advance of the enemy's troops in that quarter, while the 4th regiment galled their flank. A furious action now ensued along the entire line, in the valley, and on the hills.

Sir John Moore, while earnestly watching the result of the battle about the village of Elvina, was struck on the left breast by a cannon shot. The shock threw him from his horse with violence. He rose again in a sitting posture. His eye was still fixed on the regiments engaged in his front; and in a few moments, when he was satisfied that the troops were gaining ground, his countenance brightened, and he suffered himself to be taken to the rear. The dreadful nature of the injury he had received was then noticed; the shoulder was shattered in pieces, and the muscles of the breast torn into long strips, which were interlaced by their recoil from the strain and dragging of the shot. As the soldiers placed him in a blanket his sword got entangled, and the hilt entered the wound. Captain Hardinge, a staff officer, who was near, attempted to take it off; but the dying man stopped him, saying, "*It is as well as it is. I had rather it should go out of the field with me.*" In that manner Sir John was borne from the fight.

During this time the army was rapidly gaining ground. The reserve, overthrowing every thing in the valley, and obliging Houssaye's dragoons, who had dismounted, to retire, turned the enemy's left, and even approached the eminence upon which the great battery was erected. On the left, Colonel Nicholls, at the head of some companies of the 14th, carried Palavia Abaxo, and in the centre the obstinate dispute for Elvina terminated in favour of the British; so that when the night set in, their line was considerably beyond the position of the morning, and the French were falling back in confusion. On the other hand, to continue the action in the dark was a dangerous experiment; for the French were still the most numerous, and their ground was strong. The disorder they were in, offered so favourable an opportunity to get on board the ships, that Sir John Hope, upon whom the command of the army had devolved, satisfied with having repulsed the attack, judged it more prudent to pursue the original plan of embarking during the night: that operation was effected without delay the arrangements being complete, no confusion or difficulty occurred. The piquets kindling a number of fires covered the retreat of the columns, and were themselves withdrawn at day-break, and embarked under the protection of General Hill's brigade, which was posted near the ramparts of the town. When the morning dawned, the French, observing that the British had abandoned their position, pushed forward some battalions to the height of St. Lucie, and succeeded in establishing a battery, which, playing upon the shipping in the harbour; caused a great deal of disorder among the transports. Several masters cut their cables, and four vessels went on shore; but the troops being immediately removed by the men-of-war's boats, the stranded vessels were burnt, and the whole fleet at last got away. Thus ended the retreat to Corunna. From the spot where he fell, the General who commanded it was carried to the town by a party of soldiers; the blood flowed fast, and the torture of the wound increased, but such was the firmness of his mind that those about him expressed a hope that his hurt was not mortal. Hearing this, he looked steadfastly at the injury for a moment, and then said, "No, I feel that to be impossible." Several times he caused his attendants to stop and turn him round, that he might behold the field of battle; and when the firing indicated the advance of the British, he expressed his satisfaction, and permitted the bearers to proceed. Being brought to his lodgings, the surgeons examined the wound; but there was no hope: the pain increased, and he spake with great difficulty. His countenance continued firm, and his thoughts clear; only once, when he spake of his mother, he became agitated. The fight was scarcely ended, when his corpse, wrapped in a military cloak, was interred by the officers of his staff in the citadel of Corunna. The guns of the enemy paid his funeral honours; and Soult, with a noble feeling of respect for his valour, raised a monument to his memory.

Through the whole of this eventful retreat, I was mercifully preserved from grievous injury. The privations of the army were shared by all; and to these I was no stranger. Many miles of road through which our route lay were nearly deserted by the inhabitants, who, unknowing whom to trust, were afraid both of friend and foe: hence arose great scarcity of provisions. It often happened that long before we had appeared, tidings of our approach had induced the entire population of the district to disappear, and with it all vestiges of food. Wine might occasionally be obtained, and sometimes in profusion; but I had observed that when our men had indulged in strong liquor, with little or no solid food, the effect was injurious, so that on the following day, when the excitement had subsided, they were unable to keep our pace: diminished strength thus compelled them to drop off, and not a few were actually picked up by the French who hung on our rear. Another serious difficulty arose from the circumstance that our retreat was conducted in winter: the roads for an immense distance had been torn into deep ruts by the wheels of the baggage-waggons and cannon, and rendered rough by the trampling of cavalry horses; severe frost then set in, when the rough and rugged surface was suddenly hardened into ice. Meantime my shoes were worn out, and as they would no longer hold together, I was compelled to march bare-footed: this was severe, and the sensation produced was singularly painful. In the frozen condition of the ground every step seemed to place my feet on flint: scarcely able to move, and yet forbidden to stay, the Sergeant of my company, a worthy fellow, proposed to lend me a pair of shoes, but his kindness was unavailing; on attempting to put them on, they would not fit my feet. How it was that I was sustained under these difficulties, I knew not then; but now I know: the Almighty was my support, though I was heedless of his help. "His arm unseen conveyed me safe;" and I feel at this moment some satisfaction, which I hope may be pardoned, that though heavily pressed with the sufferings of those days, I never fell out of the line of march, or impeded the public service by imbecility of purpose, or disposition to flinch from duty. Previous to embarkation I was provided with the article needed; and, praised be the Lord, I have never wanted a pair of shoes from that day to this. On getting into the boat which conveyed me on board the ship, determined to forget my former vexations, I threw my old shoes into the sea, and there, like my past troubles, they were soon out of sight and forgotten.

CHAPTER IV

DURING a violent snow-storm, which overtook us on our march upon Corunna, several of my comrades, and myself among the rest, wearied with fatigue, took refuge one evening in a small out-house or hovel, as it afforded temporary shelter from the descending storm. There we resolved to pass the night; and having gathered a few sticks, we placed them in the middle of the shed, and kindled a fire for mutual benefit. In the course of the night we were surprised by hearing a rap at the door, accompanied by the weak tone of some one craving admission. Half a dozen voices instantly exclaimed, "Come in:" when, lo! a woman, recognised as the wife of a soldier, but hardly able to stand, crept into the shed, and asked protection from the hurricane that was loudly howling along the sierra: had Satan himself begged an entrance at such a moment, we should scarcely have been able to repress our pity. The poor wandering woman was received with rough but honest sympathy, and was invited to approach the fire. When able to speak she asked for a certain company, to which her husband belonged: we told her it was considerably in advance, and at present out of her reach. Modesty prevented the poor creature from further explanation; when; to the surprise of the men present, the weak cry of a child was heard. The fact was, the mother had in the course of the preceding day given birth to an infant while on the snowy ridge of a desolate mountainous tract, and without the company of a single human being: and yet, so far all was well:—there is One who tempers the wind to the shorn lamb. The life both of the mother and her offspring was whole; and though in a condition so extraordinary, they were likely to survive. English soldiers know how to feel, nor are they quite destitute of discretion; they may be rather rough in manner, nor can they at all times invent the

phraseology of oily compliment; but they have no part of the
bear about them except the skin, unless provoked, and then the
consequences must be abided: when virtue is in distress, none
can show sympathy with greater delicacy, or exercise benevolence
with more perfect freedom. At the appearance and sad tale of
this suffering daughter of affliction, every heart in the place was
touched: wretched as was our own condition, each man contrived
to spare something. They even parted with some article of their
own linen, much as they needed it, for the purpose of contributing
to the warmth and comfort of the sufferer: kindness of speech was
added, and it did wonders. While on our march the following day
the woman, again on her feet, was observed by one of our officers:
he was told the story of her distress, and, with kindness which none
but a great and gallant heart possesses, he alighted from his horse
and tramped with us in favour of the poor woman and child. The
animal, like his master, joined in the scheme, and carried his novel
load most comfortably. I rejoice to add, that both root and branch
were preserved, and eventually transplanted in the soil at home.

Let me be permitted here to relate the particulars of another
circumstance, the truth of which is attested by evidence which
none need doubt. But it will be as well to premise at once, that if
the fact to be disclosed should meet the eye of any person disposed
to deny the doctrine of a particular Providence, overseeing and
directing the concerns of men, to bring down the lofty, to raise
the lowly, and support the weak and feeble, the detail will be
unworthy of notice, as the instruction it conveys is based upon
the belief that from the rapt seraph that burns before the throne,
to the minutest particle of dust borne upon the eddying gale,
and in and through the all but infinite gradations of rational and
instinctive beings which lie between, al mighty goodness provides
and metes out its dispensations with justest weight and measure.
Not long before our arrival at Corunna, and in the severest part
of the retreat, Surgeon Griffith, of the Dragoons, while riding at
a rapid pace, observed a woman with a child, reclining on the
snow: the weather was tempestuous, and the advanced posts of the
enemy not far in the rear. Humanity, however, compelled him to
notice the unfortunate female: he immediately reined in his horse

and dismounted, when he discovered with regret, that the woman now stretched upon the ground had just breathed her last. She had dropped, no doubt, and perished like many others from mere exhaustion; while the infant, all unconscious of the calamity, had nestled his head close to the cold bosom of his hapless mother, and was endeavouring to suck as heretofore. The melancholy spectacle had now fully aroused the compassion of the horseman, and as relief came too late for the parent, he determined if possible to save the child. He accordingly lifted him up, and after placing him comfortably on the saddle, again mounted and rode on. The apprehended danger was soon realized: having lost time by this merciful act, he was overtaken by the enemy's cavalry, by whom he and the child were captured and ordered to the rear. This good Samaritan was, however, faithful to his charge, and he and the infant, though prisoners, were inseparable companions. After being detained so time in France, and having visited Paris, Griffith obtained his liberty on parole, and proceeded to England. The tender little child had by this time grown into a healthy boy, and was placed by the interest of his benefactor in the Military Asylum at Chelsea. Even here his kind attentions were continued; he generally paid the lad a Sabbath-day visit, and never failed to bring him a present either for his instruction or amusement, not forgetting to line his pocket with a little of the needful for passing exigencies. About three years after the occurrence just related, a soldier who had lost his wife and child in Spain, came to the Asylum at Chelsea to inquire concerning the welfare of a son of his named Hector, who had been previously placed in the establishment. The veteran had not long been engaged in conversation with Hector when the attention of the former was excited by the appearance of a younger lad, in whose countenance there were lines on which his sight seemed to be unavoidably riveted. On consideration, the features were more familiar than ever: the thought then arose, "Perhaps this may be my long-lost child who I deemed had perished in the snow." The father recollected that on a particular place just above one of the knees, his child had a scar; and on raising the boy's trousers, there it was! The two brothers, though unknown, had been playfellows, and were mutually attached. The delights of this singular recognition may be better conceived than described. Let us hope that a life so remarkably preserved was well spent. How justly might the father exclaim, "This my son, who was dead, is alive again; and he who was lost is found!"

On the 18th of January, 1809, we left the shores of Spain, and made the voyage home on board the Hindostan, of sixty-four guns, which had been partially cut down and prepared as a transport. We encountered several heavy gales during the passage, but were mercifully preserved from a watery grave. It was on a Sabbath evening that the Light-house near Plymouth became visible from deck: it is built on a ledge of rock, about eighteen miles from the harbour, and gave us cheering proof that we were nearing the land we loved. After remaining at anchor for a short time, it was judged advisable to proceed up the Channel; we accordingly weighed, and stood for Portsmouth, at which place the shattered remains of our regiment were safely landed. Aware of the deplorable figure we made, the debarkation was cleverly effected under cover of the night. The pride which urged this method was, I trust, excusable: such a legion of ragged warriors I should think never before approached this or any other land; we were therefore glad to escape observation, and march quickly into barracks. Our old clothes, by far too! bad for amendment, were speedily burned, together with a countless company of Spanish insects thereunto appertaining, and which, to our oft-repeated sorrow, we were never able fully to eject. A few weeks' residence on shore restored us to society and our friends; and in a period of time marvellously short we held ourselves ready for ser vice either at home or abroad.

Time rolled rapidly away, and though our stay in England was extended to the space of several months, such was the buoyancy of our spirits, and the general hilarity, that it had passed like a summer's day. The business of recruiting our ranks had gone on so rapidly that by the end of May we mustered a thousand rank and file; nor were our a in the least danger of contracting rust: firing at a target was an every day exercise; field-days were frequently appointed, and the note of warlike preparation was familiar and agreeable. I am sorry to say that my boasting can not extend to the morals of my friends. Cards and dice, with other games of chance, connected with the intemperance and dissipation of which they are the usual forerunners, consumed the time of most of those by whom I was surrounded. From these excesses I was preserved; and if asked by what means, I can only reply, that I felt an aversion to such practices, grounded, I firmly believe, upon the advices once received from my honoured mother, which as a warning and monitory voice pursued and protected me through life, and by which, though far away, she seemed to speak the words of wisdom. The regularity of my conduct, as a private soldier, attracted the notice of the officers, and I had the satisfaction of hearing that there was some probability of an elevation from the place I held in the ranks to that of a Corporal in the British army,—a distinction to which my wishes were earnestly directed. Having remained some time at Colchester, orders were received towards the close of May to march to the coast. We accordingly proceeded to Harwich, and immediately embarked. With the exception of the inconveniences arising from crowded berths, and provisions of very defective quality, nothing occurred to ruffle the good humour that prevailed between decks during the passage. In little more than thirty days from the time of leaving home we were released from our confinement on ship-board. It was a pleasing sound when the man on look-out exclaimed, "Land a-head." In the course of a few hours we passed the castle of St. Julian, and soon after rode at anchor in the Tagus, from whence we were conveyed in boats to Villa Franca and Santarem. The latter is a fine large town, commanding a noble view of the adjacent country. The weather was extremely hot, and water scarce. Wine was cheap, three pints of which could be obtained for about fourpence. Anxious to form a junction with the forces under Sir Arthur Wellesley, who, it was rightly conjectured, might be engaged with the enemy, our march was urged by every possible means. We suffered in consequence very severely. Over head the scorching rays of an almost vertical sun appeared to wither the face of nature, while the hot sand on which we trod blistered and inflamed our feet. By uncommon exertion we reached Abrantes, where we found a small encampment, formerly occupied, but hastily abandoned, by the French. Ready to drop as most of us were, the halt, though short, was grateful, and of great value. After a brief stay, our march was renewed with greater speed than before; and as the nights were comparatively cool, we advanced without intermission. Proofs that hard fighting had commenced now crowded on us on every side. We met several dastardly renegade Spaniards, who asserted that the British forces were defeated, and all was lost. Scattered groups of men were also occasionally seen silently retiring. The muttering of distant artillery had been heard for some time; but these indications of actual contest, so far from dispiriting our party, called forth redoubled exertions to press forward. Our pace increased to a kind of impetuous movement, which, by tacit agreement, was to be neither retarded nor turned aside. The result was, that though three thousand strong, with the exception of seventeen stragglers left behind, one of whom was well thrashed with some olive-twigs for leaving the ranks, we had, in twenty-six hours crossed the field of battle in a close and compact body, and passed over sixty-two English miles, in the hottest season of the year, each man carrying from fifty to sixty pounds weight upon his shoulders. It is not for me to boast; but if this was not stepping out with spirit, I should like to know what is.

Our arrival was hailed as an auspicious omen; for though too late to take any part in the battle of Talavera, which had just been fought, our presence served to exhilarate the army, which, though victorious, required support. The fight had been well sustained on both sides. From nine o'clock in the morning until mid-day the field of battle offered no appearance of hostility; the weather was intensely hot, and the troops on both sides descended and mingled, without fear or suspicion, to quench their thirst at the little brook which divided the positions; but at one o'clock in the afternoon the French soldiers were seen to gather round their eagles, and the rolling of drums was heard along the whole line. Half an hour later the Guards of King Joseph, the reserve, and the 4th corps, were descried near the centre of the enemy's position, marching to join the 1st corps; and at two o'clock the table-land, and the height on the French right, even to the valley, were covered with the dark and lowering masses. The Duke of Belluno, whose arrangements

were now completed, gave the signal for battle; and eighty pieces
of artillery immediately sent out a tempest of bullets before the
light troops, who, coming on swiftly, and with the violence of a
hailstorm, were closely followed by the broad black columns, in all
the majesty of war.

Sir Arthur Wellesley, from the summit of the hill, had a clear
view of the entire scene of action. He saw the 4th corps rush
forward with the usual celerity of French soldiers, and, clearing
the intrenched ground in their front, fall upon Campbell's division
with prodigious fury; but that General, assisted by Mackenzie's
brigade, and by two Spanish battalions, withstood their utmost
efforts. The English regiments putting the French skirmishers aside,
met the advancing columns with loud shouts, and, breaking in on
their front, and lapping their flanks with fire, and giving no respite,
pushed them back with terrible carnage. Ten guns were taken; but,
as General Campbell prudently forbore pursuit, the French rallied
on their supports, and made a show of attacking again, but did not
attempt it. The British artillery and musketry were directed with
vehement accuracy against their masses, and a Spanish regiment of
cavalry charging on their flank at the same time, the whole retired
in disorder, and the victory was secured in that quarter. The next
grand attack was directed to the English centre, which was thrown
into great confusion, and for some time completely broken. The
fate of the day for some moments seemed to incline in favour
of the French, when suddenly Colonel Donellan, with the 48th
regiment, was seen advancing through the midst of the disordered
masses. At first it appeared as if this regiment must be carried away
by the retiring crowds; but, wheeling back by companies, it let them
pass through the intervals, and then, resuming its firm and beautiful
line, marched against the right of the pursuing columns, plied them
with such a destructive musketry, and closed upon them with
a pace so regular and steady, that the forward movement of the
French was checked. The Guards and the Germans immediately
rallied; a brigade of light cavalry came up from the second line at a
trot; the artillery battered the enemy's flanks without intermission,
and the French, beginning to waver, soon lost their advantage, and
the battle was restored. The annals of warfare often tell us that in

all actions there is one critical and decisive moment which will give the victory to the General who knows how to discover and secure it. When the Guards first made their rash charge, Sir Arthur Wellesley, foreseeing the issue of it, had ordered the 48th down from the hill, although a rough battle was going on there, and at the same time he ordered Cotton's light cavalry to advance. These dispositions gained the day. The French relaxed their efforts by degrees; the fire of the English grew hotter; and their loud and confident shouts, sure augury of success, were heard along the whole line. The French army soon after retired to the position from whence it had descended to the attack. This retrograde movement was covered by skirmishers, and increasing fire of artillery ; and the British, reduced to less than fourteen thousand men, and exhausted by toil and want of food, were unable to pursue. The battle was scarcely over when the dry grass and shrubs taking fire, a volume of flame passed with inconceivable rapidity across a part of the field, scorching in its course both the dead and wounded. The loss of the British in the course of this severe action and previous skirmishing was upwards of six thousand men killed and wounded. That of the French, as afterwards appeared in a manuscript of Marshal Jourdan, was rather more than seven thousand three hundred.

The following morning presented a choice of disagreeables. Having taken a position along the battle field somewhat in advance of the British line, we were surrounded with the dying and the dead. The number of the latter was hourly increasing. Combatants who had mingled in the fray, belonging to either army, lay intermingled in frightful heaps. Many of the bodies, though exposed only for so short a time to the sun's rays, were offensively putrid and discoloured, so that interment without ceremony or distinction became necessary for the safety of the living. Meantime provisions were scanty, the water we had to drink was stagnant, the heat of the weather increased, and the enemy was hastily concentrating in great force in the vicinity. The 30th of July was passed by Sir Arthur in establishing hospitals at Talavera, and in fruitless endeavours to procure food, and the help required to keep the wounded men from perishing. On this occasion the Spanish behaved infamously. Not an inhabitant, although possessing ample means, would render the slightest aid, nor even assist to bury the dead. The corn secreted in Talavera alone was sufficient to support the army for a month; but the troops were starving, although the inhabitants, who had fled across the Tagus with their portable effects at the beginning of the battle, had returned. This conduct left an indelible impression on the minds of the English soldiers. From that period their contempt and dislike of the Spaniards were never effaced. The principal motive in war with these people was personal rancour: hence those troops who had behaved so ill in action, and the inhabitants, who alike withheld their sympathy and their aid from the English soldiers, to whose bravery they owed the preservation of their town, were busily engaged after the battle in beating out the brains of the wounded French, as they lay upon the field; and they were only checked by the English soldiers, who, in some instances, fired upon the perpetrators of this horrible iniquity.

Hitherto the allied Generals had paid little attention to the Duke of Dalmatia's movements; but on the 30th of July information was received that he had entered Placentia at the head of an imposing force. The danger of the British on account of their numerical inferiority was extreme; in fact, the fate of the Peninsula was suspended on a thread, which the events of a few hours might dissever; and yet it was so ordered that no irreparable disaster ensued. The Generals on each side at length became acquainted with each other's strength; and this, it will be believed, was a moment of extreme peril for the British. Their progress was barred in front, the Tagus was on their left, impassable mountains on their right, and it was certain that the retreat of the Spanish would bring down the King and Victor upon their rear. In this trying moment Sir Arthur Wellesley abated nothing of his usual calmness and fortitude. He knew not the full extent of the danger; but assuming the enemy in his front to be thirty thousand men, and Victor to have twenty-five thousand others in his rear, he judged that to continue the offensive would be rash, because he must fight and defeat those two Marshals separately within three days, which, with starving and tired troops, inferior in number, was scarcely to be accomplished. The movements of

Sir Arthur were executed with precision and success. About noon, the road being clear, the columns marched to the bridge, and at two o'clock the whole army was in position on the other side; the present danger was therefore averted, and the combinations of the enemy baffled. Our sufferings during these rapid transitions were almost intolerable. During the passage several herds of swine were met with, feeding in the woods, when the soldiers ran in among the animals, shooting, stabbing, and, like men possessed, cutting off the flesh while the beasts were yet alive. Well has it been said that hunger will break through stone walls. I had carried a sheaf of wheat for many miles on my knapsack, rubbing the ears when opportunity offered between my hands, and eating the extracted grain with rapture. At night, by way of a feast, I used to thrash a little more, by bruising the grain, having first laid my great-coat on the ground for the purpose. On one occasion a comrade, by great exertion, procured a small quantity of bullock's blood. We agreed to boil it for dinner, and halve it between us. We did so; and, though unaided even by a bit of salt, I thought it delicious. These privations occurred in our passage through an elevated and open tract of country, where shelter from the sultry heat could hardly be procured. One of these spots we called Mount Misery. Many a time we have breakfasted upon the acorns or oak-nuts beaten down by the Spanish swineherds for the use of the hogs. A goat's offal sold at this time for four dollars, or about double the usual price of the whole animal; and men and officers strove to outbid each other in the purchase of this wretched pittance. In one word, famine raged through the camp; and it was notorious that the Spanish cavalry intercepted the provisions and forage destined for the English army, and fired upon the foragers, as if they had been enemies. From Arzobispo the army moved towards Deleytoza; and our brigade, with six pieces of artillery, was directed to gain the bridge of Almarez by a forced march, lest the enemy, discovering the ford below that place, should cross the river, and seize the Puerto de Mirabete. The roads were rugged, and the guns could be drawn only by the force of men. The movement was, however, effected. The Spaniards under Albuquerque were not equally successful. The infantry were sleeping or loitering about without care or thought, when Mortier, who was charged with the direction of the attack, taking advantage of their want of vigilance, commenced the passage of the river. The French cavalry, about six thousand in number, were secretly assembled near the ford, and about two o'clock in the day General Caulincourt's brigade suddenly entered the stream. The Spanish, running to their arms, manned the batteries, and opened upon the leading squadrons; but Mortier, with a powerful concentric fire of artillery, overwhelmed the Spanish gunners, and dispersed the infantry who attempted to form. On the 20th of August the main body of the British army quitted Jaraicejo, and marched by Truxillo upon Merida. Our brigade, under General Crauford, being relieved at Almarez by the Spaniards, took the road of Caceres to Valencia de Alcantara; but the pass of Mirabete discovered how much we had suffered. Our brigade, which only a few weeks before, had traversed sixty miles in a single march, were now with difficulty, and after many halts, only able to reach the summit of the Mirabete, although only four miles from the camp; and the side of that mountain was covered with baggage, and the carcases of many hundred animals that died in the ascent. In this eventful campaign of two months, the loss of the army was considerable. Above three thousand five hundred men had been killed, or had died of sickness, or had fallen into the hands of the enemy. Fifteen hundred horses had perished for want of food; and, to fill the bitter cup, the pestilent fever of the Guadiana, assailing those who by fatigue and bad nourishment were predisposed to disease, made frightful ravages. Dysentery, that scourge of armies, also raged, and in a short time above five thousand men died in the hospitals.

Passing by the details of successive conflicts sustained with unequal success by the Spanish forces in opposing their invaders, it may be sufficient generally to state, that their inability to maintain the defensive positions assumed, without English cooperation, was evident. An attempt was at length made by the French forces, under Marshal Victor, to gain possession of Cadiz, situate in the Isle of Leon, in Andalusia, the finest port in Spain, with a mercantile and wealthy population of an hundred and fifty thousand inhabitants. For this purpose preparations of

extraordinary magnitude were made. The assaulting army was
spread quite round the margin of the harbour. Works of contrav-
allation were constructed not less than twenty-five miles in extent,
and strong batteries frowned upon the city wherever they could
be erected with advantage to the besiegers. The lines of blockade
were connected by a covered way concealed by thick woods, and
when finished mounted three hundred guns. On the other hand,
the Spanish troops under Albuquerque, composing the garrison,
were in a miserable condition. The whole had been long without
pay, and the greater part without arms or accoutrements. Men
were placed in command destitute of energy or local influence,
and private traffic was unblushingly pursued with the public stores.
Albuquerque was afterwards sent Ambassador to England, where
he died soon after of a phrenzy, brought on, it is said, by grief and
passion at the unworthy treatment he received. In this deplorable
state of affairs, British troops again appeared, and the surrender
of the city by that means was averted. On the 11th of February,
1810, General Stewart arrived in Cadiz with three thousand men,
who were received with enthusiastic joy. On the 17th of the same
month, thirteen hundred Portuguese arrived, and Spanish troops
in small bodies came in daily. Two ships of war, the Euthalion and
Undaunted, arrived from Mexico, with six millions of dollars: and
other British troops having appeared, the whole force assembled
behind the Santa Petri was not fewer than eighteen thousand
effective men. The worst symptom was, that among the Spaniards
there was little enthusiasm, and not a man among the citizens had
been enrolled or armed, or had volunteered either to labour or fight.
General Stewart's first measure was to recover Matagorda, a most
important point, about four thousand yards from the city, which
the Spaniards had foolishly dismantled and abandoned. In the night
of the 22d a detachment, consisting of fifty marines and seamen,
twenty-five artillery-men, and sixty-seven of the 94th regiment,
the whole under the command of Captain M'Lean, pushed across
the channel during a storm, and took possession of the dismantled
fort, before morning effected a solid lodgment, and al though
the French cannonaded the work with field artillery all the next
day, the garrison was immoveable. Early in March a more minute

survey of the general state of the defensive works was made, when
it appeared that the force then assigned was quite inadequate, and
that to secure it against the efforts of the enemy, twenty thousand
soldiers, and a series redoubts and batteries, requiring the labour
of four thousand men for three months, were absolutely necessary;
and yet an unaccountable apathy prevailed. In vain did the English
engineers present plans, and offer to construct works; the Spaniards
would never consent to pull down a house, or destroy a garden;
and had the enemy been then prepared to press onward vigorously,
the city must have been lost by procrastination so fatal. One word
more for Matagorda. The capture of this place by a few intrepid
men has been mentioned. Though frequently cannonaded, it had
been held fifty five days, and contributed to prevent the completion
of the enemy's works at the Troccadero point. This small fort, of a
square form, without a ditch, with bomb-proofs insufficient for the
garrison, and with one angle projecting towards the land, was little
calculated for resistance; and, as it could only bring seven guns to
bear, a Spanish seventy-four, and an armed flotilla, were moored on
the flanks to co-operate in the defence. The French had, however,
raised great batteries behind some houses on the Troccadero, and,
as day-light broke on the 21st of April, a hissing shower of heated
shot falling on the seventy-four, and in the midst of the flotilla,
obliged them to cut their cables and take shelter under the works
of Cadiz. Then the fire of forty-eight guns and mortars of the
largest size was concentrated upon the little fort of Matagorda, and
the feeble parapet disappeared in a moment before this crashing
flight of metal. The naked rampart, and the undaunted hearts of
the garrison, remained; but the troops fell fast, the enemy shot
quick and close; a staff, bearing the Spanish flag, was broken six
times in an hour, and the colours were at last fastened to the angle
of the work itself; while the men, especially the sailors, besought
the officers to hoist the British ensign, attributing the slaughter to
their fighting under a foreign flag. Thirty hours the tempest lasted,
and sixty-four men out of one hundred and forty were down,
when General Graham sent boats to carry off the survivers. The
bastion was then blown up, under the direction of Major Lefebre,
an engineer of great promise; and he also fell,—the last man whose

blood wetted the ruins thus abandoned. An action must be here recorded truly heroic. A Sergeant's wife, named Retson, was in a casemate with the wounded men, when a very young drummer was ordered to fetch water from the well of the fort. Seeing the child hesitate, she snatched the vessel from his hand, braving the terrible cannonade herself; and although a shot cut the bucket-cord from her hand, she recovered the vessel, and fulfilled her mission. In July, the British force in Cadiz was increased to eight thousand five hundred men, and Sir Richard Keats arrived to take the command of the fleet. The operations of the besiegers were thus greatly checked; and the mighty lines, constructed with so much labour and skill, led to little or nothing.

As the spring of the year advanced, the operation of the campaign became increasingly extended and important. Reinforcements from France continued to crowd the roads. The command of these collected forces, which included seventeen thousand of the Imperial Guards, was entrusted to Massena, Prince of Essling, on account of his great name in arms. Under his auspices Ney commenced the first siege of Ciudad Rodrigo; and if he expected to carry it without delay, it only shows that, like some of his predecessors, he was liable to mistake. The present Governor, Don Andreas Herrasti was a veteran of fifty years' service, whose silver hairs, dignified countenance, and courteous manners excited respect; and whose courage, talents, and honour were worthy of his venerable appearance. His garrison amounted to six thousand fighting men, besides the citizens; and the place, built on a height over hanging the northern bank of the Agueda river, was amply supplied with artillery and stores of all kinds. The works were, however, weak. There were no bomb-proofs, and Herrasti was obliged to place his powder in the church for security. The country immediately about Ciudad Rodrigo, although wooded, was easy for troops, especially on the left bank of the Agueda, to which the garrison had access by a stone bridge within pistol shot of the castle-gate. But the Agueda itself rising in the Sierra de Francia, and running into the Douro, is subject to great and sudden floods; and six or seven miles below the town, near San Feliceo, the channel deepens into one continued and frightful chasm, many hundred feet deep, and overhung with huge desolate rocks. Towards the end of April a French camp was formed, upon a lofty ridge five miles eastward of the city; and in a few days a second, and then a third arose. These portentous clouds continued to gather on the hills until June, when fifty thousand fighting men came down into the plain, and, throwing two bridges over the Agueda, begirt the fortress. In the night of the 22d, Julian Sanchez, with two hundred horsemen, passed silently out of the castle-gate, and, crossing the river, fell upon the nearest French posts, pierced their line in a moment, and reached the English light division then behind the Azava, six miles from Ciudad Rodrigo. We cheerfully received the party, and three days after this, feat the batteries opened. The assailants were warmly received. Three of their magazines, by the fire of the besieged, blew up, and killed above a hundred men. On the 27th the Prince of Essling arrived in the camp, and summoned the Governor to surrender. Herrasti answered in the manner to be expected from so good a soldier; and the fire was resumed, until the 1st of July, when Massena, sensible that the mode of attack was faulty, directed the engineers to raise counter-batteries, to push on their parallels, work regularly forward, blow in the counterscarp, and pass the ditch in form. On the 9th of July the besiegers' batteries re-opened with terrible effect. In twenty-four hours the fire of the Spanish guns was nearly silenced, part of the town was in flames, a reserve magazine exploded on the walls, the counterscarp was blown in by a mine, on an extent of thirty-six feet, the ditch filled by ruins, and a broad way made into the place. At this moment three French soldiers, suddenly running out of the ranks, mounted the breach, looked into the town, and having thus in broad day-light proved the state of affairs, discharged their muskets, and with singular success retired unhurt. The columns of assault immediately assembled. The troops, animated by the presence of Ney, were impatient for the signal to advance. A few minutes would have sent them raging into the midst of the city; when the white flag waved on the rampart, and the venerable Governor was seen standing alone on the ruins, and signifying by his gestures that he desired to capitulate. The defence made did no discredit to the parties. Every one lent a hand. The inhabitants contributed largely in maintaining the vigour and resolution of the garrison. Women and children, and even the blind, were earnestly engaged in providing necessaries for the fighting men. Those who were unable to bear arms encouraged those who could. Indeed, it was to the spirit of determined resistance prevailing among the people generally within the walls, that the powerful force without was so long detained there. Above forty thousand shells had been thrown into the place, and not a house remained uninjured.

One of the favourite designs of Napoleon at this period was to establish his power in Portugal. This the British Government was determined, if possible, to prevent; and the person selected to direct the defence of our ancient ally was Lord Wellington. Confidence was felt in no other; and it was a question whether any other military leader was in all respects properly qualified for the arduous under taking. When his Lordship required thirty thousand men for the defence of Portugal, he considered the number that could be fed rather than what was necessary to fight the enemy. On this principle he asserted that success must depend on the exertions and devotedness of the native forces. Two points were to be secured at the very onset. One was, to concert measures by which sustenance might be secured for the united British and Portuguese army; and the other, to devise plans by which the enemy should be deprived of supplies, whenever and wherever he entered the country. In effecting this latter purpose it was demanded, (for the exactions of war are necessarily rigorous,) that the people should destroy their mills, remove their boats, break down their bridges, lay waste their fields, abandon their dwellings, and carry off their property, on whatever line the invader should penetrate; while the entire population, converted into soldiers and closing on the rear and flanks, should cut off all resources, excepting those carried in the midst of the troops. These were hard sayings; but they were dictated by stern necessity, and were positively required for the safety of the kingdom. The call was obeyed. Part of the public property was sacrificed, in order that the whole might, in some form or other, eventually be restored and rendered safe. In pursuance of the comprehensive plans adopted by the British leader, it was necessary to find a position, covering Lisbon, where the allied forces could neither be turned by the flanks, nor forced in front by numbers, nor reduced by famine. The mountains filling the tongue of land upon which Lisbon is situated, furnished this key-stone to the arch of defence. Lord Wellington then conceived the design of turning these vast mountains into one stupendous and impregnable citadel, on which to deposit the independence of the whole Peninsula. The works were forthwith commenced. Intrenchments, inundations, and redoubts, covered more than five hundred square miles of mountainous country, lying between the Tagus and the ocean. The actual force under Lord Wellington cannot be estimated higher than eighty thousand men, while the frontier he had to defend, reckoning from Bragansa to Ayamonte, was four hundred miles long. The British forces included in the above were under thirty thousand. Every probable movement of the enemy was previously considered: at the same time the English Commander was aware how many counter-combinations were to be expected in a contest with eighty thousand French veterans, having a competent General at their head. Hence, to secure embarkation in the event of disaster, a third line of entrenchments was prepared, and twenty-four thousand tons of shipping were constantly kept in the river to receive the British forces.

Where all behaved so well, distinctions are unnecessary, and may appear invidious. Perhaps, however, I may be allowed to claim at least an equal share of the honours of a successful campaign for the division of the British army under the command of General Crauford, in which was included the 43d regiment. Without attempting to institute any comparison between him and the Commander-in-chief, the comprehensiveness and strength of whose capacity in the direction of extensive movements was unrivalled, it may be safely averred, that for zeal, intrepidity of spirit, and personal prowess, Crauford was not inferior to any General of division in the forces. His men partook in a great measure of the qualities of their leader. Inured to almost every species of warlike toil, they were formidable either for assault or defence; and never were the energies of fighting men more thoroughly tested than those of this very corps in the course of the few succeeding months.

In the midst of March, Crauford lined the banks of the Agueda with his Hussars for a distance of twenty-five miles, following the course of the river. The infantry were disposed in small parties in the villages between Almeida and the Lower Agueda. Two battalions of Portuguese Cacadores (Riflemen) soon afterwards arriving, made a total of four thousand men, and six guns. While therefore the Hussars kept a good watch at the two distant bridges, the troops could always concentrate under Almeida before the enemy could reach them on that side; and on the side of Barba del Puerco the ravine was so profound that a few companies of the 95th were considered capable of opposing any numbers. This arrangement was suitable while the Agueda was swollen; but that river was capricious, often falling many feet in a night, without visible cause. When it was fordable, Crauford always withdrew his outposts, and concentrated his division; and his situation demanded a quickness and intelligence in his troops, the like of which has never been surpassed. Seven minutes sufficed for the division to get under arms in the middle of the night; and a quarter of an hour, night or day, to bring it in order of battle to the alarm-posts, with the baggage loaded and assembled at a convenient distance in the rear, and this not upon a concerted signal, or as a trial, but at all times, and to a certainty. Our condition at that season was no unapt epitome of what the Christian ought to be. With a foe so vigilant as his spiritual adversary, the godly man should be all eye and ear, ready to gather himself up for action every moment, both by night and day!; not by way of experiment and trial, but as matter of constant and universal practice. The waters of carnal security are sadly deceptive: the enemy may find some fordable spot when least expected. If the heaven-bound pilgrim east behind his worldly load, and place it in the rear, as we did our baggage, he would find himself so much the more free to give and take manfully. This is a digression: but men have souls to save though they wear red coats; and an occasional halt to look at eternal things through the vista of temporalities may not, after all, produce much loss of time. But to return: We soon found that our caution was called for. On the 19th of March General Ferey, a bold officer, attempted to surprise us, for which purpose he collected six hundred Grenadiers close to the bridge of San Felices, and just as the moon rising behind him east long shadows from the rocks, and rendered the bottom of the chasm dark, he silently passed the bridge, and, with incredible speed ascending the opposite side, bayoneted the sentries, and fell upon the piquet so fiercely, that friends and enemies went fighting into the village of Barba del Puerco, while the first shout was still echoing in the gulf below. So sudden was the attack, and so great the confusion, that the British companies could not form, but each soldier encountering the nearest enemy, fought hand to hand; and their Colonel, Sydney Beckwith, conspicuous by his lofty stature and daring actions, a man capable of rallying a whole army in flight, urged the contest with such vigour, that in a quarter of an hour the French column was borne back, and pushed over the edge of the descent. Soon after this the whole army was distressed for money; and Crauford, notwithstanding his prodigious activity, being unable to procure food for the division, gave the reins to his fiery temper, and seized some church plate, with a view to the purchase of corn. For this impolitic act he was immediately rebuked, and such redress granted that no mischief ensued. The proceeding itself was not, however, altogether useless, as it convinced the Priests that our distress was real.

Nothing could be more critical than our position. From the Agueda to the Coa the whole country, although studded with woods, and scooped into hollows, was free for cavalry and artillery, and there were at least six thousand horsemen and fifty guns within an hour's march of our position; and yet, trusting to his own admirable arrangements, and to the surprising discipline of his troops, Crauford still maintained his dangerous position, thus encouraging the garrison of Ciudad Rodrigo, and protecting the villages in the plain. The fall of that fortress was, however, soon announced. A Spaniard, eluding the French posts, brought a note from old Herrasti, the Governor, claiming assistance. It contained these words,—"O venir luego! Luego! a secorrer esta plaza." (O come now, now, to the succour of this place!) But the gallant old man could not be relieved.

Soon after this I had the misfortune to fall into bad hands. Having had occasion to visit a neighbouring village on regimental business, and to make some small purchases for one of the officers, I was detained rather late in the evening, and on attempting on my return to cross a mountainous district without a guide, I lost my way. After wandering in various directions among rocks and low brushwood, two large dogs, singularly fierce and powerful, used by the Spaniards to protect their cattle from wolves, suddenly appeared in the attitude of springing at me. Putting on a bold front, I stepped back, and drew my bayonet, when, to my surprise, they seemed to dislike my appearance, and recoiled. Concluding that some human abode was nigh, I followed the track of the dogs, and presently arrived at an open space, where a few glowing embers indicated that a fire had recently been there. While gazing on the spot my attention was arrested by a rushing noise quite close to my ear, and, in almost the same instant, three men darted through an adjoining copse, and were on me with incredible violence. One of them, who was armed with a halbert, made a desperate plunge with his formidable weapon; and had I not parried it, that moment would have ended my life. The others joined in this unmanly and unaccountable attack; but though roughly used, I escaped without mortal injury. I at first imagined that the fellows were part of a banditti, living by rapine and plunder, and that, disappointed of booty, they had wreaked their resentment by violent usage. I found afterwards that they were cattle-owners; and what aggravated their conduct, a report was spread through their agency that I had a design upon their property, than which nothing was further from my thought. The outrage being reported to our Commander, Major M'Leod, a Sergeant, with his piquet of men, was sent to investigate the truth. On arriving at the place, there they found me, unable to move from the ill treatment I had received. I stated exactly what had taken place, and requested that the men might be secured, and taken to quarters, so that I might confront them before the Major. This was acceded to, and being permitted to answer for myself, I produced the proper pass, still in my possession, and soon convinced the board that I had been within the line of duty, was the only injured party, and deserved some compensation for the treatment I had received. This was immediately granted; so that with the exception of a few bruises, which grew better under the agreeable remedy just glanced at, I came off with flying colours, while the Dons paid for the entertainment.

At the beginning of July, the enemy began to appear in numbers; but, obstinate in maintaining every inch of ground, our division remained firm. The troops were marched in succession slowly, and within sight of the French, hoping that they would imagine the whole British army was come up. By this manœuvre two days were gained, but on the 4th a strong body of the enemy assembled at Marialva; and a squadron of horse, crossing the ford below that bridge, pushed at full force towards Gallegos, driving back the piquets. The enemy then passed the river, and the British retired, skirmishing upon Almeida, leaving two guns, a troop of British, and one of German Hussars, to cover the movement. This rear-guard drew up on a hill, half cannon-shot from a streamlet with marshy banks, which crossed the road to Almeida: in a few moments a column of French horsemen was observed coming on at a charging pace, diminishing its front as it approached the bridge, but resolute to pass, and preserving the most perfect order in spite of some well-directed shots from the guns. Captain Krauchenberg, of the Hussars, proposed to charge: the English officer did not conceive his order warranted it, but the gallant Captain rode full speed against the head of the advanced column with his single troop, and with such a shock that he killed the leading officer, overthrew the front ranks, and drove the whole back. This skirmish was followed by another on the 11th: on this occasion two French parties were observed, the one of infantry near Villa de Puerco, the other of cavalry at Barquillo. An open country on the right would have enabled the six squadrons to get between the infantry in Villa de Puerco and their point of retreat: this was circuitous, and Crauford preferred pushing straight through a stone enclosure as the shortest road. The enclosure proved difficult, the squadrons were separated, and the French, 200 strong, had time to draw up in a square on a rather steep rise of land; yet so far from the edge as not to be seen till the ascent was gained. The two squadrons which first arrived galloped in upon them; and the charge was rough and pushed home, but failed. The troopers received the fire of the square in front and on both sides, and in passing saw and heard the French Captain, Gauche, and his Sergeant-major, exhorting the men to shoot carefully. Meanwhile Colonel Talbot, mounting the hill with four squadrons of the 14th Dragoons, bore gallantly in upon Captain Gauche; but the latter again opened such a fire that Talbot himself and fourteen men went down close to the bayonets, and the stout Frenchman made good his retreat. Crauford fell back to Almeida, apparently disposed to cross the Coa; yet nothing was further from his thoughts. Braving the whole French army, he had kept, with a weak division, for three months within two hours march of sixty thousand men, appropriating the resources of the plains entirely to himself. Had he been satisfied with this feat, it would have shown him to be master of some prudence; but forgetting that his stay beyond the Coa was a matter of sufferance rather than real strength, he resolved with ambition not easily excusable, in defiance of reason and the repeated order of his General, to fight again on the right bank,—a piece of rashness for which we dearly paid.

Upon a calm review of the circumstances under which this engagement took place, I consider it little short of a miracle that a single British soldier survived to describe it. The troops we had to oppose were those of a well-disciplined army, they were commanded by officers of approved talent and courage, and out-numbered us at least in the proportion of four to one. Nor, mingled as I was among the most furious combatants, can I conceive how it happened that I escaped unhurt: to be sure, this is talking as if God and his providence were banished from the earth. Danger and death were undoubtedly averted by the unperceived, but almighty, agency of the divine protection; that delivered my soul from perdition, my eyes from tears, and my feet from falling, in order that in future my days, so singularly lengthened, should be devoted to his service. He gave his angels charge concerning me: such, at least, is my conviction. Millions of spiritual creatures walk the earth, both when we wake and when we sleep: these are all ministering spirits sent forth to minister to those who are the heirs of salvation; and as I humbly raise my claim for a share therein, why should it be thought a thing incredible that the Almighty was my special defence

> And turn'd aside the fatal blow,
> And lifted up my sinking head!

The most dangerous crisis had now arrived: this was on the evening of the 24th of July, which was stormy, and proved to be a memorable period. Our whole force under arms consisted of four thousand infantry, eleven hundred cavalry, and six guns; and the position occupied was about one mile and a half in length, extending in an oblique line towards the Coa. The cavalry piquets were upon the plain in front, the right on some broken ground, and the left resting on an unfinished tower eight hundred yards from Almeida: the rear was on the edge of the ravine forming the channel of the Coa, and the bridge was more than a mile distant in the bottom of the chasm. The lightning towards midnight became unusually vivid. Having been under arms for several hours, we were drenched with rain: as the day dawned a few pistol-shots in front, followed by an order for the cavalry reserve and the guns to advance, gave notice of the enemy's approach; and as the morning cleared, twenty-four thousand French infantry, five thousand cavalry, and thirty pieces of artillery were observed marching from Turones. Our line was immediately contracted, and brought under the edge of the ravine: in an instant four thousand hostile cavalry swept the plain, and our regiment was unaccountably placed within an enclosure of solid masonry at least ten feet high, situate on the left of the road, with but one narrow outlet about half musket-shot down the ravine. While thus shut up the firing in front redoubled, the cavalry, the artillery, and the Cacaderes successively passed by in retreat, and the sharp clang of the 95th Rifle was heard along the edge of the plain above. A few moments later and we should have been surrounded; but here, as in every other part of the field, the quickness and knowledge of the battalion officer remedied the faults of the General. In little more than a minute, by united effort, we contrived to loosen some large stones, when, by a powerful exertion, we burst the enclosure, and the regiment, reformed in column of companies, was the next instant up with the Riflemen. There was no room to array the line, no time for anything but battle; every Captain carried off his company as an independent body, the whole presenting a mass of skirmishers, acting in small parties and under no regular command, yet each confident in the courage and discipline of those on his right and left, and all regulating their movements by a common discretion. Having the advantage of ground and number, the enemy broke over the edge of the ravine; their guns, ranged along the summit, played hotly with grape; and their Hussars, galloping over the glacis of Almeida, poured down the road, sabring everything in their way. The British regiments, however, extricated themselves from their perilous situation. Falling back slowly, and yet stopping and fighting whenever opportunity offered, they made their way through a rugged country, tangled with vineyards, in despite of the enemy, who was so fierce and eager, that even the horsemen rode in among the enclosures, striking at us, as we mounted the walls, or scrambled over the rocks. Just then, I found myself within pistol-shot of the enemy, while my passage was checked by a deep chasm or ravine: as not a moment was to be lost, I contrived to mount to the edge, and, having gained the opposite side, put myself in a crouching position, and managed to slide down the steep and slippery descent without injury. On approaching the river, a more open space presented itself; but the left wing being harder pressed, and having the shortest distance, the bridge was so crowded as to be impassable: here therefore we made a stand. The post was maintained until the enemy, gathering in great numbers, made a second burst, when the companies fell back. At this moment the right wing of the 52d was seen marching towards the bridge, which was still crowded with the passing troops, when M'Leod, a very young man, immediately turned his horse round, called to the troops to follow, and, taking off his cap, rode with a shout towards the enemy. The suddenness of the thing, and the distinguished action of the man, produced the effect he designed we all rushed after him, cheering and charging as if a whole army were behind to sustain us; the enemy's skirmishers, amazed at this unexpected movement, were directly checked. The conflict was tremendous: thrice we repulsed the enemy at the point of the bayonet. M'Leod was in the hottest of the battle, and a ball passed through the collar of his coat; still he was to be seen with a pistol in his right hand, among the last to retire. At length the bugle sounded for retreat: just then, my left-hand man, one of the stoutest in the regiment, was hit by a musket shot,—he threw his head back, and was instantly dead. I fired at the fellow who shot my comrade; and before I could

reload, my pay-serjeant, Thomas, received a ball in the thigh, and
earnestly implored me to carry him away. As the enemy was not far
off, such a load was by no means desirable: but he was my friend; I
therefore took him up; and though several shots were directed to us,
they all missed, and I was able, though encumbered with such
weight, to carry him safely over the bridge. At length the assistance
of another soldier was procured: we then carried the wounded man
between us, when he was placed on a car. He returned me sincere
thanks, and, what was just then much better, gave me his canteen,
out of which I was permitted to take a draught of rum: how
refreshing it was, can be fully known only to myself. As the
regiments passed the bridge, they planted themselves in loose order
on the side of the mountain; the artillery drew up on the summit,
and the cavalry were disposed in parties on the roads to the right,
because two miles higher up the stream there were fords, and
beyond them the bridge of Castello Bom. The French skirmishers,
swarming on the right bank, opened a biting fire, which was
returned as bitterly the artillery on both sides played across the
ravine, the sounds were repeated by numberless echoes; and the
smoke, rising slowly, resolved itself into an immense arch, sparkling
with the whirling phases of the flying shells. The enemy despatched
a Dragoon to try the depth of the stream above; but two shots from
the 52d killed man and horse, and the carcases floating down the
river discovered that it was impassable. The monotonous tones of a
French drum were than heard; and in another second the head of a
column was at the long narrow bridge. A drummer, and an officer
in splendid uniform, leaped forward together, and the whole rushed
on with loud cries. The depth of the ravine at first deceived the
soldiers' aim on our side, and two-thirds of the passage were won
before an English shot had brought down an enemy. A few paces
onward the line of death was traced, and the whole of the leading
French section fell as one man. Still the gallant column pressed
forward, but no foot could pass that terrible line: the killed and
wounded rolled together, until the heap rose nearly to a level with
the parapet. Our shouts now rose loudly, but they were confidently
answered; and in half an hour a second column, more numerous
than the first, again crowded the bridge. This time the range was

better judged, and ere half the distance was passed, the multitude was again torn, shattered, dispersed, and slain: ten or twelve men only succeeded in crossing, and took shelter under the rocks at the brink of the river. The skirmishing was renewed, and a French surgeon, coming down to the very foot of the bridge, waved his handkerchief, and commenced dressing the wounded under the hottest fire: the appeal was heard; every musket turned from him, although his still undaunted countrymen were preparing for a third attempt. This last effort was comparatively feeble, and soon failed. The combat was nevertheless continued by the French, as a point of honour to cover the escape of those who had passed the bridge, and by the English from ignorance of their object. One of the enemy's guns was dismantled; a powder magazine blew up; and many continued to fall on both sides till four o'clock, when a heavy rain caused a momentary cessation of fire: the men among the rocks returned unmolested to their own party, the fight ceased, and we retired behind the Pinkel river. On our side upwards of three hundred were killed or wounded. The French lost more than a thousand men.

During the march that ensued, which of necessity was rapid, my mind was deeply impressed with the occurrences of the preceding eventful day. Many of my valued friends were missing, and their remains lay unburied on the spot where they fell. Colonel Hull, who had joined the regiment only the day before the action, was killed; and I afterwards saw his body, with the face downwards, thrown across the back of a mule, for conveyance to some place of interment: the Colonel's nephew was also badly wounded in the mouth, and obliged to return to England. Despondency is not, however, the fitting mood for a soldier. Tears for the dead were soon brushed away, and, to secure our own preservation, thought was soon diverted from musing on the past, to the active operations before us. Unremitted exertions were made by the Commissariat to provide us with necessaries. Grapes were plentiful; vegetables also were within reach. Bread in sufficient quantities, with a pipe of wine in front for regimental use, afforded an agreeable prospect; and the evening after the arrival of this welcome reinforcement was spent in a good-humoured review of dangers gone by.

CHAPTER V

THE Captain of the company in which I served being in want of a servant, I had the honour of being engaged in that capacity: my place, however, was no sinecure, and often amounted to a rather dangerous distinction. The duties enjoined were heavy, and contributed not a little to increase the severity of general military service. When my master dismounted from his horse, I had to hold the animal, or lead him by the bridle along roads through which it was difficult to drag myself; and the horse, chafed by rough usage, and deficient feed, was frequently so restive that my employment was both irksome and laborious: this horse became an eventual favourite. Having been placed for a short time at large, he thought proper to escape, and accordingly scoured away over hill and dale, with the saddle and accoutrements of his master, including a pair of pistols in the holster, and change of clothing behind. He was observed by a party of French, who tried to secure him, but, strange to say, he was determined they should not. By a kind of instinct, to me an entire enigma, the horse chose the road in which he apparently knew his old associates were to follow; and when we had crossed the bridge, to my surprise, he was there beforehand, and waiting our arrival. A rare and unpleasant circumstance took place here. The discipline and good order of the 43d were proverbial: the matter was therefore so much the more vexatious. Being placed for a brief period in the vicinity of a village, the landlady of a Spanish house of entertainment had broached a puncheon of wine, which she retailed at a stipulated price. One of our men, with more wit than wisdom, got behind the cask unperceived by the lady, and having pierced the hinder end with his bayonet, drew away both for himself and friends. In an evil hour the unlucky wight was detected, and next morning was punished in presence of the regiment. That the man did wrong, is clear; but being a good soldier, and of an excellent temper withal, the event excited great regret, and the humiliating spectacle was witnessed with reluctance. One day a bullock was killed for our use, and afforded a luxurious repast; but we were obliged to make haste about it. Scarcely had we finished a hasty meal, when the advance of the enemy was announced. The men were unwilling to lose even a fragment of viands so scarce; and several were afterwards observed, collecting bundles of the long dry grass and making a fire, over which they frizzled pieces of meat, impaled on the end of a ramrod. The hardships we endured in the prosecution of this retreat were increasingly severe. Personal comforts were out of the question. No change of linen could be procured; and as to a pair of stockings, the luxury was not to be thought of. As mine were worn to tatters, I contented myself without a new supply. Snatches of broken slumber were all we could obtain, though ready to stumble with weariness. The physical energies both of myself and comrades have, since that period, often appeared wonderful, even to myself. Many a time I have marched eight or ten miles on the nourishment afforded by a little water; and even then, with a pipe and good company, we talked away dull care, and were able with three cheers to face about, and with a determined volley warn away the following foe. We were much hurt by exposure to extremes, After the exhaustion arising from a forced march, pursued for hours, during the meridian heat of this burning climate, we lay down to rest for the night; and on the following morning such was the copiousness of the fallen dew, that our blankets appeared as if dipped in water. Rising from the ground in such a condition, it will be easily imagined that our sensations were not of an enviable cast. Even then I thought of thee, my native land; of thy rivers and vales, all so peaceful and beauteous, and they arose fairer than ever: and I thought of thee, my mother, who so often hadst cared and watched for me. But these meditations were dismissed. Had they been long indulged, my heart would have melted within me; and the time was at hand, when the sterner faculties were likely to be tried to the uttermost.

A sad disaster happened at this period. Almeida was besieged by Massena in person, at the head of a powerful army. The place, though regularly constructed with six bastions, ravelines, an excellent ditch and covered way, was extremely defective: with the exception of some damp casemates in one of the bastions, there was no magazine for the powder. The garrison consisted of about four thousand men. On the 18th of July the trenches were begun; and on the morning of the 26th, the second parallel being commenced, sixty-five pieces of artillery mounted on ten batteries threw in their fire. Many houses were soon in flames, and the garrison was unable to extinguish them; the counter fire was, however, briskly maintained, little military damage was sustained, and towards evening the cannonade slackened on both sides; but just after dark; the ground suddenly trembled, the castle burst into a thousand pieces, and gave vent to a column of smoke and fire: presently the whole town sunk into a shapeless mass of ruin. Treason or accident had caused the magazine to explode; and the devastation was incredible. Five hundred persons were struck dead on the instant; only six houses remained standing; and the surviving garrison, aghast at the terrible commotion, disregarded all exhortations to rally. An immediate surrender was the necessary result.

The invasion of Portugal by the French now assumed a most serious aspect. Massena's command extended from the banks of the Tagus to the Bay of Biscay, and the number of his troops exceeded a hundred and ten thousand men. The view was discouraging, and was so felt by the British Ministry at home. Massena could bring sixty thousand veterans into the field, while the British force was scarcely fifty thousand, more than half of which consisted of untried men. The Sierra Busaco was the place on which Lord Wellington fixed for his position. A succession of ascending ridges lead to this mountain, which is separated from the last by a chasm so profound, that the unassisted eye could hardly distinguish the movement of troops in the bottom. When this formidable position was chosen, some officers expressed their fears that Massena would not assail it. "But if he do, I shall beat him," was the reply of the English leader; who was well assured that the Prince would attack. Massena was in fact anxious for a battle, and indulged in a vision, in which he beheld the allies fly before his face.

On the 22d of September we fell back exactly a league, and encamped in a pine-wood. One night there happened among us an extraordinary panic, for which none of us, either then or since, could assign any reasonable cause. No enemy was near, nor was any alarm given, yet suddenly large bodies of the troops started from sleep, as if seized with a phrenzy, and dispersed in every direction; some climbed the trees, they knew not why: nor was there any possibility of allaying this strange terror, until some person called out that the enemy's cavalry were among them, when the soldiers mechanically fell into something like order, and the illusion instantly vanished. On the 25th the enemy's cavalry were seen gathering in front, and the heads of three infantry columns were visible on the table-land above Mortagas, coming on abreast, and at a most impetuous pace; while heavy clouds of dust, rising and loading the atmosphere for miles behind, showed that the whole French army was in full march to attack. The cavalry skirmishers were already exchanging pistol-shots, when Lord Wellington, suddenly arriving, ordered the division to retire, and, taking the personal direction, covered the retreat with the 52d and other troops. Nor was there a moment to lose: the enemy with great rapidity brought up both infantry and guns, and fell on so briskly, that all the skill of the General, and the readiness of the rear-guard, where I was placed, could scarcely prevent the division from being seriously engaged. Before three o'clock, forty thousand French infantry were in position on the two points, and the sharp musketry of the skirmishers arose from the gloomy chasms beneath. The allies had now taken their stand; and along the whole of their front, skirmishers were thrown out on the mountain side, and about fifty pieces of artillery disposed upon the salient points. In the evening, in order to facilitate the approaching attack, the light French troops were observed stealing by twos and threes into the lowest parts of the valley, endeavouring to make their way up the wooded dells and hollows, and to establish themselves unseen, close to the piquets of the light division. Some companies of Rifle corps and Cacadores checked this; but similar attempts made with more or less success, at different points of the position, seemed to indicate a night attack, and excited all the vigilance of the troops. Had it not been so, none but veterans tired of war could have slept. The weather was calm and fine, and the dark mountain masses rising on either side were crowned with innumerable watch-fires, around which, more than a hundred thousand brave men were gathered.

The attack began on the following morning before day-break. Three columns were led by Ney, and two by Reynier, the points being about three miles asunder. The resistance was spirited, and six guns played along the slope with grape; but in less than half an hour the French were close upon the summit, so swiftly did they scale the mountain, overthrowing every thing that opposed their progress. The leading battalions immediately established themselves upon the higher rocks, and a confused mass wheeled to the right, intending to Sweep the summit of the sierra; but at that moment Lord Wellington directed two guns to open with grape upon their flank, while a heavy musketry was poured into their front; and in a little time the 45th and 88th regiments charged so furiously that even fresh men could not have withstood them. The French, quite spent with their previous exertion, opened a straggling fire, and both parties, mingling together, went down the mountain side with mighty clamour and confusion; the dead and dying strewing the way, even to the bottom of the valley. Meanwhile the French who had first gained the summit had re-formed their ranks, with the right resting upon a precipice overhanging the reverse side of the sierra; and thus the position was in fact gained, if any reserve had been at hand; but just then General Leith, who saw what had taken place, came on rapidly. Keeping the Royals in reserve, he directed the 38th to turn the right of the French; but the precipice prevented this; and meanwhile Colonel Cameron, informed by a staff officer of the critical state of affairs, formed the 9th regiment in line under a violent fire, and, without returning a single shot, ran in upon and drove the Grenadiers from the rocks with irresistible bravery, and yet with excellent discipline; refraining from pursuit, lest the crest of the position should be again lost, for the mountain was so rugged that it was impossible to judge clearly of the general State of the action.

On that side, however, the victory was secure. Ney's attack was equally unsuccessful. From the abutment of the mountain on which the light division was placed, the lower parts of the valley could be discerned. The table-land was sufficiently hollow to conceal the 43d and 52d regiments, drawn up in a line; and a quarter of a mile behind them, but on higher ground, and close to the convent, a brigade of German infantry appeared to be the only solid line of resistance on this part of the position. In front of the two British regiments, some rocks over-hanging the descent furnished natural embrasures, in which the guns of the division were placed, and the whole face of the hill was planted with the skirmishers of the Rifle corps, and of the two Portuguese Cacadore battalions. While it was yet dark, on listening attentively, we heard a straggling musketry in the deep hollows separating the armies; and when the light broke, the three divisions of the 6th corps were observed entering the woods below, and throwing for ward a profusion of skirmishers soon afterwards. The French ascended with wonderful cheerfulness, and though the light troops plied them unceasingly with musketry, and the artillery bullets swept through their ranks, the order of advance was never disturbed. Ross's guns were worked with incredible swiftness, yet their range was contracted every round, and the enemy's shot came singing up in a sharper key, until the skirmishers, breathless, and begrimed with powder, rushed over the edge of the ascent, when the artillery suddenly drew back, and the victorious cries of the French were heard within a few yards of the summit. Crauford, who, standing alone on one of the rocks, had been intently watching the progress of the attack, then turned, and in a quick shrill tone desired the two regiments in reserve to charge. The next moment eighteen hundred British bayonets went over the hill. Our shouts startled the French column; and yet so truly brave were the hostile leaders, that each man of the first section raised his musket, and two officers and ten men fell before them, so unerring was their aim. They could do no more: we were on them with resistless impetuosity. The head of their column was violently overturned, and driven upon the rear; both flanks were lapped over by our wings; and three terrible discharges at five yards distance completed the rout. In a few minutes a long line of carcases and broken arms indicated the line of retreat. The main body of the British stood fast, but several Companies followed in pursuit down the mountain. Before two o'clock, Crauford having assented to a momentary truce, parties of both armies were mixed amicably together, searching for the wounded men. Towards evening, however, a French company having impudently seized a village within half musket-shot of our division, and refusing to retire, it so incensed Crauford, that, turning twelve guns on the village, he overwhelmed it with bullets for half an hour. A company of the 43d was then sent down, who cleared the place in a few minutes. An affecting incident, contrasting strongly with the savage character of the preceding events, added to the interest of the day. A poor orphan Portuguese girl, about seventeen years of age, and very handsome, was seen coming down the mountain, and driving an ass loaded with all her property through the midst of the French army. She had abandoned her dwelling in obedience to the proclamation; and now passed over the field of battle with simplicity which told she was unconscious of her perilous situation, and scarcely understanding which were the hostile and which the friendly troops, for no man on either side was so brutal as to molest her. In this battle of Busaco, the French, after astonishing acts of valour, were repulsed. General Graind'orge, and about eight hundred men, were slain, beside nearly five thousand wounded; while the loss of the allies did not exceed thirteen hundred. After this trial, Massena judged the position of Busaco impregnable, and to turn it by the Mondego impossible, as the allies could pass that river quicker than himself. But a peasant informed him of the road leading from Mortagas to Boyalva, and he resolved to turn Lord Wellington's left. To cover this movement the skirmishing was renewed with such vigour on the 28th, that many thought a general battle would take place; and yet the disappearance of baggage and the throwing up of intrenchments on the hill, covering the roads to Mortagas, indicated some other design. It was not till evening, when the enemy's masses in front being sensibly diminished, and his cavalry descried winding over the distant mountains, that the project became quite apparent.

On the 1st of October, our outposts were attacked but the French, on entering the plain of Coimbra, suffered some loss from a cannonade; and the British cavalry were drawn up in line, but with no serious intention of fighting, and were soon after withdrawn across the Mondego. The light division then marched hastily to gain the defiles of Condeixa, which commences at the end of the bridge. At this juncture all the inhabitants of the place rushed simultaneously out, who had not before quitted the place, each with what could be caught up in the hand, and driving before them a number of animals loaded with sick people or children. At the entrance to the bridge the press was so great that the troops halted for a few moments, just under the prison. The jailer had fled with the keys; the prisoners, crowding to the windows, were endeavouring to tear down the bars with their hands, and even with their teeth; some were shouting in the most frantic manner, while the bitter lamentations of the multitude increased, and the pistol-shots of the cavalry, engaged at the fords below, were distinctly heard. Captain William Campbell burst the prison doors, and released the wretched inmates, while the troops forced their way over the bridge; yet, at the other end, the up-hill road, passing between high rocks, was so crowded, that no effort, even of the artillery, could make way. At last some of the infantry opened a passage on the right flank, and by great exertions the road was cleared for the guns; but it was not until after dusk that the division reached Condeixa, although the distance was less than eight miles. Hitherto the marches had been easy, the weather fine, and provisions abundant; nevertheless, the usual mischievous disorders of a retreat had shown themselves. In Coimbra, a quantity of harness and intrenching tools lay scattered in the streets; at Leiria, the magazines were plundered by the troops and camp followers; and at Condeixa a magazine of tents, shoes, spirits, and salt meat was destroyed, or abandoned to the enemy; and the streets were flowing ankle-deep with wasted rum, while the Portuguese division, only a quarter of a mile distant, could receive only half the usual supply of liquor. It is with some regret I reflect, that at this period, though exposed to dangers so imminent, I was carried away in some degree with the torrent of prevailing dissipation. Not that during any period of my active service I ever suffered the pleasure of conviviality, so called, to interfere with my duty. I was indeed often astonished to notice the reckless gaiety of my companions in arms, many of whom would crowd around the evening card-table, though aware that by dawn of day they might be engaged in mortal combat. In the midst of examples so contaminating, certain principles of morality, aided perhaps by a little natural gravity, were never totally subverted; and, under the blessing of God, preserved me from the grosser vices. Had I been favoured with an able and enlightened Christian teacher, it is probable, even then, that my mind might have received the light of Gospel truth. Insensible and ungrateful indeed I must have been not to have perceived and felt the mercies of divine Providence; for during the entire period of my active service, though exposed to perils almost unnumbered, I was not only preserved alive, but had been exempted from sickness, and therefore able, without a single exception, to maintain my place in the division.

Massena resumed his march on the 4th. Leaving his sick and wounded with a slender guard at Coimbra, amounting altogether to four thousand seven hundred men, he resumed his march by Condeixa and Leiria. His hospital was established at the Convent of Santa Clara, on the left bank of the river; and all the inhabitants who were unable to reach the lines, came down from their hiding-places in the mountains. But scarcely had the Prince left the city, when Trant, Miller, and Wilson, with nearly ten thousand militia, closed upon his rear, occupying the sierras on both sides the Mondego, and cutting off all communication with Almeida. The English army retreated; the right by Thomar and Santarem, the centre by Batalha and Rio Mayor, the left by Olobaca and Obidos; and at the same time a native force under Colonel Blunt was thrown into Peniché. Massena followed in one column, by the way of Rio Mayor; but mean while a capital exploit, performed by a partisan officer, convicted the Prince of bad generalship, and shook his plan of invasion to the base. Colonel Trant reached Milheada, and, believing that his arrival was unknown at Coimbra, he resolved to attack the French in that city. Having surprised a small post at Fornos, early in the morning of the 7th, he sent his cavalry at full gallop through the streets of Coimbra, with orders to pass the bridge, and cut off all communications with the French

army. Mean time his infantry penetrated at different points into
the principal parts of the town; and the enemy, astounded, made
little or no resistance. The convent of St. Clara surrendered at
discretion; and thus, on the third day after the Prince of Essling
had quitted the Moudego, his depots and hospitals, with nearly
five thousand prisoners, wounded and unwounded, among which
there was a company of the marines of the Imperial Guard, fell
into the hands of a small militia force. But Crauford, who had
reached Alemguer on the 9th, was still there at three o'clock
on the afternoon of the 10th. The weather being stormy, we
were placed under cover, and no indication of marching was
given. The cavalry had already filed into the lines; yet no guards
were posted, no patroles sent forward, nor any precautions taken
against surprise, although the town, situated in a deep ravine, was
peculiarly favourable for such an attempt. It was clear to me, and
others, that our officers were uneasy at this posture of affairs; the
height in front was anxiously watched, and about four o'clock
some French Dragoons on the summit were observed. The alarm
was given, and the regiments got under arms; but the posts of
assembly had been marked on an open space very much exposed,
and from whence the road led through an ancient gateway to
the top of the mountain behind. The enemy's numbers increased
every moment, and they endeavoured to create a belief that their
artillery was come up: this feint was easily seen through, but the
General desired the regiments to break, and reform on the other
side of the archway, out of gun-range; and immediately all was
disorder. The baggage animals were still loading, the streets were
crowded with the followers of the division, and the whole in one
confused mass rushed or were driven headlong to the archway.
Several were crushed, and with worse troops general panic must
have ensued; but the greater number of the soldiers, ashamed of
the order, stood firm in their ranks until the confusion abated.
Nevertheless the mischief was sufficiently great; and the enemy's
infantry, descending the heights, endeavoured, some to turn
the town on the left, while others pushed directly through the
streets in pursuit; and thus, with our front in disorder, and our
rear skirmishing, the retreat was commenced. The weather was,

however, so boisterous that the firing soon ceased, and a few
wounded, with the loss of some baggage, was all the hurt sustained.
I was on this occasion on the verge of considerable personal
danger. Having been ordered by an officer to procure forage for
his horse, I incautiously ventured too near the enemy; and being
further tempted by some clusters of fine grapes, accidentally
noticed, I remained some little time to discuss them. On a sudden
I found that the last column of the British was out of sight, while
imperceptibly to myself the advanced horsemen of the French
had nearly hemmed me in. Fully aware of my danger, which I
felt conscious had been increased by my agreeable but untimely
repast, I was aroused to instant exertion, and was happy enough to
elude surrounding scouts and reach my division. Having, however,
exceeded my commission, by taking care of myself as well as the
horse, and exposed both to extreme jeopardy, I was glad to resign
the animal to his owner, and resume my musket and place in the
ranks with out notice: and had no objection to perceive that my
error had been unnoticed both by foes and friends. The Captain
of the company in whose service I had engaged myself, like many
others, had not much time to spare. When an alarm was given
of the enemy's approach, we were preparing for dinner. Three
or four officers messed together; and on that day another or two
were expected, by way of a small party. Culinary preparations on a
moderate scale were going on, and I had just opened the Captain's
trunk, and taken out some table-linen, when, lo! the well-known
bugle sounded to arms. Aware that something unexpected had
happened, I ran up stairs, and on looking out at a back window,
I saw the enemy on the brow of a mountain, a column of whom
were rapidly descending into the town. Coming down in haste,
I found the dinner ready; but there is many a slip between the
cup and the lip; and, reaching across the table, which was ready
garnished, I swept the whole—utensils, food, and all—into the
orifice of a large travelling-bag, and made my way with it into
the street. Confusion and disorder are terms too weak to describe
the condition of the public thoroughfare. This time, thought I,
we shall be surely taken. The Captain clamoured for his horse: I
was as urgent for a mule to carry the baggage: every minute of

delay seemed an hour. At length, by uncommon effort, we cleared the town, and though the roads were bad, reached a small village within the lines, before midnight. I was billeted, with several officers, in a gentleman's house: it was well furnished; but I regret to add, that in a few days most of the moveables were destroyed: the proprietor, it would appear, had a presentiment of approaching injury; for previous to our actual entrance on the premises, he and his family had decamped.

I have already made some allusion to the lines of Torres Vedras, thrown up for the defence of Lisbon by Lord Wellington. These lines consisted of three distinct ranges of defence. The first, extending from Alhandra on the Tagus to the mouth of the Zizandre on the sea-coast, was, following the inflections of the hills, twenty-nine miles long. The second, traced at a distance varying from six to ten miles in rear of the first, stretched from Quintella, on the Tagus, to the mouth of the St. Lorenzo, being twenty-four miles in length. The third, intended to cover a forced embarkation, should it become necessary, extended from Passo d'Arcos, on the Tagus, to the tower of Junquera, on the coast. Here an outer line, constructed on an opening of three thousand yards, enclosed an entrenched camp, designed to cover the embarkation with fewer troops, should the operation be delayed by bad weather: and within this second camp, Fort St. Julian's, whose high ramparts and deep ditches defied an escalade, was armed and strengthened to enable a rear-guard to protect both itself and the army. Of these stupendous lines, the second, whether regarded for its strength or importance, was the principal, and the others only appendages; the one as a final place of refuge, the other as an advanced work to stem the violence of the enemy, and to enable the army to take up its ground on the second line without hurry or pressure. The aim and scope of all the works were to bar those passes, and to strengthen the favourable fighting positions between them, without impeding the movements of the army. The fortifications extended to the space of fifty miles: there were one hundred and fifty forts, and not fewer than six hundred pieces of artillery mounted within them, while the river was protected by gun-boats manned with British marines.

Massena was astonished at the extent and strength of works, the existence of which had only become known to him five days before he came upon them. He employed several days in examining their nature, and was as much at a loss at the end of his inspection as at the beginning. The heights of Alhandra he judged unattackable; but the valleys of Calandrix and Aruda attracted his attention. There were here frequent skirmishes with the light division to oblige Crauford to show his force; but by making Aruda an advanced post, he rendered it impossible to discover his true position without a serious affair; and in a short time the division, with prodigious labour, secured the position, in a manner which was spoken of with admiration. Across the ravine on the left, a loose stone wall, sixteen feet thick, and forty feet high, was raised: and across the great valley of Aruda, a double line of abattis was drawn; not composed, as is usual, of the limbs of trees, but of full grown oaks and chestnuts, dug up with all their roots and branches, dragged by main force for several hundred yards, and then reset and crossed, so that no human strength could break through. Breast-works at convenient distances, to defend this line of trees, were then cast up; and along the summit of the mountain, for the space of nearly three miles, including the salient points, other stone walls, six feet high, and four in thickness, with banquettes, were built, so that a good defence might have been made against the attacks of twenty thousand men. The increased strength of the works in general soon convinced Massena that it was impracticable to force the lines without great reinforcements; and towards the end of October the hospitals, stores, and other incumbrances of the French army, were removed to Santarem. On the 31st of the month two thousand men forded the Zezere above Punheta, to cover the construction of a bridge; and a remarkable exploit was performed by a Sergeant of the 16th Dragoons, named Baxter. This man, having only five troopers, came suddenly upon a piquet of fifty men, who were cooking. The Frenchmen ran to their arms, and killed one of the Dragoons; but the rest broke in amongst them so strongly, that Baxter with the assistance of some countrymen, made forty-two captives. On the 19th the light division entered the plain between the Rio-Mayor and the Tagus, and advanced against the heights by a sedgy marsh. The columns on our side were formed for attack, and the skirmishers of the light division were exchanging shots with the enemy, when it was found that the guns belonging to Pack's brigade had not arrived; and Lord Wellington, not quite satisfied with the appearance of his adversary's force, after three hours' demonstrations, ordered the troops to retire to their former ground. It was indeed evident that the French were resolved to maintain their position. Every advantageous spot of ground was fully occupied, the most advanced sentinels boldly returned the fire of the skirmishers, large bodies of reserve were descried, some in arms, others cooking; the strokes of the hatchet, and the fall of trees, resounded from the woods upon the hills; and the commencement of a triple line of abattis, and the fresh earth of entrenchments, were discernible in many places. Our active light division was, however, again in motion. General Crauford thought that the hostile troops who had shown themselves, amounted merely to a rear-guard of the enemy. His eager spirit could not bear to be restrained; and seizing a musket, he advanced in the night along the causeway, followed only by a Serjeant, and commenced a personal skirmish with the French piquets, from whose fire he escaped by miracle, convinced at last that the enemy were not in flight. Lord Wellington judged it best to remain on the defensive, and strengthen the lines. With this view the light division, supported by a brigade of cavalry, occupied Valle, and the heights overlooking the marsh and inundation; the bridge at the end of the causeway was mined; a sugar-loaf shaped hill, looking straight down the approach, was crowned with embrasures for artillery, and laced in front with a zig-zag covered way, capable of containing five hundred infantry. Thus the causeway being blocked, the French could not, while the inundation was maintained, make any sudden irruption from Santarem. About this period, a column of French, six thousand strong, scoured all the country beyond the Zezere, and contrived to secrete a quantity of food near Pedragoa, while other detachments arriving on the Mondego, below Coimbra, even passed that river, and carried off four hundred oxen and two thousand sheep intended for the allies. These excursions gave rise to horrible excesses, which broke down the discipline of the

French army, and were not always executed with impunity. The British cavalry at various times redeemed many cattle, and brought in a considerable number of prisoners.

Finding the drudgery of servitude, when added to my customary military duty, greater than I could well sustain, I requested permission to resign my situation with the Captain; and we parted, mutually satisfied with past acquaintance, and on the fairest terms. While in the vicinity of Santarem, the unarmed French and English soldiers, while procuring wine for the respective forces, were frequently intermingled in the same cellar, when there seemed to exist a tacit understanding that all animosity was suspended. The liquor was, however, sometimes too powerful; and one of our men who had been a good soldier, after a sad debauch, relapsed into a fit of despondency: the inordinate cup was then resorted to, but as usual, it lifted him up, only to throw him into lower depths of misery. He then deserted; and when taken, seized an opportunity of placing the muzzle of a musket to his mouth, and setting his foot upon the trigger, blew his head to atoms.

The French in their retreat from Santarem, had either consumed or destroyed every particle of food that came within their reach, so that the country was a spacious desert. During a sharp day's march in pursuit, a horrible calamity was unexpectedly disclosed. While passing over a desolate mountain, a large house standing alone, and apparently deserted, was discovered near the line of our route. Prompted by curiosity, several men turned aside to inspect the interior, where they found a number of famished wretches crowded together, for no other conceivable purpose but to die in company. Thirty women and children had perished for want of food, and lay dead upon the floor; while about half that number of survivors sat watching the remains of those who had fallen. Of those who thus perished the bodies were not much emaciated, but the muscles of the face were invariably drawn transversely, giving the appearance of a smile, and presenting the most ghastly sight imaginable. Most of the living were unable to move; and it had been by great exertion that they had crawled to a little distance from the group of death. The soldiers offered some refreshment to these unfortunate persons; but one man only had sufficient strength to eat. The women seemed patient and resigned, and even in this distress had arranged the bodies of those who first died with decency and care.

The blockade of Cadiz was now prosecuted with unusual vigour by the French forces. The chain of forts they had built was perfected. The batteries at the Trocaderos were powerful, and the flotillas ready for action. Soult repaired in person to San Luear; and in the last night of October thirty pinnaces and gun-boats slipped out of the Guadalquivir, eluded the allied fleet, passed along the coast to Rota, and from thence, aided by shore-batteries, fought their way to Santa-Maria and the San-Pedro. The flotilla was afterwards transported over-land; and in the ensuing month one hundred and thirty armed vessels and transports were assembled in the Trocadero canal. At that celebrated point there were immense batteries, and some notable pieces of ordnance, called cannon-mortars, or Villantroys, after the inventor. These huge engines were east in Seville, and, being placed in slings, threw shells with such prodigious force as to range over Cadiz, a distance of more than five thousand yards; but to obtain this flight, the shells were partly filled with lead, so that the charge of powder was proportionately of less effective explosion. While Cadiz was thus begirt, a furious engagement took place at Cerra de Puereo, called by the English the heights of Barossa, about four miles from the sea-mouth of the Santa-Petri. Barossa is a low ridge creeping in from the coast about a mile and a half, and overlooking a high and broken plain of small extent. Graham, who commanded the British, was extremely desirous of holding the Barossa height, as the key both to offensive and defensive movements. Our Spanish allies on this occasion behaved scandalously; indeed nothing but the unflinching firmness and courage of the English troops could have saved the army from entire ruin. Major Brown, seeing the general confusion arising from the defeat of the Spaniards, and being unable to stem the torrent, slowly retired into the plain, sending notice of what was passing to Graham, and demanding orders. That General, being then near Bermeja, answered that he was to fight; and instantly facing about himself, regained the plains with the greatest celerity, when, to his surprise, he beheld the Spanish rear-guard and baggage flying in confusion, the French cavalry between the summit and the sea, and Laval close on his own left flank. In this desperate situation he felt that to retreat upon Bermeja, and thus bring the enemy pell-mell with the allies on that narrow bridge, must be disastrous: hence, without a moment's hesitation, he resolved to attack, although the key of the field of battle was already in the enemy's possession. Ten guns, under Major Duncan, instantly opened a terrific fire against Laval's column, while Colonel Barnard, with the Riflemen, and the Portuguese companies, running out to the left, commenced the fight. The remainder of the British troops, without any attention to regiments or brigades, so sudden was the affair, formed two masses, one of which, under General Dukes, marched hastily against Ruffin, and the other, under Colonel Wheatley, against Laval. Duncan's guns ravaged the French ranks; Laval's artillery replied with spirit; Ruffin's batteries took Wheatley's columns in flank; and the infantry on both sides pressed forward eagerly and with a pealing musketry; but when near together, a fierce, rapid, prolonged charge of the British overthrew the first line of the French, and, notwithstanding its extreme valour, drove it in confusion over a narrow dip of ground upon the second, which was almost immediately broken in the same manner, and only the chosen battalion, hitherto posted on the right, remained to cover the retreat. Meanwhile Brown, receiving his orders, had marched headlong against Ruffin. Nearly half of his detachment went down under the enemy's last fire; yet he maintained the fight until Dilkes's column, which had crossed a deep hollow and never stopped even to re-form the regiments, came up, with little order indeed, but in a fierce mood, when the whole ran up towards the summit. There was no slackness on any side, and at the very edge of the ascent their opponents met them. A dreadful, and for some time a doubtful fight ensued. Ruffin and Chaudron Rousseau, commanding the chosen Grenadiers, both fell, mortally wounded. The English bore strongly onward; and their incessant slaughtering fire forced the French from the hill, with the loss of three guns and many brave men. The defeated divisions retired concentrically, and having soon met, they endeavoured with great energy to re-form and renew the action; but the fire of Duncan's guns, close, rapid, and destructive, rendered the attempt vain. Victor was soon in full retreat; and the British, having been twenty-four hours under arms, were too exhausted to pursue. In this brief but desperate fight upwards of twelve hundred British soldiers, and more than two thousand Frenchmen were killed or wounded: from the latter, six guns, an eagle, and two Generals, both mortally wounded, were taken, together with four hundred other prisoners.

The activities of this spirited campaign were maintained in other places. Badajos was sorely pressed by the French. Early in March, the second parallel being completed, and the Pardaleras taken into the works, the approaches were carried by sap to the covered way; mines were also prepared to blow in the counterscarp; and yet Rafael Menacho, the Governor, was not dismayed: his sallies were frequent and vigorous; he constructed new entrenchments where necessary; and every thing went on prosperously till the evening of the 2d, when in a sally, in which the nearest French batteries were carried, the guns spiked, and trenches partly ruined, Menacho was killed, and the command fell to Imas, a man so unworthy that a worse could not be found. At once the spirit of the garrison died away; for cowardice is often contagious: the besiegers' works rapidly advanced, the ditch was passed, a lodgment was made on one of the ravelines, the rampart was breached, and, the fire of the besieged being nearly silenced, on the 10th of March the place was summoned in a peremptory manner: not that there was the least need to surrender. A strong body of British and Portuguese were in full march for the relief of the place: this information had been communicated by telegraph; besides which Imas had been informed by a confidential messenger, that Massena was in full retreat. The breach was not practicable, provisions were plentiful, the garrison above eight thousand strong; the French army reduced by sickness and the previous operations to fewer than fourteen thousand men. Imas, how ever, instantly surrendered; but he also demanded that his Grenadiers should march out of the breach: this was granted, and he was obliged to enlarge the opening before they could do so. Yet this man, so overwhelmed with opprobrium, was never punished.

Massena continued to retreat; and a skirmish, attended with some loss on both sides, unexpectedly took place at Pombal. The

Commander just named was so closely followed by our division, that, the streets being still encumbered, Ney drew up a rear-guard on a height behind the town, and threw a detachment into the old castle. He had, however, waited too long: the French army was moving in some confusion, and in an extended column of march, by a narrow defile between the mountains and the Soire river, which was fordable; while the British divisions were in rapid motion on the left bank, with the design of crossing lower down, and cutting Massena's line of retreat; but darkness came on, and the operation terminated in a sharp conflict at Pombal, whence the 95th and the 3d Cacadores drove the French from the castle and town with such vigour, that the latter could not destroy the bridge, though it was mined for the purpose. Daybreak on the 12th saw both armies in movement; and eight miles of march brought the head of the British into a hollow way leading to a high table-land, on which Ney had disposed five thousand infantry, a few squadrons of cavalry, and some light guns. His centre was opposite to the hollow road; his wings were covered by the woody heights which he occupied with light troops. Behind him arose the village of Redhina, situated on low ground; in front of which were posted a division of infantry, a regiment of cavalry, and a battery of heavy guns, all so skilfully disposed as to give the appearance of considerable force. After examining the enemy's position for a short time, Lord Wellington first directed the light division to attack the wooded slopes covering Ney's right; and in less than an hour these orders were executed. The woods were presently cleared, and our skirmishers advanced even to the open plain beyond: just then, the French battalions, supported by four guns, opened a heavy rolling fire, and at the same moment, Colonel Farriere, of the 3d French Hussars, charged and took fourteen prisoners. This officer, during the whole campaign, had never failed to break in upon the skirmishers in the most critical moments; sometimes with a squadron, sometimes with only a few men: he was, however, sure to be found in the right place. The British light division, commanded by Sir William Erskine, consisted of five battalions of infantry, and six guns, and was formed so that it out-flanked the French right.

It was also reinforced with two regiments of Dragoons: meanwhile Picton seized the woody heights protecting the French left, and thus Ney's position was exposed. Nevertheless, that Marshal, observing that Lord Wellington, deceived as to his real numbers, was bringing the mass of the allied troops into line, far from re treating, even charged Picton's shirmishers, and continued to hold his ground with astonishing confidence. In this posture both sides remained for about an hour, when three shots were fired from the British centre as a signal for a forward movement, and a most splendid spectacle of war was exhibited. The woods seemed alive with troops, and in a few moments thirty thou sand men, forming three gorgeous lines of battle, were stretched across the plain; but bending on a gentle curve, and moving majestically forward, while horsemen and guns springing simultaneously onward from the centre and left wing, charged under a volley from the French battalions: the latter were instantly hidden by the smoke; and when that cleared away, no enemy was to be seen. Ney keenly watched the progress of this grand formation, and having opposed Picton's foremost skirmishers with his left, withdrew the rest of his people with such rapidity that he gained the village before the cavalry could touch him: the utmost efforts of Picton's skirmishers and of the horse artillery scarcely enabled them to gall the hind most of the French. One howitzer was, indeed, dismounted close to the bridge, but the village of Redhina was in flames. The Marshal was hard pressed, for the British were thundering at his rear; and the light troops of the 3d division, chasing like heated blood-hounds, passed the river almost at the same time with the French: Ney, at length, fell back upon the main body at Condeixa. The mind is sometimes impressed by trifling occurrences, especially when they take place unexpectedly, or are at all out of the common way. I remember that in the midst of the clangor and firing just described, a hare emerged from the woods, and for some time amused herself by sundry doubles and evolutions between the hostile lines at length, as if satisfied that enough had been seen, she suddenly disappeared. The other event is, that the tallest man I ever saw had been a private in the French ranks at Redhina: he was lying dead on the road side. Our forces continued to drive the enemy. Massena, in repairing to Fonte-Coberta, had left orders to fire Condeixa at a certain hour: these gentlemen left nothing willingly behind them, but ruin and desolation. In a few days we came up with the rear. Picton contrived to wind round the bluff side of a mountain about eight miles distant: as he was already beyond the French left, instant confusion pervaded their camp. The British immediately pushed forward; their advance was extremely rapid, and it is affirmed that the Prince of Essling, who was on the road, only escaped capture by taking the feathers out of his hat, and riding through some of the light troops. Condeixa being thus evacuated, the British cavalry pushed towards Coimbra, and cutting off Montbrun, captured part of his horsemen. The rest of the army kindled their fires, and the light division, in which, as usual, I was stationed, planted piquets close up to the enemy; but about ten at night the French divisions, whose presence was unknown to Lord Wellington, stole out, and passing along the front of the British posts, made for Miranda de Corvo.

The noise of their march was heard, but the night was dark it was imagined to be the moving of the French to the rear, and being so reported to Sir William Erskine, that officer put the light division in march at day-light on the 14th: our movements partook of extraordinary rashness; and what increased the danger, we were insensible of it. The morning was so obscured that nothing could be distinguished at the distance of a hundred feet, but the sound of a great multitude was heard on the hills in front, and it being evident that the French were there in force, many officers represented the impropriety of thus advancing without orders, and in such a fog: but Erskine, with what is deemed astounding negligence, sent the 52d forward in a simple column of sections, without a vanguard or other precaution, and even before the piquets had come in from their posts. The road dipped suddenly, descending into a valley, and the regiment was immediately lost in the mist, which was so thick that the troops, unconsciously passing the enemy's outposts, had nearly captured Ney himself, whose bivouac was close to the piquets. The riflemen followed in a few moments, and the rest of the division was about to plunge into the same gulf, when the rattling of musketry, and the booming of round shot was heard;

and when the vapour slowly rose, the 52d were seen on the slopes of the opposite mountain engaged, without support, in the midst of the enemy's army. At this moment Lord Wellington arrived, and the whole of the light division were pushed forward to sustain the 52d. The enemy's ground was so extensive, and his skirmishers so thick and so easily supported, that in a little time the division was necessarily stretched out in one thin thread, and closely engaged in every part without any reserve; nor could it even thus present an equal front, until Picton sent the Riflemen of the 60th to prolong the line. The fight was vigorously maintained amidst the numerous stone enclosures on the mountain-side; some advantages were gained, and the right of the enemy was partially turned, yet the main position could not be shaken until Picton and Cole had turned it by the left. Ney then commenced his retreat, retiring from ridge to ridge with admirable precision, and for a long time without confusion and with very little loss. Towards the middle of the day, however, the British guns and the skirmishers got within range of his masses, and the retreat became more rapid and less orderly; yet he finally gained the strong pass of Miranda de Corvo, which was secured by the main body of the French. The loss in the light division this day was eleven officers and a hundred and fifty men, and about a hundred prisoners were taken.

On the 15th the weather was so obscure that the allies could not reach the Ceira before four o'clock in the afternoon, and the troops as they came up proceeded to kindle fires for the night. The French right rested on some thick and wooded ground, and their left on the village of Fons d'Aronce; but Lord Wellington, having cast a rapid glance over it, directed the light division, who were seldom forgotten when honour was to be obtained, to hold the right in play, and at the same moment the horse artillery, galloping forward to a rising ground, opened with great and sudden effect. Ney's left wing, being surprised and overthrown by the first charge, dispersed in a panic, and fled in such confusion towards the river that some, missing the fords, were drowned, and others, crowding on the bridge, were crushed to death. On the right the ground was so rugged and close that the action resolved itself into a skirmish; and thus Ney was able to use some battalions to check the pursuit of his left; but meanwhile darkness came on, and the French troops in their disorder fired upon each other. Only four officers and sixty men fell on the side of the British: the enemy's loss was not less than five hundred, of which one half were drowned; and an eagle was afterwards found in the bed of the river when the waters had subsided. Ney maintained the left bank of the Ceira until every incumbrance had passed, and then, blowing up seventy feet of the bridge, sent his corps on. Thus terminated the first part of the retreat from Santarem, in which, though the ability of the French Commander was conspicuous, it revealed much that savoured of a harsh and ruthless spirit. Almost every horror that could make war hideous attended this dreadful march. Death was dealt out in all modes. Unpitying vengeance seemed to steel every breast. Lives were lost by wounds, by fatigue, by fire, by water, besides the numerous victims of famine. One of my comrades going out at dusk in search of provisions, on turning a corner stumbled over the body of a recently murdered man. The natives were of course excited to retaliate, and Colonel Napier once saw a peasant cheering on his dog to devour the dead and dying; the spirit of cruelty once unchained, smote even the brute creation. On the 15th, the French General, in order to diminish the incumbrances on his march, ordered a number of beasts of burden to be destroyed. The inhuman fellow charged with the execution, who, if known, would have long since been hooted from society, ham-stringed five hundred asses, and left them to starve; and thus they were found by the British army. The acute, but deep expression of pain, visible in these poor creatures' looks, wonderfully aroused the fury of the soldiers; and so little weight has reason with the multitude, when opposed by momentary sensation, that had prisoners been taken at that moment, no quarter most assuredly would have been given.

CHAPTER VI

AT day-light on the 3d of April our nearness to the enemy indicated the approach of another collision. The English General, having ten thousand men pivoted on the 5th division at Sabugal, designed to turn Reynier's left, and surround him before he could be succoured. This well-concerted plan was marred by one of those accidents to which war is always liable, and brought on the combat of Sabugal, one of the hottest in which I was ever engaged. The morning was so foggy that the troops could not gain their respective posts of attack with that simultaneous regularity which is so essential to success. Colonel Beckwith, who commanded the first brigade, halted at a ford to await orders, and at that moment a staff officer rode up, and somewhat hastily asked why he did not attack. The thing appeared rash; but with an enemy in front he could make no reply; and instantly passing the river, which was deep and rapid, mounted a steep wooded hill on the other side. Many of the men were up to their middle in water; and a dark heavy rain coming on, it was impossible for some time to distinguish friends from foes. The attack was thus made too soon; for owing to the obscurity, none of the divisions of the army had reached their respective posts; and Beckwith having only one bayonet regiment, and four companies of Riflemen, was advancing against more than twelve thousand infantry supported by cavalry and artillery. Scarcely had the Riflemen reached the top of the hill, when a compact and strong body of French drove them back upon the 43d. The weather cleared at that instant, and Beckwith at once saw and felt all his danger; but, well supported as he was, it was met with a heart that nothing could shake. Leading a fierce charge, he beat back the enemy, and the summit of the hill was attained; but at the same moment two French guns opened with grape, at the distance of a hundred yards: a fresh body appeared in front, and considerable forces fell upon either flank of the regiment. Fortunately, Reynier, little expecting to be attacked, had, for the convenience of water, placed his principal masses in the low ground, behind the height on which the action commenced; his renewed attack was therefore uphill; yet the musketry, heavy from the beginning, now increased to a storm. The French mounted the acclivity with great clamour; and it was evident that nothing but the most desperate fighting could save the regiment from destruction. Captain Hopkins, commanding a flank company of the 43d, immediately ran out to the right, and with admirable presence of mind seized a small eminence close to the French guns and commanding the ascent by which the French troops were approaching. His first fire was so sharp that the assailants were thrown into confusion: they rallied, and were again confounded by the volleys of this company: a third time they endeavoured to form an attack, when Hopkins, with a sudden charge, increased the disorder; and at the same moment the two battalions of the 52d regiment, which had been attracted by the fire, entered the line. Meantime the centre and left of the 43d were furiously engaged, and excited beyond all former precedent. Beckwith, wounded in the head, and with the blood streaming down his face, rode amongst the foremost of the skirmishers, directing all with ability, and praising the men in a loud, cheerful tone. I was close to him at the time. One of our company called out, "Old Sydney is wounded." Beckwith heard the remark, and instantly replied, "But he wont leave you: fight on, my brave fellows; we shall beat them." The musket bullets flew thicker and closer every instant; but the French fell fast: a second charge cleared the hill, a howitzer was taken, and the British skirmishers were even advanced a short way down the hill, when small bodies of French cavalry came galloping in from all parts, and obliged them to take refuge in the main body of the regiment.

Having brought down a Frenchman by a random shot, I advanced close to the poor fellow as he lay on his side. Never shall I forget the alarm that was pictured on his countenance: he thought I was going to bayonet him, to avert which he held out his knap sack, containing most likely all his worldly substance, by way of appeasing my wrath. Unwilling to injure a fallen foe, I did not take his life, and in a few seconds he was protected by a charge of cavalry.

The English line was now formed behind a stone wall above; yet one squadron of Dragoons surmounted the ascent, and with incredible desperation, riding up to this wall, were in the act of firing over it with their pistols, when a rolling volley laid nearly the whole of them prostrate. By this time, however, a second and stronger column of infantry had rushed up the face of the hill, endeavouring to break in and retake the howitzer, which was on the edge of the descent, and only fifty yards from the wall. But no man could reach it and live, so deadly was the 43d's fire. One of my comrades, having previously passed the howitzer, took a piece of chalk from his pocket, and, as he said, marked it as our own, and we were determined to keep it. Reynier, convinced at last, that he had acted unskilfully in sending up his troops in small parties, put all his reserves, amounting to nearly six thousand infantry, with artillery, and cavalry into motion, and outflanking the division on the left, appeared resolved to storm the contested position. At this critical period the 5th division passed the bridge of Sabugal, the British cavalry appeared on the hills beyond the enemy's left, and General Colville with the leading brigade of the 3d division, issued out of the woods on Reynier's right, and opened a fire on the flank that directly decided the fate of the day. The loss of the allies in this sanguinary contest, which did not last quite an hour, was nearly two hundred killed and wounded: that of the enemy was enormous,—three hundred dead bodies were heaped together on the hill, the greater part round the captured howitzer; and more than twelve hundred were wounded,—so unwisely had Reynier managed his masses, and so true and constant was the English fire. Lord Wellington afterwards observed that this was one of the most glorious actions that British troops ever sustained. If by this term we are to understand that a numerous and well-disciplined force was signally repulsed by one of numerical inferiority, and that on the British side our national honour was upheld, he was right. In any other sense, the glories of war are, I am afraid, of a cast rather ambiguous. I scarcely ever before saw such determined firmness in our troops. It amounted almost to invincibility. During the action there was through our ranks to be observed a fierce and terrible anger, before the breakings forth of which the enemy quailed and fled. Our fire was given with singular exactness and rapidity. This fine conduct arose partly from a sense of extreme personal danger,—for of that not a man was insensible; and partly from the desire which I believe pervaded every breast, of properly supporting the officers engaged. Among others, I had been unusually excited, and had dealt out wounds and destruction with an unsparing hand. In endeavouring to reach the enemy, all concern for my own preservation was forgotten. Just as the action commenced, a round shot struck a horseman close to my side, and brought him down. Daniel Lowry, an intimate friend, who was also within a few paces, was slain. My old Captain was hit and badly wounded: his place was, however, well supplied by Lieutenant Brown, who succeeded in the command of the company. After the action had ceased, the latter officer was pleased to take special notice of my conduct, and by his recommendation I was made Corporal in one of the companies of the regiment. We halted on the field of battle during the succeeding day; some of our men were quartered in a chapel which had been recently occupied by French troops. Nearly the whole of the interior fittings were destroyed. As the place had been used for Roman Catholic worship, saints and images, attired in fanciful vestments, "black, white, and grey, with all their trumpery," had been abundant. These petty divinities, despite of their alleged virtues, were upset and destroyed: some were prostrate on the floor; others were broken and disfigured; not a few had been consumed; and all that remained of many were a few glowing embers. As food now became dreadfully scarce, a small party, of which I was one, went in search of bread or any other article of sustenance we could procure. After wandering at least ten or twelve miles from the camp ground, we observed a young heifer, to which we immediately gave chase; but the animal was so timid, and withal so swift of foot, that after a weary pursuit the game was lost. The French soldiers had, in fact, laid waste the land. Having spread themselves over the surface of many a league, they had, like a devastating army of locusts, devoured every particle of food within reach; and what in some respects is worse, what they did not eat was destroyed. On ascending an eminence, we saw the smoke of several burning villages. One of the men discovered also, at a moderate distance, what appeared to be two or three huts; we accordingly made for them: on arriving near the spot, we found they were tents, pitched apparently for temporary use. Two or three women and some children presently appeared, when we asked if they had any bread and wine to sell; telling them at the same time, to secure their favour, that we were English soldiers. They were inexorable and declared they had nothing: but one of our party, not disposed to credit the ladies, forced his way into the tent, and dragged out a leathern bottle, containing perhaps twenty or thirty gallons of liquid. We flattered ourselves it was wine, but on inspection it was filled with oil. Several loaves of bread were, however, discovered, with which we made free; but had nearly paid a high price for the liberty taken. All on a sudden the whole party of women and children set up a dismal piercing shout, and almost at the same instant a numerous and armed party of men were observed rapidly coming down the mountain-side upon us. We were few in number, and unfortunately were without our muskets. Sensible that if overtaken, our lives were forfeited, a hasty retreat became necessary. We were chased for several miles; but owing to our superior speed, we at length left our pursuers behind. When out of the reach of danger, we halted, almost dead with fatigue, and divided our spoil. It amounted to a small piece of bread for each; but how sweet that morsel was, no man can tell but he who has been driven to desperate acts by the call of biting hunger. The next day our division took the route of Valdespina, to look out for the enemy on the side of the passes leading upon Coria; but Massena was in full retreat for Ciudad Rodrigo; and on the 5th he crossed the frontier of Portugal; so that Lord Wellington now stood victorious on the confines of that kingdom, having executed, what to others had appeared incredible and vain.

The pursuit was continued. When Massena reached the Agueda, his cavalry detachments, heavy artillery, and convalescents, again augmented his army to more than fifty thousand men; but the fatigue of the retreat, and want of provisions, would not suffer him to show a front to the allies: he therefore fell back to Salamanca, and Lord Wellington invested Almeida. Our division occupied Gallegos and Espeja, and the rest of the army were disposed in villages on both sides of the Coa. Here Colonel Waters, who had been taken near Belmonte, rejoined the army. His escape was most extraordinary. Confident in his own resources, he had refused his parole; but when carried to Ciudad Rodrigo, he rashly mentioned his intention to the Spaniard in whose house he was lodged. This man betrayed him; but a servant, detesting his master's treachery, secretly offered his aid, and Waters coolly allowed him to get the rowels of his spurs sharpened. When the French army was near Salamanca, Waters, being in the custody of Gendarmes, waited until their chief, who rode the only good horse in the party, had alighted; then, giving the spur to his own beast, he galloped off. This was an act of astonishing resolution and hardihood; for he was on a large plain, and before him, and for miles behind, the road was covered with the French columns. His hat fell off, and thus distinguished, he rode along the flank of the troops, some encouraging him, others firing at him, and the Gendarmes, sword in hand, close at his heels; but suddenly breaking at full speed between two columns, he gained a wooded hollow, and having baffled his pursuers, evaded the rear of the enemy's army. The beautiful village of Fuentes d'Onoro was now destined to suffer. It had escaped all injury during the previous warfare, though occupied alternately for above a year by both sides. Every family in it was known to our division; and it was therefore a subject of deep regret to find that the preceding troops had pillaged it, leaving only the shells of houses where, three days before, a friendly population had been living in comfort. This wanton act was so warmly felt by the whole army, that eight thousand dollars were afterwards collected by general subscription for the poor inhabitants; yet the injury sunk deeper than the remedy. The allies occupied a fine table-land, lying between the Turones and the Dos-Casos; the left at Fort-Conception, the centre towards the village of Alameda, the right at Fuentes d'Onoro, the whole distance being five miles. The first and third divisions were concentrated on a gentle declivity,

about a cannon-shot behind Fuentes d'Onoro, where the line
of ground occupied by the army turned back, and ended on the
Turones. The French came up in three columns abreast. General
Loison fell upon Fuentes d'Onoro, which was occupied by five
battalions of chosen troops. Most of the houses in this village were
at the bottom of the ravine; but an old chapel, and some buildings
on a craggy eminence, overhung one end. The low parts were
vigorously defended; yet the violence of the attack was so great,
and the cannonade so heavy, that the British abandoned the streets,
and could scarcely maintain the upper ground; and the fight was
becoming perilous, when three fresh regiments, coming down
from the main position, charged with so little ceremony, that the
French were forced back, and, after a severe contest, finally driven
over the stream of, Dos-Casos. On the 4th Massena arrived; and,
having examined all the line, made dispositions for the next day.
Forty thousand infantry, and five thousand horse, with thirty
pieces of artillery, were under arms; and they had shown, in the
action of the 3d, that their courage was not abated. The position
of the English was, on the other hand, not at all desirable; and it
required no common resolution to receive battle on ground so
dangerous. The action began by severe cavalry fighting; and the
British horsemen, being overmatched, retired behind the light
division, which threw itself into squares; but the main body of the
French were upon the seventh division, before the like formation
could be effected: nevertheless the troops stood firm, and,
although some were cut down, the Chasseurs Britanniques, taking
advantage of a loose wall, received the attack with such a fire,
that the enemy recoiled. Immediately after this, a commotion was
observed among the French squadrons: men and officers closed in
confusion towards one point, where a thick dust was arising, and
where loud cries, and the sparkling of blades, and the flashing of
pistols, indicated some, extraordinary occurrence. Suddenly the
multitude was violently agitated; an English shout arose, the mass
was rent asunder, and Norman Ramsey burst forth at the head of
his battery, his horses on full stretch, and his guns bounding along
like things of no weight, with the mounted gunners in close and
compact order protecting the rear. But while this brilliant action

was passing in one part, the enemy were making progress in the wood, and it was evident that the battle would soon be lost if the original position was not immediately regained.

In this posture of affairs, Lord Wellington directed the seventh division to cross the Turones and move down the left bank to Frenada. General Crauford, who had resumed the command of the light division, first covered the passage of the seventh, and then retired slowly over the plain in squares, having the British cavalry principally on the right flank. He was followed by the enemy's horse, which continually outflanked him, and near the wood surprised and sabred an advanced post of the Guards, making Colonel Hill and fourteen men prisoners. Several times Montbrun seemed disposed to storm the light division squares, but we were too formidable to be meddled with: yet, on the authority of Colonel Napier, there was not during the war a more dangerous hour than this for England. The whole of that vast plain, as far as the Turones, was covered with a confused multitude, amidst which the squares appeared but as specks. The seventh division was separated from the army by the Turones; five thousand French cavalry, with fifteen pieces of artillery, were close at hand, impatient to charge; the infantry of the eighth corps was in order of battle behind the horsemen; the wood was filled with the skirmishers of the sixth corps; and, if the latter body had issued forth, our division was in imminent danger of being broken. No effort of the sort was made: Montbrun's horsemen merely hovered about our squares; the plain was soon cleared, the cavalry took post behind the centre, and the light division formed a reserve, sending the Riflemen among the rocks to connect it with the seventh. At sight of this new front, so deeply lined with troops, the French stopped short, and commenced a heavy cannonade, which did great execution from the closeness of the allied masses; but twelve British guns replied with vigour, and the violence of the hostile fire abated. All this time a fierce battle was raging at Fuentes d'Onoro. Massena had directed Drouet to carry this village, at the very moment when Montbrun's cavalry should turn the right wing: it was, however, two hours later when the attack began. The three British regiments made a desperate resistance, but, overpowered by numbers, they were pierced and divided; two companies of the 79th were taken, Colonel Cameron was mortally wounded, and the lower part of the town was carried: the upper part was, however, stiffly held, and the rolling of musketry was incessant. In this manner the fight lasted till the evening, when the lower part of the town was abandoned by both parties; the British maintaining the crags, and the French retiring a cannon-shot from the stream. Fifteen hundred men and officers; of which three hundred were prisoners, comprised the loss of the allies: that of the enemy was computed at five thousand, but this I have reason to believe was an exaggerated statement. The night after the action, I was stationed on the line of-sentinels, not far from the French front, and at the extreme verge of our own: this service, which demands perpetual vigilance, requires also, on account of its wearisome and continued toil, no ordinary degree of physical energy, as the safety of the army itself often depends upon the caution and alertness with which the outposts are preserved. Often when pacing some doubtful position, at dead of night, I have applied my ear to the ground, to try if by that means a distant footstep could be heard. At the precise time to which I now refer, the feeble voice of many a poor wounded fellow, calling for help, might be heard: these were, however, removed by the par ties on both sides without delay, after which the dead were buried with as much decency and respect as circumstances allowed. A pile of about one hundred and thirty dead bodies, of which one-third were British, was discovered on a small space at Fuentes d'Onoro; and several large excavations or graves were formed, in which the remains of our fallen friends were deposited.

Soon after this period the French were compelled to evacuate Almeida; but by a singular and ingenious train of operations, the men who defended it contrived to effect their escape. During the battle of Fuentes d'Onoro, General Brennier, the Governor of Almeida, with his garrison of fifteen hundred, skirmished boldly with the blockading force, and loud explosions, supposed to be signals of communication with the relieving army, were frequently heard. When all hope of succour vanished, a soldier, named Tillet, contrived with extraordinary courage and presence of mind to penetrate, although in uniform, through the posts of the blockade, carrying Brennier's orders to evacuate the fortress. The blockade, it would appear, was imperfectly maintained: this was noticed by Brennier, who prepared to force his way through the encircling troops. An open country and a double line of troops greatly enhanced the difficulty; yet Brennier was resolved not only to cut his own passage, but to render the fortress useless to the allies. To effect this, he ruined all the principal bastions, and kept up a constant fire of his artillery, so directed that the mouth of one piece crossed that of another; while therefore some shots flew towards the besiegers, and a loud explosion was heard, others destroyed pieces without attracting notice. At midnight, on the 10th, all being ready, he sprung his mines, sallied forth in a compact column, broke through the piquets, and passed the quarters of the reserves, with a nicety that proved at once his talent of observation, and his coolness. General Pack followed, with a few men collected at the instant, and plied him with a constant fire; yet nothing could shake or retard his column, which in silence, and without returning a shot, gained the rough country upon Barba del Puerco. Here it halted for a moment, just as daylight broke: and Pack, who was at hand, hearing that some English Dragoons were in a village, sent an officer to bring them out, thus occasioning a slight skirmish, and consequent delay. The troops of the blockade had paid little attention at first to the explosion of the mines, thinking them a repetition of Brennier's previous practice; but Pack's fire having aroused them, the 36th regiment was close at hand; and the 4th also, having heard the firing at Valde-Mula, was rapidly gaining the right flank of the enemy. Brennier, having driven off the cavalry, was again in march; yet the British regiments, having thrown off their knapsacks, followed at such a pace that they overtook the rear of his column in the act of descending the deep chasm of Barba del Puerco, killed and wounded many, captured about three hundred, and even passed the bridge in pursuit. Lord Wellington, it is said, was stung by this event, and issued a remonstrance to the army, couched in terms which no one could misunderstand.

When Marmont had thus recovered the garrison of Almeida, he withdrew the greater part of his army to Salamanca. Lord Wellington also set out for that province; but before he could arrive, a great and bloody battle had closed the operations. Beresford held a conference with the Spanish Generals at Valverde, on the 13th, when it was resolved to abide the enemy's attack at Albuera. The position taken by the allied forces was, it is said, singularly defective. It was occupied by thirty thousand infantry, above two thousand cavalry, and thirty-eight pieces of artillery; but the brigade of the fourth division being still absent, the British infantry, the pith and strength of the battle, did not amount to seven thousand. The French had fifty guns, and above four thousand veteran cavalry, but only nineteen thousand chosen infantry; yet being of one nation, obedient to one discipline, and animated by one spirit, their excellent composition amply compensated for inferiority of numbers: beside which, it is acknowledged by military men, that the talents of their General were immeasurably greater than those of his adversary. Soult examined Beresford's position without hinderance on the evening of the 15th, and having detected the weaknesses of the entire arrangement, resolved to attack the next morning. Passing by the varied evolutions which preceded the contest, it may be sufficient to observe, that a little before nine in the morning, Godinet's division issued from the woods in one heavy column of attack, preceded by ten guns. He was flanked by the light cavalry, and followed by Werle's division of reserve; and, making straight towards the bridge, commenced a sharp cannonade, attempting to force the passage. The allies' guns, on the rising ground above the village, answered the fire of the French, and ploughed through their columns, which were crowding without judgment towards the bridge, although the stream was fordable above and below. Beresford, convinced that the principal effort would be on the right, sent Blake orders to form a part of the first, and all the second, line of the Spanish army on the broad part of the hills, at right angles to their actual front. Soon after, the enemy's columns began to appear on the right; and Blake, moving at last, proceeded in the evolution with such pedantic slowness, that Beresford, impatient of his folly, took the direction in person. Great was the confusion and delay thus occasioned; and before the troops could be put in order, the French were among them. In one short half hour Beresford's situation was rendered nearly desperate.

Two thirds of the French were in compact order of battle, on a line perpendicular to his right, and his army, disordered, and composed of different nations, was still in the difficult act of changing its front. The Spaniards were already in disorder; some had given way; and Soult, thinking that the whole army was yielding, pushed forward his columns, while his reserves also mounted the hill, and all the batteries were placed in position. At this critical moment, General Stewart arrived with Colonel Colborne's brigade, which formed the head of the second division. The Colonel seeing the confusion above, desired to form in order of battle previous to mounting the ascent; but Stewart, carried away by the impetuosity of his feelings, led up without any delay in column of companies, and attempted to open out his line in succession as the battalions arrived at the summit. Being under a destructive fire, the foremost charged to gain room, but a heavy rain prevented any object from being distinctly seen; and four regiments of Hussars and Lancers, which had passed the right flank in obscurity, came galloping in upon the rear of the line, at the instant of its developement and slew or took two-thirds of the brigade. In the tumult, a Lancer fell upon Beresford; but the Marshal, a man of great strength, putting his spear aside, cast him from his saddle; and a shift of wind blowing aside the mist and smoke, the mischief was perceived from the plains by General Lumley, who sent four squadrons out upon the Lancers, and cut many of them off. During this unhappy effort of the second division, so great was the confusion that the Spanish line continued to fire, although the British were before them; on which Beresford, finding his exhortations to advance fruitless, seized an Ensign, and bore him and his colours by main force to the front: yet the troops would not follow, and the man went back again on being released. At this juncture, Sir William Stewart once more advanced: and the weather having cleared, he poured a dreadful fire into the thickest of the French columns, convincing Soult, that whatever might be the result, the day was not yet won. Houghton's regiments soon got footing on the summit; Dickson placed the artillery in line; the remaining brigade of the second division came up on the left; and two Spanish corps at last moved forward. The enemy's infantry then recoiled; yet soon recovering, renewed the fight with greater violence than before. The cannon on both sides discharged showers of grape at half range, and the peals of musketry were incessant, and often within pistol-shot. But the close formation of the French embarrassed their battle, and the British line would not yield them one inch of ground, nor a moment of time, to open their ranks: their fighting was, however, fierce and dangerous. Stewart was twice hurt; Colonel Duckworth of the 48th was slain; and the valiant Houghton, who had received many wounds without shrinking, fell, and died in the act of encouraging his men. Still the combat raged with unabated fury. Colonel Inglis, twenty-two officers, and more than four hundred men, out of five hundred and seventy that had ascended the hill, fell in the 57th alone: and the other regiments were much the same in loss; not one-third were standing in any. Ammunition failed; and as the English fire slackened, the enemy established a column in advance upon the right flank the play of Dickson's artillery checked them for a moment, but again the Polish Lancers charged, and captured six guns. In this desperate crisis, Colonel Hardinge boldly ordered Cole to advance; and then riding to Colonel Abercrombie, who commanded the remaining brigade of the second division, directed him also to push forward into the fight. The die being thus cast, the terrible battle was continued. The field was heaped with carcases; the Lancers were riding furiously about the captured artillery on the upper slope of the hill; and on the lower parts a Spanish and an English regiment, in mutual error, were exchanging volleys; behind all, some Portuguese, in withdrawing from the heights above the bridge, appeared to be in retreat. All now appeared to be lost, when all was in a few minutes gained, by the conduct of a few brave and unconquerable men. Colonel Arbuthnot pushing between the fire of the mistaken troops, enlightened their minds; while Cole, with the Fusileers, flanked by a battalion of the Lusitanian legion, mounted the hill, dispersed the Lancers, recovered the captured guns, and soon appeared on the right of Houghton's brigade.

Such a gallant line, issuing from the midst of the smoke, and rapidly separating itself from the confused and broken multitude, startled the enemy's heavy masses, which were increasing and pressing onwards as to an assured victory: they wavered, hesitated, and then vomiting forth a storm of fire, hastily endeavoured to enlarge their front, while a fearful discharge of grape from all their artillery whistled through the British ranks. Myers was killed; Cole, and the three Colonels, Ellis, Blakeny, and Hawkshawe, fell wounded; and the Fusileer battalions, struck by the iron tempest, began to reel. In that moment, when the last particle of energy appeared to be gone, they arose in almost unprecedented might, and surpassed their former selves. Closing at once with their enemies, the strength and intrepidity of a British soldier were exhibited in deeds seldom seen. In vain did Soult, by voice and gesture, animate his Frenchmen; in vain did the hardiest veterans, extricating themselves from the crowded columns, sacrifice their lives to gain time for the mass to open out, on so fair a field; in vain did the mass itself bear up, and, fiercely striving, fire indiscriminately upon friends and foes, while the horsemen, hovering on the flank, threatened to charge the advancing line. Nothing could stop that astonishing infantry: their eyes were bent on the dark columns in front; their firm, heavy, and measured tread shook the ground; their dreadful volleys swept away the head of every formation; their deafening shouts overpowered the dissonant cries that broke from all parts of the tumultuous crowd, as foot by foot, and with horrid carnage, it was driven by the vigour of the attack to the extreme edge of the hill. Here the last stand was made, with the hope of averting this mountain torrent. But it was in vain: the effort only served to increase the irremediable confusion; and the mighty mass giving way, like a loosened cliff, went headlong down the ascent. The rain flowed after in streams discoloured with blood; and of six thousand British soldiers who performed these wonders, fifteen hundred unwounded men were all that remained upon the fatal hill. The serious fighting had endured only four hours; and in that space of time nearly seven thousand of the allies, and above eight thousand of their antagonists, were struck down. Three French Generals were wounded, two slain, and eight hundred soldiers so badly hurt as to be left on the field. On Beresford's side, beside the loss of the British already named, two thousand Spaniards, and six hundred Germans and Portuguese, were killed or wounded. The trophies of the French were five hundred unwounded prisoners, a howitzer, and several stand of colours: the British had nothing of that sort to display; but the piles of carcases within their lines told, with convincing eloquence, who were the conquerors; and all the night the rain poured down, and the rivers, and hills, and woods resounded with the groans of dying men. On the 18th Soult retreated.

Towards winter I was charged with a mission to fetch clothing from Lisbon for the use of the regiment. One description of article was flannel shirts, of which I received six hundred, for the approaching winter wear. On returning, I met with an accident, which had nearly deprived me of sight. One of our party, with consummate carelessness, placed his powder-horn upon the table, fully charged, and by some accident the whole quantity exploded: my face was sadly scorched, but providentially the organs of vision received no lasting injury. On returning with the property for the army, I found my way into considerable trouble. Our party consisted of six or seven persons: of these, three were Corporals; and of these three I was senior, and therefore sustained the responsibility of every act. Having to pass over several mountains of vast height, our progress was necessarily slow. One evening, having ascended the slope of a stupendous hill, on which the snow was deep, we were unable to move the cars on which the stores were carried. Having also but an imperfect knowledge of the pass, we found ourselves compelled to spend the night in that bleak and desolate region. All the shelter we could procure was to creep under the cars. Two of the men, were soon after seized with ague, and suffered extremely. The silence which prevailed in this elevated region was singularly impressive. After a wearisome night, which appeared almost endless, we were happy to perceive the first morning ray. We soon after discovered a man coming our way, driving two bullocks: I thought the omen a happy one; and in the spirit of the national war then raging I ordered the man to stop, and without hesitation pressed the animals into our service, by yoking them to our cars. The driver demanded my authority for so doing: I told him to look at my musket. To my dismay I afterwards found that some of the troops had been in the habit of laying violent hands upon cattle, having no other object in view than to extort money from

the owners when they applied to reclaim their property. To put
down this practice, Lord Wellington had issued a proclamation, of
which, unfortunately, I had not heard, denouncing these excesses
in terms of great severity. In fact, strange as it appeared to myself,
who had no intention of violating general orders, on my arrival
at quarters, I was handed over to the Provost-Marshal, deprived of
my arms and accoutrements, and thrown into confinement among
some of the most ill-favoured vagabonds that ever infested man or
beast. The officer in whose custody I was placed, proved himself
one of Job's comforters. He gave me to understand, that not long
since a man in the 52d had been shot for the exact crime of
which I was guilty: he then closed the prison-door and departed.
Conscious, however, that I had intended neither to rob nor injure,
my mind was supported. Let me tell an old-fashioned secret: the
Almighty has always been my guide and defence. What is more,
He always will. But, says an objector, this is rank fanaticism. That I
cannot help: such is the truth; nor can it be altered by the coinage
of any term, whether of approval or reproach. On the occasion
now described, I was released as if nothing had happened. After
my enlargement had taken place, I found that my worthy comrades
had been to the owner of the animals, and had exhausted the entire
circle of a soldier's pleading on my behalf. I was young; had not
heard of the late order; knew no better; used no violence; asked for
no money; was an Irishman: beside which they gave him to under
stand that I was a good Catholic; to which I believe they subjoined
a little cash in hand: these two latter arguments were irresistible,
and the matter was smoothly settled.

The new year opened with uncommon effort on the side of
the British forces in Spain. Lord Wellington, whose means of
collecting information were extensive and correct, had discovered
that a considerable reduction had taken place in the French army.
The Imperial Guards, seventeen thousand strong, were required
for the Russian war, and had returned to France; so that the force
in the Peninsula was diminished by sixty thousand men. Marmont
was also deceived, by what appeared to him the careless winter
attitude of the allies, and Ciudad Rodrigo was left unprotected.
The Frenchman was mistaken; and Wellington resolved to show

that he was, by grasping at that fortress. The troops disposable for the attack of Ciudad Rodrigo were about thirty-five thousand, including cavalry. From the scarcity of transports, only thirty-eight guns could be brought to the trenches, and these would have wanted their proper supply of ammunition, if eight thousand shot had not been found among the ruins of Almeida. When the place was closely examined, it was found that the French, in addition to the old works, had fortified two convents. They had also constructed an enclosed and pallisadoed redoubt upon the greater Teson; and this redoubt, called Francisco, was supported by two guns and a howitzer, placed upon the flat roof of the convent of that name. On minutely inspecting these enlarged works, it was resolved to storm Fort Francisco, and, opening the first parallel along the greater Teson, to form counter-batteries, with which to ruin the defences, and drive the besieged from the convent. Meanwhile, to cover the siege, Julian Sanchez, and Carlos d'Espana, were posted in observation of the enemy. On the 8th of January, the eighth division and some Portuguese forded the Agueda near Caridad, three miles above the fortress, and making a circuit took post beyond the great Teson. As there was no regular investment, the enemy did not believe that the siege was commenced; but in the evening the troops stood to their arms, and Colonel Colborne, commanding the 52d, having assembled two companies from each of the British regiments of the light division, stormed the redoubt of Francisco: of this party I had the honour to make one. The attack was so rapid and furious that the assailants appeared to be at one and the same time in the ditch, mounting the parapets, fighting on the top of the rampart, and forcing the gorge of the redoubt, where the explosion of one of the French shells had burst the gate open. The post was taken with the loss only of twenty-four men and officers; and working parties were set to labour on the right of it, for the fort itself was instantly covered with shot and shells from the town. This tempest continued through the night; but at day-break the parallel, six hundred yards in length, was sunk three feet deep, and four wide: the communication over the Teson to the rear was completed, and the progress of the siege was hastened several days by this well-managed assault. I was exposed to the fire of the enemy for some time previous to our arrival at the fort, but sustained no injury. We were discovered when about a hundred and fifty yards from the fort. After the redoubt had been taken, I was employed with several others in escorting the prisoners to a place of safety. The garrison, it seems, had no expectation of this unceremonious visit; and when we entered the place I observed several packs of cards, with which the men had been amusing themselves. On returning, I unexpectedly came in contact with a French soldier, who by some means or other had escaped notice. I called out instantly, desiring him to surrender, which he did; but while in the act of conducting him to the others, a British Sergeant, who deserves to be named, but on whom compassionate silence shall be shown, stopped the prisoner for the sake of plunder. Enraged at this unjust and discreditable interference, I placed my gun on the ground, determined to knock down the interloper, and secure my captive. A scuffle accordingly ensued; when, in an instant, we found, to our dismay, that further contention was needless. The Frenchman, observing our quarrel, instantly took to his heels, and, being exceedingly alert, was out of sight before I could fire at him. On the 12th we were employed in the trenches, from whence we picked off the enemy's gunners. The Riflemen also, taking advantage of a thick fog, did great execution; but in the night the weather was so cold, and the besieged shot so briskly, that little progress was made. Two days afterwards, the enemy, having observed that the men in the trenches went off in a disorderly manner on the approach of the relief, made a sally, and overturned the gabions of the sap; they even penetrated to the parallel, and were upon the point o entering the batteries, when a few of the workmen getting together, checked them until a support arrived, and thus the guns were saved. This affair, together with the death of the engineer on duty, and the heavy fire from the town, delayed the opening of the breaching batteries; but at half-past four in the evening, twenty-five heavy guns battered the rampart and two pieces were directed against the convent of Francisco. The spectacle was sublime. The enemy replied by more than fifty pieces; the bellowing of eighty large guns shook the ground far and wide; the smoke rested in heavy columns upon the battlements of the place; the walls crashed to the blow al the bullet; and when night put an end to this turmoil! the quick clatter of musketry was heard like the pattering of hail after a peal of thunder; for the 40th regiment assaulted and carried the convent of Francisco, and established itself on the suburb on the left of the attack. On the 17th the firing on both side was very heavy, and the wall of the place was beaten down in large cantles; but several of the besiegers' guns were dismounted, their batteries injured, and many of their men killed. General Borthwiek, the Commandant of the artillery, was wounded, and the sap was entirely ruined. Even the Riflemen in the pits were at first overpowered with grape; yet towards evening they recovered the upper hand, and the French could fire only from the more distant embrasures. In the night the battery intended for the lesser breach was armed, and that on the lower Teson raised, so as to afford cover in the day-time. On the 19th it was reported that both breaches were practicable, and a plan of attack was immediately formed.

All the troops reached their different posts without seeming to attract the attention of the enemy; but be fore the signal was given, and while Lord Wellington was still at the convent of Francisco, the attack on the right commenced, and was instantly taken up along the whole line. The space between the army and the ditch was then ravaged by a tempest of grape from the ramparts. The storming parties of the third division jumped out of the parallel when the first shout arose; but so rapid had been the movements on their right, that before they could reach the ditch, three regiments had already scoured the fausse-braye, and were pushing up the great breach, amid the bursting of shells, the whistling of grape and muskets, and the shrill cries of the French, who were driven fighting behind the retrenchments. There, however, they rallied, and, aided by the musketry from the houses, made hard battle for their post; none would go back on either side, and yet the British could not get for ward; and men and officers, filling in heaps, choked up the passage, which was incessantly raked with grape from two guns flanking the top of the breach at the distance of a few yards. It was now our turn. We had three hundred yards to clear; but, impatient of delay, we did not wait for the hay-bags, but swiftly ran to the crest of the glacis, jumped down the scarp, a depth of eleven feet, and rushed up the fausse braye, under a smashing discharge of grape and musketry. The bottom of the ditch was dark and intricate, and the forlorn hope took too much to their left; but the storming party went straight to the breach, which was so contracted, that a gun placed lengthwise across the top nearly blocked up the opening. Here the forlorn hope rejoined the stormers; but when two-thirds of the ascent were gained, the leading men, crushed together by the narrowness of the place, staggered under the weight of the enemy's fire. Our Commander, Major Napier, was at this moment struck to the earth by a grape-shot, which shattered his arm, but he called on his men to trust to their bayonets; and all the officers simultaneously sprang to the front, when the charge was renewed with a furious shout, and the entrance was gained. The supporting regiments then came up in sections abreast, and the place was won. During the contest, which lasted only for a few minutes after the fausse-braye was passed, the fighting had continued at the great breach with unabated violence; but when the 43d, and the stormers of the light division, came pouring down on the right flank of the French, the latter yielded to the storm; at the same mo the explosion of three wall-magazines destroyed many persons, and the third division with a mighty effort broke through the retrenchments. The garrison fought for a short time in the streets, but finally fled to the castle, where an officer, who, though wounded, had been amongst the foremost at the lesser breach, received the Governor's sword. The allies now plunged into the streets from all quarters; after which, throwing off the restraints of discipline, frightful excesses were committed. The town was fired in three or four places; the soldiers menaced their officers, and shot each other; many were killed in the market-place; intoxication soon in creased the disorder; and at last, the fury rising to an absolute madness, a fire was wilfully lighted in the middle of the great magazine, when the town, and all in it, would have been blown to atoms, but for the energetic courage of some officers and a few soldiers, who still preserved their senses. Three hundred French had fallen; fifteen hundred were made prisoners; and beside the immense store of ammunition, above one hundred and fifty pieces of artillery were captured in the place. The whole loss of the allies was about twelve hundred soldiers, and ninety officers; and of these above six hundred and fifty men, and sixty officers, had been slain or hurt in the breaches. General Crauford and General Mackinnon were killed. With these died many gallant men; and amongst others, a Captain in the regiment to which I belonged. Of him it was felicitously said, that "three Generals and seventy other officers had fallen; but the soldiers fresh from the strife only talked of Hardyman." Unhappily, the slaughter did not end with the battle; for the next day, as the prisoners and their escort were marching out by the breach, an accidental explosion took place, and numbers of both were blown into the air. The personal sufferings of the soldiers were severe, as the service had been unusually dangerous. While in the front ditch near the glacis, a live shell exploded within a few paces of the spot on which I stood: we threw ourselves flat on the ground, but, though nearly suffocated by the dust it threw around, no material injury was inflicted either on myself or comrades. The station I was ordered to take on the following day was of a melancholy cast. It was in the ditch, among the unburied dead. Nothing struck me more forcibly than the conduct of a soldier's widow. Suspecting that her husband had fallen, she traversed this vale of death to seek him. Never shall I forget the anguish of her soul when she discovered the much-loved remains. The brave man had fallen covered with wounds. His countenance was sadly disfigured, and suffused with blood. She fell upon his face, and kissed his faded lips. She then gazed at the lifeless form, repeated her embraces, and gave way to the wild and ungovernable grief which struggled for expression. Sin! what hast thou done? Nor can I forbear observing, that a noble disregard for suffering, and fortitude of no common kind, were frequently shown both by officers and men, those severely hurt and disabled. None retired to the rear, until compelled by stern necessity. This resolute disposition to surmount, and if possible forget, all surmountable difficulties, re minds me of a French royalist officer, in the late revolutionary war. Being engaged in a desperate action, he had the misfortune to have both his legs carried away by a cannon-ball. While lying on the ground, a wounded soldier indulged in loud and clamorous complaints: "Peace, friend," said the officer: "our God died upon the cross; our King perished on the scaffold; and I have lost my limbs. Revere the Almighty, and be patient."

The siege of Ciudad Rodrigo lasted twelve days. When the Commander-in-chief terminated his order for the assault, with this sentence, "Ciudad Rodrigo must be stormed this evening," he knew well that it would be nobly understood. The difficulties we had to encounter were great. The principal breach was cut off from the town by a perpendicular descent of six teen feet; and the bottom was planted with sharp spikes, and strewed with live shells. The houses behind were all loop-holed and sprinkled with musketeers.

The French had left their temporary bridges, but behind were parapets so powerfully defended, that it was said the third division could never have carried them, had hot the light division taken the enemy in flank. To recompense an exploit so boldly undertaken and so nobly finished, Lord Wellington was created Duke of Ciudad Rodrigo, by the Spaniards, Earl of Wellington, by the English, and Marquis of Torres Vedras, by the Portuguese.

CHAPTER VII

SOON after the close of the siege just described, I received, in conjunction with others who were similarly entitled, my share of prize-money, on account of the property captured some years before at Copenhagen. Some arrears of pay were also supplied by the hands of Major Wells. A little good advice was kindly subjoined. We were exhorted to save our money, to avoid excesses, and spend with economy. But alas! how hardly shall they that are rich keep in the path of moderation and humility. The cash burnt in our pockets. The intimations so civilly given were altogether wasted, and might as well have been addressed to our knapsacks. No sooner did opportunity offer, than the wine-houses washed away, not only all our good advices, but the whole of our hard-earned pittance so recently distributed. When a man is determined to indulge in liquor, he is almost sure to find some justification for it. It is commonly of Dean Aldrich's sort, more wordy than wise:

> Good wine, old friends, or being dry,
> Or that he may be by and by,
> Or any other reason why.

I am sorry to admit that I was carried away with the torrent of sensuality, which at this time set in with a kind of powerful flood-tide. Every good impression was well nigh obliterated from my mind. The nice mental perception of right and wrong, which I retained as a valued relic, resulting from my mother's advices, was nearly blunted; and my subsequent experience has shown me, that when once the barrier between vice and virtue is weakened, or is dimly visible, great danger is at hand. Among other habits unhappily contracted was that of profane swearing; which, connected with

singing licentious ballads, and free living, completed the depravity
of my conduct. And yet I was more proud of my religion than ever;
and had any one called in question the infallibility of the Pope, I
should have instantly challenged him to fight for the insolence of
the thing.

It has been observed by an acute military writer, that the
talents of Lord Wellington rose with his difficulties; and notwithstanding the serious impediments which obstructed the measure,
he resolved to subdue the important fortress of Badajos. He
accordingly proceeded to Elvas, which he reached on the 11th
of March, and arrangements were immediately commenced for
the formal investment of the place. Badajos is a regularly fortified
town. The garrison, composed of French, Hessian, and Spanish
troops, was now near five thousand strong. Phillipon, the Governor,
had greatly improved the defences of the place. A second ditch
had been dug at the bottom of the great one, which was also
in some parts filled with water. The gorge of the Pardaleras was
inclosed, and that outwork was connected with the body of the
place, from whence powerful batteries looked into it. The three
western fronts were mined; and on the east, the arch of the bridge
behind the San Roque was built up to form an inundation two
hundred yards wide, which greatly contracted the space by which
the place could be approached by troops; and all the inhabitants
had been compelled, on pain of being sent away, to lay up food for
three months; The plan fixed upon by the besiegers was, to attack
the bastion of Trinidad, because the counter-guard there being
unfinished, the bastion could be battered from the hill on which
Picurina stood. Of nine hundred gunners present, three hundred
were British, the rest Portuguese; and there were one hundred and
fifty sappers, volunteers from the third division. In the night of the
17th eighteen hundred men broke ground one hundred and sixty
yards from the Picurina. A tempest, which happened to arise, stifled
the sound of their pickaxes; and though the work was commenced
late, a communication four thousand feet in length was formed,
and a parallel of six hundred yards, three feet deep, and three feet
six inches wide, was opened. However, when the day broke, the
Picurina was reinforced; and a sharp musketry, interspersed with

discharges from some field-pieces, aided by heavy guns from the body of the place, was directed on the trenches. On the 19th Lord Wellington, having secret intelligence that a sally was intended, ordered the guards to be reinforced. Nevertheless, at one o'clock, some cavalry came out by the Talavera gate; and thirteen hundred infantry, under the command of General Vielland, filed unobserved into the communication between the Picurina and the San Roque. These troops, jumping out, at once drove the workmen before them, and began to demolish the parallel. Previous to this outbreak the French cavalry, forming two parties, had commenced a sham-fight on the right of the parallel; and the smaller party, pretending to fly, and answering Portuguese to the challenge of the piquets, were allowed to pass. Elated by the success of their stratagem, they then galloped to the engineers' park, which was a thousand yards in the rear of the trenches, and there cut down some men,—not many, for succour soon came; and meanwhile the troops at the parallel, having rallied upon the relief which had just arrived, beat the enemy's infantry back, even into the castle. In this hot fight the besieged lost above three hundred men and officers, the besiegers only one hundred and fifty; but Colonel Fletcher, the chief engineer, was badly wounded; and several hundred trenching-tools were carried off;—for Phillipon had promised a high price for each: yet this turned out ill; for the soldiers, instead of pursuing briskly, dispersed to gather the tools. After the action, a squadron of Dragoons, and six field-pieces, were placed as a reserve-guard behind St. Michael and a signal-post was established on the Sierra de Venta, to give notice of the enemy's motions.

On the 24th the fifth division invested the place, on the right bank of the Guadiana: the weather was fine, and the batteries were heavily armed. The next day at eleven o'clock, the pieces opened but were so vigorously opposed, that one howitzer was dismounted, and several artillery and engineer officers were killed. Nevertheless, the San Roche was silenced; and the garrison of the Picurina was so galled by the marksmen in the trenches, that no man dared look over the parapet. Hence, as the external appearance of the fort did not indicate much strength, General Kempt was charged to assault it in the night. The outward seeming of the Picurina was, however,

fallacious: the fort was very strong; the fronts were well covered
by the glacis; the flanks were deep; and the rampart, fourteen feet
perpendicular from the bottom of the ditch, was guarded with thick
slanting pales above; and from thence to the top there were sixteen
feet of an earthen slope. Seven guns were mounted on the works,
the entrance to which, by the rear, was protected with three rows
of thick paling; the garrison was above two hundred strong, and
every man had two muskets. The top of the rampart was furnished
with loaded shells, to pushover; and finally some small mines, and
a loop-holed gallery under the counter scarp intended to take the
assailants in rear, were be gun, but not finished. Five hundred men
of the third division being assembled for the attack, General Kempt
ordered two hundred, under Major Rudd, to turn the fort on the
left; an equal force, under Major Shaw, to turn the fort by the right;
and one hundred from each of these bodies were directed to enter
the communication with San Roche, and intercept any succours
coming from the town. The engineers, with twenty-four sappers
bearing hatchets and ladders, guided these columns; and fifty men
of the light division, provided also with axes, were to move out of
the trenches at the moment of attack.

The night was fine, the arrangements clearly and skilfully made,
and about nine o'clock the two flanking bodies moved forward.
The distance was short, and the troops quickly closed on the fort,
which, black and silent before, now seemed one mass of fire: then
the assailants, running up to the palisades in the rear, endeavoured
to break through; and when the destructive musketry of the
French and the thickness of the pales rendered their efforts useless,
they turned against the faces of the work, and strove to break in
there; but the depth of the ditch, and the slanting stakes at the top
of the brick-work, baffled them.

At this time, the enemy firing incessantly and dangerously, the
crisis appeared imminent; and Kempt sent the reserve headlong
against the front: thus the fight was continued strongly; the carnage
became terrible; and a battalion coming out from the town to
succour the fort, was encountered, and beaten by the party on
the communication. The guns of Badajos and of the castle now
opened; the guard of the trenches replied with musketry; rockets

were thrown up by the besieged; and the shrill sound of alarm-bells, mixing with the shouts of the combatants, increased the tumult. Still Picurina sent out streams of fire, by the light of which dark figures were seen furiously struggling on the ramparts; for Powis first escaladed the place in front, where the artillery had beaten down the pales; and the other assailants had thrown their ladders on the flanks, in the manner of bridges, from the brink of the ditch to the slanting stakes; and all were fighting hand to hand with the enemy. Meanwhile the axe-men of the light division, compassing the fort like prowling wolves, discovered the gate, and hewing it down, broke in by the rear. Yet the struggle continued: Powis Holloway, Gips, and Oats, of the 88th, fell wounded in or beyond the rampart. Nixon, of the 52d, was shot, two yards within the gate; Shaw, Rudd, and nearly all the other officers, had fallen outside: and it was not until nearly half the garrison were killed, that Gasper Thiery, the Commandant, and eighty-six men surrendered, while a few rushing out of the gate endeavoured to cross the bridge, and were drowned. This intrepid assault, which lasted an hour, cost four officers and fifty men killed, fifteen officers and two hundred and fifty men wounded; and so vehement was the fight throughout, that the garrison either forgot or had not time to roll over the shells and combustibles arranged on the rampart.

On the 3d of April it was evident that the crisis of the siege drew nigh. The British guns being all turned against the curtain, the masonry crumbled rapidly away; in two hours a yawning breach appeared; and Lord Wellington, having examined the points of attack in person, gave the order for assault. The soldiers then made themselves ready for the approaching combat, one of the most fierce and terrible ever exhibited in the annals of war. Posterity will find it difficult to credit the tale, but many who are still alive know that it is true. The British General was so sensible of Phillipon's firmness, and of the courage of his garrison, that he spared them the affront of a summons; yet, seeing the breach strongly entrenched, and the enemy's flank fire still powerful, he would not in this dread crisis trust his fortune to a single effort. Eighteen thousand soldiers burned for the signal of attack, and as he was unwilling to lose the Services of any, to each division he gave a task such as few Generals would have the hardihood to contemplate. Nor were the enemy idle, for while it was yet twilight some French cavalry issued from the Pardaleras, escorting an officer, who endeavoured to look into the trenches, with a view to ascertain if an assault was intended; but the piquet on that side jumped up, and, firing as it ran, drove him and his escort back into the works. The darkness then fell, and the troops awaited the signal.

With respect to myself, I could not help largely sharing in the general desire to advance: indeed, our duty in the trenches had been so severe, that, in spite of approaching peril, we had no objection to move. I had been stationed in battery number six, and was frequently exposed to a terrific raking fire from the besieged. Directions, I remember, were given on one occasion to fill a quantity of sand-bags. Poor Woollams, a private in the regiment, and myself, worked together; he held the mouth of the sack open, while I threw in the sand with a shovel: before we had been long thus engaged, a shell struck his knee, and in an instant severed his leg, which dropt on the ground: he fell backwards, while the shell, which lodged in the earth at a few feet distance, had burnt nearly to the exploding point. Aware of the approaching danger, I threw myself on my face; and I had scarcely taken the precaution when the shell burst with ruinous effect. Stones, dust, and fragments of timber were scattered in all directions; and among other substances whirled into the air, was the lost limb of my comrade. I knew it while descending by the pattern of the gaiter. As the leg was useless, I ran to the sufferer to whom it had belonged, tied my coat-strap round his thigh to check the effusion of blood, and, after placing him in a blanket, carried him to the nearest hospital, where surgical assistance was promptly afforded. On my return to the trenches, another friend was borne off greatly hurt: a comrade was loading his musket, and while the ramrod was in the barrel, the piece was accidentally discharged. The ramrod pierced through his body, and so firmly was the worm-end fixed near the backbone, that the strongest man among us was unable to move it. He was conveyed to the infirmary, and things went on as usual, as no calamity of this sort could be allowed to interfere with the duties then before us. The fine young man, whose case is just recorded, recovered from the wound, but was, I believe, eventually drowned in a river near Salamanca. At another time, during a violent cannonade from the besieged, I had been conversing with a man on the trenches, when our discussion was closed by a round shot, which took away the head of the respondent, as smoothly as if it had been sabred. I was also informed that another of our men had been killed merely by the wind of a cannon-bullet; but as I did not witness the circumstance, I will not vouch for its correctness. Not long before the storming parties were selected, a sad in of the fatal effects of intemperance occurred. One of our company was ordered out on duty, but, being in a state of inebriety, durst not appear. We afterwards missed him altogether; and some time after, we found his lifeless body coiled up in a blanket, in a crouching posture, behind one of the tents. Our opinion was, that he had crept there for secrecy, and by some means or other was smothered. All that remained in our power we did, which was to consign his remains to the parent earth. The day on which we proceeded to Badajos I received a letter from my brother in Ireland, in which he recommended me to an officer named Carey. After some search I found the gentleman, who received me with genuine kindness, and promised his future patronage when the town was taken; an engagement on which, from his frank and generous bearing, I at once felt it was safe to depend. But, Lord, what is man, or the best of men? My newly-acquired friend fell while leading on his men; so that our brief intercourse was the first and last which this world afforded.

We were now selected and classified for the actual assault. The difficulty was, not to procure men enough, but how to refuse applications,—for all were ready. Nor were these offers founded in ignorance of the nature of the expected service: the candidates were not such novices. The watch-word of Nelson was not forgotten,—"England expects every man to do his duty;" and the resolution which everywhere prevailed, was entered into with a thorough consciousness that life was then scarcely worth an hour's purchase. And yet every countenance was bright, for every heart was firm; and it was clear that the elevation and strength of mind so universally prevalent, was the effect of principle, well considered, and approved. Indeed, there was no stimulus at hand, to produce superficial excitement; no drops of Scheidam, to generate Dutch courage: the men were kept in the utmost silence and order. It is true, here and there a soldier might be perceived stealing from the trenches, with a little refreshment in his canteen for the friend with whom he was to part; and in return, more than one message, the last to be delivered on earth, was sent from many a brave man to mother, wife, or some other valued relative, with directions that if killed, the knapsack of a certain number, with its contents, should be duly forwarded. The night was dry, but clouded; the air thick with watery exhalations from the river; the ramparts and the trenches were unusually still, yet a low murmur pervaded the latter, and in the former, lights were seen to flit here and there; while the deep voices of the sentinels at times proclaimed that all was well in Badajos. The French, confiding in Phillipon's direful skill, watched from their lofty station the approach of enemies, whom they had twice before baffled, and now hoped to drive a third time, blasted and mined, from the walls. At ten o'clock the whole of the works were to have been simultaneously assailed, and it was hoped that the strength of the enemy would shrivel before this fiery girdle; but the disappointments of war are many. An unforeseen accident delayed the attack of the 5th division; and a lighted carcass thrown from the castle falling close to where the men of the 3d division were drawn up, discovered their array, and obliged them to anticipate the signal by half an hour. Then, every thing being suddenly disturbed, the double columns of the 4th and light divisions also moved silently and swiftly against the breaches; and the guard of the trenches rushing forward with a shout, encompassed the San Roque with fire, and broke in so violently that scarcely any resistance was made. General Kempt passed the Rivellas in single files by a narrow bridge, under a terrible musketry; and then re-forming and running up the rugged hill, had reached the foot of the castle, when he fell severely wounded, and being carried back to the trenches, met Picton, who hastened forward to take the command. Meanwhile his troops spreading along the front reared their ladders, some against the lofty castle, some against the adjoining front on the left, and with incredible courage ascended amidst showers of heavy stones, logs of wood, and bursting shells rolled off the parapet; while from the flanks the enemy plied his musketry with fearful rapidity, and in front with pikes and bayonets stabbing the leading assailants, or pushed the ladders from the walls; and all this attended with deafening shouts, and the crash of breaking ladders, and the shriek of soldiers crushed by violent falls. Still, swarming round the remaining ladders, these undaunted veterans strove who should first climb; until all being overturned, the French shouted victory, and the British, baffled but untamed, fell back a few paces, and took shelter under the rugged edge of the hill. Here, when the broken ranks were somewhat re-formed, the heroic Colonel Ridge, springing forward, called with stentorian voice on his men to follow; and seizing a ladder, once more raised it against the castle, yet to the right of the former attack, where the wall was lower, and an embrasure offered some facility. A second ladder was soon placed alongside the first, by the Grenadier officer Canch; and the next instant he and Ridge were on the rampart: the shouting troops pressed after them; the garrison, amazed, and in a manner surprised, were driven fighting through the double gate into the town, and the castle was won. A reinforcement sent from the French reserve then came up a sharp action followed, both sides fired through the gate, and the enemy retired; but Ridge fell,—and no man died that night with greater honour.

During these events, the tumult at the breaches was such, as if the very earth had been rent asunder, and its central fires were bursting up uncontrolled. The two divisions had reached the glacis in silence; as yet no stir was heard, and darkness covered the breaches. Some hay-packs were then thrown, several ladders placed, and the forlorn hopes and storming parties of the light division, about five hundred in all, had descended into the ditch without opposition, when a bright flame shooting upwards displayed all the terror of the scene. The ramparts, crowded with dark figures, and glittering arms, were on the one side; and on the other the red columns of the British, deep and broad, were coming on like streams of burning lava. A crash immediately followed, and the storming parties were dashed to pieces with incredible violence by the explosion of hundreds of shells and powder barrels. The place which fell to my lot was just in the centre of this hurly-burly. With what similitude to illustrate our condition at that moment, I know not. The regular discharge of musketry at given distances, and the usual clash of arms, infield-warfare, is rather rough, to say the least of it; but the collision of hostile forces in open space, where the combatants may evade approaching ruin, is civil pastime compared with this deadly ditch-conflict. Each of the men fought as if the issue of the assault depended on his single arm. As to timidity, the thing was unknown: every drum-boy acted well. Shielded by Eternal Mercy, all undeserving as I was, my life was preserved. Not that it then appeared even to myself worth consideration. All thought of self-protection was banished from the corps in general. Every nerve and muscle was strained to the utmost tension in the struggle; among the whole body there appeared to be only one heart; and in the attempt to reach the ramparts all other considerations merged. But what an assemblage of furies; the excitement was indescribable. Fancying that the man immediately behind myself did not press forward with sufficient energy, I turned round, and with imprecations of which the bare remembrance causes regret, I declared that if he did not push on I would shoot him. Most likely I was wrong, not only in language but in opinion: I have since thought the man did his best; but in the raging of such a tempest, mistakes were easily made, and the mere notion of defective effort ignited the passions. For one instant we stood on the brink of the ditch, amazed at the terrific sight; then with a shout that matched even the sound of the explosion, the men flew down the ladders, or, disdaining their aid, leaped, unmindful of the depth, into the gulf below. The fourth division came running after, and followed with like fury: there were, how ever, only five ladders for both columns, which were close together; and a deep cut made in the bottom of the ditch as far as the counter-guard of the Trinidad, was filled with water from the inundation; into this watery snare the head of the fourth division fell, and it is said that above a hundred of the Fusileers, the men of Albuera, were there smothered. Great was the confusion at this juncture; for now the ravelin was crowded with men of both divisions, and while some continued to fire, others ran down and jumped towards the breach; many also passed between the ravelin and the counter-guard of the Trinidad; the two divisions got mingled; and the reserves, who should have remained at the quarries, also came pouring in, until the ditch was quite filled,—the rear still crowding forward, and all cheering vehemently. The enemy's shouts were also loud and terrible; and the bursting of shells and of grenades, the roaring of the guns from the flanks, answered by the iron howitzers from the battery of the parallel, the heavy rolls and explosion of the powder-barrels, the flight of the blazing splinters, the loud exhortations of the officers, and the continued clatter of the muskets, made a maddening din.

Impatient of delay, a heavy column now bounded up the great breach; but across the top glittered a range of sword-blades, sharp-pointed, keen-edged on both sides, and firmly fixed in ponderous beams, which were chained together and set deep in the ruins; and for ten feet in front the ascent was covered with loose planks studded with sharp iron points, on which the feet of the foremost being set, the planks moved, and the unhappy soldiers, falling forward on the spikes, rolled down upon the ranks behind. Then the French men, exulting at the success of their stratagem, and leaping forward, plied their shot with terrible rapidity; for every man had several muskets, and each musket, in addition to its ordinary charge, contained a small cylinder of wood, stuck full of leaden slugs, which scattered like hail when they were discharged. At the beginning of this dreadful conflict, Colonel Andrew Barnard had, with prodigious efforts, separated his division from the other, and preserved some degree of military array: but now the tumult was such that no command could be heard distinctly, except by those close at hand; and the mutilated bodies, heaped on each other, and the wounded, struggling to avoid being trampled upon, broke the formations. Order was unattainable: yet officers of all stations, followed more or less numerously by the men, were seen to start out, as if struck by sudden madness, and rush into the breach. In one of these attempts, Colonel M'Leod, of our regiment, a young man, whose feeble body would have been quite unfit for war, had it not been sustained by an unconquerable spirit, was killed. Wherever his voice was heard, there his soldiers gathered; and with such a strong resolution did he lead them up the fatal ruins, that when one behind him in falling plunged a bayonet in his back, he complained not, and, continuing his course, was shot dead within a yard of the sword-blades. Two hours spent in these vain efforts convinced the soldiers that the breach of the Trinadad was impregnable. Gathering in dark groups, and leaning on their muskets, they looked up with sullen desperation; while the enemy, stepping out on the ramparts, and aiming their shots by the light of the fire-balls which they threw over, asked, as their victims fell, "why they did not come into Badajos!"

About midnight, when two thousand brave men had fallen, Wellington, who was on a height close to the quarries, sent orders for the remainder to retire, and re-form for a second assault; for he had just then heard that the castle was taken, and, thinking the enemy would still hold out in the town, was resolved to assail the breaches again. This retreat from the ditch, however, was not effected without further carnage and confusion; for the French fire never slackened, and a cry arose that the French were making a sally from the distant flanks, which caused a rush towards the ladders. Then the groans and lamentations of the wounded, who could not move, and expected to be slain, increased; many officers, who had not heard of the order, endeavoured to stop the soldiers from going back, and so would even have removed the ladders, but were unable to break through the crowd.

All this time, the third division was lying close to the castle; and, either from the fear of risking the loss of a point which ensured the capture of the place, or that the egress was too difficult, made no attempt to drive away the enemy from the breaches. On the other side, however, the fifth division had commenced the false attack on the Pardaleras; and on the right of the Guadiana, the Portuguese were sharply engaged at the bridge. Thus the town was begirt; for General Walker's brigade, having pressed on during the feint on the Pardaleras, was escalading the distant bastion of San Vincente. His troops had advanced along the banks of the river, and reached the French guard-house at the barrier gate undiscovered, for the ripple of the waters smothered the sound of their footsteps; but

just then the explosion at the breaches took place, the moon
shone out, and the French sentinels, discovering the columns, fired.
The British troops, immediately springing forward under a sharp
cover of musketry, began to hew down the wooden barrier at the
covered way, while the Portuguese, being panic-stricken, threw
down the scaling-ladders. Nevertheless, the others snatched them
up again, and forcing the barrier, jumped into the ditch; but the
guiding engineer officer was killed; and when the foremost man
succeeded in reaching the ladders, the latter were found too short,
for the walls were generally above thirty feet high. Meanwhile the
fire of the French was deadly, a small mine was sprung beneath the
soldiers' feet, beams of wood and live shells were rolled over on
their heads, showers of grape from the flank swept the ditch, and
man after man dr6pped dead from the ladders. Fortunately, some
of the defenders having been called away to aid in recovering the
castle, the ramparts were not entirely manned; and the assailants,
having discovered a corner of the bastion where the scarp was only
twenty feet high, placed three ladders there, under an embrasure
which had no gun, and was only stopped with a gabion. Some
men with extreme difficulty got up, for the ladders were still too
short; and the first man who gained the top was pushed up by
his comrades, and then drew others after him, until many had
gained the summit; and though the French shot heavily against
them from both flanks, and from a house in front, they thickened
and could not be driven back. Half the 4th regiment entered the
town itself to dislodge the enemy from the houses while the others
pushed forward towards the breach, and by dint of hard fighting
successively mastered three bastions. In this disorder a French
reserve, under General Viellande, drove on the British advance
with a firm and rapid charge, and pitching some men over the
walls, and killing others outright, again cleared the ramparts even
to the San Vincente. There, however, Colonel Nugent had taken
his station with a battalion of the 38th, as a reserve; and when
the French came up, shouting and slaying all before them, this
battalion, about two hundred strong, arose, and with one close
volley destroyed them. The panic then ceased; the soldiers rallied,
and in compact order once more charged along the walls towards

the breaches; but the French, although turned on both flanks, did not yield. Meanwhile the detachment of the 4th regiment, which had entered the town when the San Vincente was first carried, was strangely situated; for the streets were empty, and brilliantly illuminated, and no person was seen; yet a low murmur or whisper was occasionally heard, lattices were now and then gently opened, and from time to time shots were fired from underneath the doors of the houses. However, the troops, with bugles sounding, advanced towards the great square of the town; and in their progress captured several mules going with ammunition to the breaches. At length the French were beaten back, other parties entered the place; and finally, General Viellande, and Phillipon, who was wounded, seeing all ruined, passed the bridge with a few hundred soldiers, and entered San Cristoval, where they all surrendered early the next morning, upon summons, to Lord Somerset, who had with great readiness pushed through the town to the draw-bridge before they had time to organize further resistance.

In these protracted conflicts many of the finest soldiers in the British army met their fate, and fell in the firm and vigorous discharge of their duty. Of these, numbers might have been preserved had they chosen to have fallen back; but it was with them a point of honour to gain the breach or die on the spot. So wonderful is the resolution of a noble heart; and so much the more is it to be regretted, that power, so morally invincible, should be employed in the sad purpose of human destruction. For my own part, my mind had been unhesitatingly made up from the first shot that was fired, that so long as life and consciousness continued, I would fulfil my commission to the best of my ability. As the battle grew hot I caught the contagion that burned all around, and in this desperate and murderous mood advanced to the breach of Trinidad. My pride perhaps wanted to be repressed; and while in the act of marching, I was wounded in the left thigh by a musket-shot, which remains unextracted to this day, and will probably go with me to the grave. At first, not disposed to heed the casualty, I affected to despise such a trifle, and continued to fight on. Nature, however, refused her support; and after firing a few times, I felt myself getting weak and feverish. What rendered my situation worse, was, that at that precise moment the report of an unexpected sally of the French was circulated. Had that been realized, my doom would have been sealed, as I could neither resist nor retreat. In this condition, faint with loss of blood, I contrived to descend into the ditch with the help of my musket. Meanwhile the depth of water by some added inundation had been increased, and no ladder was to be discovered for my ascent on the opposite side. Unwilling to die there, I made another effort, and at length observed a ladder standing in front of the ditch. Unable to get up with my musket, I reluctantly left that behind, and scrambled up with extreme difficulty. Numerous shots were fired at me while ascending, and I perceived bullets whistling through the rounds of the ladder, but not one of them struck me. But I was sadly grieved at the loss of my musket: it had been a faithful friend to me. I seldom knew it to fail in the hour of need: the number on it was seventy-seven. Having succeeded in gaining the summit, I found, to my surprise, a young man belonging to the gallant Napier's company, who kindly offered his arm, and supported me to the field-hospital. May the Almighty think upon and reward this timely benefactor! He was amongst the bravest where all were brave, and, though unhurt, had stood in the fore-front and pinnacle at the severest point of strife. With so large an influx of patients, it will be supposed that the hospital attentions were not very prompt: I was placed on the ground, with many others in a worse condition than myself, to await my turn for surgical assistance. After some hours I found that unless my wound ceased bleeding I should not long survive: this, with a little contrivance, I managed to effect. But the most intolerable sensation was that of raging thirst: all my worldly substance, ten times valued, would have been no price at all for a draught of water. Mean time the frost was so severe, that my limbs appeared to be deprived of flexibility and motion. In the course of the night, hearing a deep moan at a little distance, I called out, "Who is there?" and was answered, "It's me, Tom." The voice was familiar, and I found it was that of Patrick Murphy, an old comrade and countryman, in Dalzell's company, who had fought most nobly through several campaigns. He had been miserably burnt while endeavouring to force the breach, and suffered extremely. In the course of a day or two we were placed in military spring waggons, and conveyed to Elvas. We were after wards transferred to bullock-carts: a mode of conveyance not remarkable either for comfort or speed; the carriages were clumsily constructed, and ensured very little in the way of easy riding; added to which, we moved only at the rate of about one mile an hour.

I have to add with sorrow that the conquest of Badajos was attended with excesses that tend to tarnish the soldier's character. All, indeed, were not alike, for hundreds risked and many lost their lives in striving to stop the violence; but the madness of ungovernable licentiousness generally prevailed and as the worst men were leaders here, all the dreadful passions of human nature were displayed: shameless rapacity, brutal intemperance, savage lust, cruelty and murder, shrieks and piteous lamentations, groans, shouts, curses, the hissing of fires bursting from the houses, the crashing of doors and windows, and the reports of muskets used in violence, resounded for two days and nights in the devoted town. Five thousand men and officers fell during the siege; and of these, including seven hundred Portuguese, three thousand five hundred had been stricken in the assault,—sixty officers and more than seven hundred men being slain on the spot. Five Generals were wounded; about six hundred men and officers fell in the escalade of San Vincente, as many at the castle, and more than two thousand at the breaches,—each division there losing about twelve hundred. Let any man picture to himself this frightful carnage taking place in a space of less than a hundred square yards. Let him consider that the slain died not all suddenly, nor by one manner of death; that some perished by steel, some by shot, some by water, that some were crushed and mangled by heavy weights, some trampled upon, some dashed to atoms by fiery explosions; that for hours this destruction was endured without shrinking; and that the town was won at last;—let any man consider this, and he must admit that a British army is by no means deficient either in physical or moral excellence. And it would be unjust to withhold the meed of praise from the French; the garrison stood and fought manfully and with good discipline, behaving worthily. Some of the instances of personal valour on each side were wondrous. A soldier of the

95th, in his resolution to win, thrust himself beneath the chained sword-blades, and there suffered the enemy to dash his head in pieces with the ends of their muskets; and the foremost man who entered the Santa Maria was an intrepid Portuguese Grenadier, who was killed on the spot. Ferguson, of the 43d, had received two deep wounds in former assaults; and yet, though not half cured, he was here leading the stormers of his regiment, the third time a volunteer, and the third time wounded. In a former action a French officer was observed in the heat of battle in the act of striking at the gallant Felton Harvey, of the 14th Dragoons, when, on perceiving that he had only one arm, the high-minded Gaul, with a rapid movement, brought down his sword into a salute, and passed on. Traits like this are worth preservation.

On alighting from our vehicles at Elvas, we were at first placed in a dark, uncomfortable apartment, adjoining the fortifications; the roof was of arched masonry, and so damp on the inner side, that water fell on us in large drops. Our attendants were also nothing to boast of; for under pretence of bringing our haversacks containing provisions, they walked away with them altogether,— an evil against which we knew no remedy, being unable, through weakness, to search for the depredators, or procure more food. The confusion in this unhappy lazar-house was extreme. Every man naturally thought his own case the most serious, and that it demanded care before all others. We were not, however, destined to remain long in these unsuitable quarters: orders were received directing our removal to Estramores, and our journey thither was commenced the same night. The procession was rather melancholy: several times we had to halt in order to bury some poor creature, who, exhausted by suffering, had fled away. On our arrival at Estramores, we found accommodation more suited to the exigencies of the invalided guests: a convent, sufficiently spacious, had been fitted up as a military hospital, and was well adapted for the purpose. When able to look around, I discovered several of my former associates. Here lay the man through whose body a ramrod had forced its way. On another couch reposed Patrick Marr, a daring fellow, but of bad character. He, with others, had led on the forlorn hope, and was violently struck with a

musket-bullet. Then there was a young man named Forbes, who
volunteered with myself into the 43d: in a short period he died.
Having an excellent constitution, I soon recovered my health, and
in the course of a few weeks was pronounced convalescent.—In
the winter of 1812 I was stationed at Gallegos; and on the 13th
of January, 1813, was promoted to the rank of Sergeant, in the
place of one Hicks, who had recently died at Lisbon. Soon after
this professional lift, one of the army physicians was desirous of
inspecting such of the non-commissioned officers and men as had
been wounded, or who, through length and severity of service,
were supposed to require rest: among these, I was one. On entering
the room, Surgeon Gilchriest related several particulars concerning
my past experience, when my name was included in a list of men
who were directed to return to England. We then proceeded,
without loss of time, to Lisbon, escorted by a detachment of the
95th. Mules were provided for us as far as Abrantes, after which
we proceeded by water. I am sorry to observe, that several of our
party, thus indulged, ill requited the kindness shown, by drinking
to excess; and am sorrier still to add, that I was weak enough to
swell the number. The consequence was, that after a halt, when the
detachment was ready to proceed, we were unprepared. The officer
in command, a very young man, mildly remonstrated with me on
the impropriety of such conduct: I answered with unbecoming
rudeness; on which he drew his sword, and I flourished my cane.
Several men, wiser than myself, then interfered, and mischief was
prevented. My opinion is, that a man altogether overcome with
strong liquor is beside himself, and should be consigned to the care
of his friends, if he have any, until he is *compos mentis* and may be
safely trusted in social society. Next day I saw my error, and made
an apology for the rudeness of the preceding day. When we had
arrived to within six leagues of Lisbon, we landed for a short time,
waiting for the return of tide, leaving in our boat a man named
Latimer, in company with a Portuguese waterman. During that
interval, Latimer, who was in jesting humour, amused himself by
soliciting the poor Portuguese to give him cigars. Not receiving
what he expected, he foolishly took up a musket, forgetting it was
loaded, and presented the muzzle to his unfortunate companion,

jocularly observing, at the same time, that if he did not give him a cigar he would shoot him. He accordingly snapped the lock, and blew out the man's brains, which, with part of his skull, were scattered about the boat. On arriving at Lisbon, I was half afraid that the officer with whom I had taken an unwarrantable liberty might call me to serious account for the misdemeanour, especially as it had taken place so soon after my promotion, when better things were expected; but I had the happiness to find that he knew both how to forget and forgive. He was an English officer; which in every correct vocabulary means a gentleman, and no mistake. He parted with me in excellent humour, and presented me with a small pecuniary balance at that time due for arrears of pay. Soon after my arrival at Lisbon, three soldiers were sentenced to death for desertion; and while waiting for conveyance to England, I was ordered, among others, to mount guard at the execution. One of the men, being a Roman Catholic, was attended by Priest of that community; the other two were assisted by a Protestant Clergyman. On arriving at the appointed spot, which was on the sands near Belem Castle, a party of soldiers, who were to fire at the culprits, was drawn up in front, with their pieces loaded. The sufferers were ordered to kneel at the usual distance; and in sight of all were the graves prepared for their reception. Just before the signal was given to fire, a Dragoon galloped up with a reprieve for the Roman Catholic. The man, however, was so enfeebled and overcome, that he was unable, for some time, to rise from his knees, or take the least notice of this extraordinary deliverance. The other two men were shot. Why the distinction was made, I know not; but with out doubt, there were circumstances in the conduct of each, that called for lenity in the one instance, and severity in the other two.

Our embarkation was immediately after effected; and, having put to sea, we were favoured with a brief and agreeable voyage to the Isle of Wight, at which place we landed, and marched into Albary barracks. In the month of May, 1813, I again joined the 2d battalion of the 43d. Nothing surprised me more than the number of new faces in the corps: such had been the ravages arising from accident, death, and other mischances of active warfare, that few only of my old associates remained, so that the regiment as to me nearly strange and new. My old ragged coat, fairly worn out, was exchanged for a new and handsome dress, ornamented with the professional insignia of my recently acquired rank; and the first time I appeared on parade with the men, was on the 4th of June, a day at that time of cheerful and loyal celebration, being the birthday of the then reigning Monarch, George the Third.

In the course of the summer, wishing to see my friends, I applied to the Colonel of the regiment for a furlough granting permission for that purpose. Leave was given; and, that the service might at the same time be promoted, I was charged with the command of a party of men who were to proceed to, and be stationed at, Castlebar, in Ireland. None but those who have visited and been detained in foreign lands, can conceive aright of the intense desire that arises in the mind, at intervals, to visit the country of their forefathers.

> Breathes there a man with soul so dead,
> Who never to himself hath said,
> This is my own, my native land?

The supposition is incredible. Indeed, any circumstance which, while in Spain, induced me to think of Ireland, was affecting; and I well remember the emotion felt on one occasion, merely because, on commencing a march, the band struck up the national air of "Saint Patrick's day in the morning." Being directed to embark at Liverpool, I hastened there with the detachment, without delay; and having engaged passages on board the packet for Dublin, our luggage was shipped. My evil genius once more prevailed, and was so far present, as to seduce me, and, of course, the soldiers under my direction, to enter a public house of entertainment for refreshments, which might perhaps have been dispensed with. Forgetting ourselves, which those who love the potent glass are sure to do, we remained too long, so that on walking to the pier, we discovered, to our no small dismay, that the packet had sailed. As negligence of this sort amounted to a breach of orders, I was apprehensive, in addition to the disappointment personally felt, of incurring the displeasure of my superior officer; beside which, our property was on board the vessel. Not a moment was to be lost. I therefore engaged a boat then on the beach, told the master to name his own price, and directed him to crowd all his canvass and strive to overtake the packet. We were instantly on board and under sail, standing out to sea in the track of the departed ship. Unfortunately the wind rose considerably, which created a great swell, so that after long and wearisome exertion, we had gained but little on the packet. We were at length perceived by the Captain, who civilly shortened sail, lay to, and received us on board. Such are the penalties to be paid for unguarded delay. Next evening I was refreshed beyond measure by a sight of the Pigeon-House in the Bay of Dublin; and soon after placed my feet on Irish soil. One whole week, which seemed to be endless, expired before I had an opportunity of seeing my relatives. At the end of that time I could no longer refrain, and made a forced march to the neighbourhood, with a heart as light and devoid of care as may be desired. Every object was delightful. There was nothing like it any where else: the shrubs were so green; the sky was so bright and blue; the air so sweet; and even the earth was more soft and verdant than in other regions of the globe. Having to pass near the residence of a beloved sister, who, with her husband and family, occupied a farm at Philipstone, I formed a little plan, and pleased myself with it, of taking her by surprise. I accordingly walked slowly to the house, as a wandering veteran in search of lodgings. As I expected, she did not know me; and no wonder. When last in her company, I was a mere gay and laughing youth: now she saw the weather-beaten sunburnt visage of an unknown soldier, with his knapsack and side-arms, on whose countenance middle age had begun to limn a few serious lines. I began by informing her that my billet directed me to her house for quarter. "I take no soldiers here; you cannot be received." "But you will not be so hard as to turn me away! See how late it is." "Perhaps it may be; but I cannot provide for the like of you." "Surely that is not what you mean to say: some of your family are, likely enough, gone soldiering; and what would you think if either of them were served so?" "That cannot happen. I had one brother, younger than myself, who listed in the army; but we shall never see him again: he was killed in battle." "Indeed!

Perhaps I might have known him: pray what was his name?" "Why, if it can be of any consequence to you, it was Thomas." "To be sure it was, sister; and here he is now. What! do you not know your brother!" I need not describe the raptures of the interview. I kissed her; she wept for joy; explanations, inquiries, and wonderments, almost without measure or end, succeeded. In a few minutes the report of my arrival got abroad: some thought it unlikely; others were sure it was impossible, unless the dead could be raised. Indeed, I discovered that letters had been received, stating that I had been slain at Badajos. Ocular demonstration, however, soon settled all debate; and congratulations, such as few but an Irishman yields, were tendered with true sincerity and friendship.

I proceeded without loss of time to my mother's residence. Having been misled by the report of my decease, she could scarcely credit the testimony of her senses when I appeared before her: great indeed was her exultation and my pleasure at meeting once more on earth. Nor did the time occupied by this social visit hang heavily upon my hands. Among other enterprises which attracted my notice, I made proposals of marriage to an excellent young woman, who was generous enough to listen; the preliminaries were soon arranged; we were shortly after united and to this day, I have reason to be thankful for the choice then made. Beside all this, I had to detail my adventures to numerous groups of listeners, each of whom must have a new version of the strange man's tale. The thirst was unquenchable for notices

> Of breaches, ambuscadoes, Spanish blades,
> Of healths five fathom deep;

with all the other vanities and circumstance of war. Being in high spirits, aided it is likely with a little vanity, so likely to cleave to a man who seeks to recommend himself by feats of arms, I had no objection to dwell occasionally upon the perils and deliverances of bygone time. But during the whole of this season my spirit was not humbled by the least sense of moral defect. I knew nothing of myself. Indeed, such was the loftiness of carriage which I thought it right to assume, that it was with me a point of honour never to sustain an affront unavenged. And yet, on looking back, I can trace an invisible but resistless influence, which even then guided me aright, and saved me from various threatening dangers: what I mean is, I was never utterly abandoned to my own devices. My furlough having expired, I returned to England, and landed at Liverpool, in the winter of 1814; which was remarkable for one of the hardest frosts known in this country for many preceding years. Here I received orders from the Paymaster to proceed to Kent, with a party of recruits destined for that district: and as most of the young fellows were rude and unruly, and strangers to military restraint, it required no common share of firmness, tempered with discretion, properly to conduct and manage them. I arrived, without missing a man, in the vicinity of Maidstone. Just before entering the town, one of the most ungovernable of the squad contrived to dip his hands in mischief; nor was his mouth entirely guiltless. Having run up a score at one of the road-side inns, for liquors had and drunk, he was unable to pay the reckoning; when, being minus his ready cash, he proposed leaving some valuable equivalent in the hands of the landlord, as a temporary deposit, to be shortly redeemed: this consisted of a bundle, containing, he averred, much valuable property. We had not proceeded far on our journey, when poor Boniface came running after us, stating, that on opening the package it contained nothing but a few worthless rags. Meantime the shuffler, apprehensive of detection, and no doubt conscience-stricken, had purposely out-walked us, and was considerably in advance when the plaintiff over took us. We could only pity his sad case, and preach caution for the future. The troublesome personage just adverted to was the author of more mischief. At our next halt, under the influence, it is probable, of the late excesses, he quarrelled with the servants in the house; and being a powerful man, of about six feet two inches in height, soon cleared the public room of its inmates: getting into the street, he threw off his coat, and gave a general challenge for a fight. The invitation was properly rejected; and, like many other violent spirits, he was eventually subdued, and marched quietly to quarters. Here I received unexpected orders to proceed to Plymouth. On my arrival there, I was stationed in the citadel. My removal was providential. I here met with an old friend, by whose side I had fought in Spain: he had received a commission as Captain in the 2d battalion. The last time we had met was on the ramparts of Ciudad Rodrigo, where he was dreadfully scorched by an explosion of combustibles. He introduced me in a very handsome manner to several officers in the garrison, and made honourable mention of my former conduct; by his influence I was also appointed Colour-Sergeant to the company. While at Plymouth, an order was issued which gave the soldiers liberty to attend such places of public worship as they thought fit, only it was expected that each should keep to his own community. When the order was read, I fell out for the Roman Catholic, where I continued some time to attend. The truth is, it mattered little by what name my religion was designated; for it was utterly worthless. I recollect that, one wet Sunday morning, it was my turn to march the Catholic party to Stonehouse chapel. The piety of the others was about equal to mine. Finding ourselves rather damp from the rain, it was proposed, that instead of going to mass, we should adjourn to the next public house. This was agreed to without a division; and there we remained till night-fall. Meanwhile I was a mighty advocate for Papacy; indeed few were louder than myself if challenged on the score of my religion. In the month of March, 1817, the second battalions of several regiments, in order to reduce them to the peace establishment, were disbanded; and that in which I served was of the number. We were inspected, previously to dismission, by the medical officer; and though my services had not extended the length required by rule, yet, in consideration of the wounds I had received, I was placed upon the pension-list for an allowance or one shilling *per diem*. Thus disengaged from the toil of military avocation, I felt desirous of directing my steps homeward again: I accordingly crossed the Channel, and arrived safely at Portarlington, Queen's County, in the month of May.

Coming events again introduced me to the army. In November, 1819, the pensioners were called up for examination, that those who were fit for service might be enrolled as a veteran battalion. For that purpose I went to Carlow, and was deemed by the inspector fit for the duty required. After continuing there several weeks, directions were received, ordering that the whole of the

Sergeants, excepting four or five, should be dispensed with. The matter was decided among us by lot, and the decision happened to be against me. As I was placed by this event in disadvantageous circumstances, and excluded from the rank to which I felt myself entitled, I at once enlisted in the 7th foot, intending to serve my full period of time, and be thus ultimately entitled to an increased pension. With this view I resolved to conduct myself with strict propriety. But what are human resolutions? Can the Ethiop change his skin, or the leopard her spots? Just as soon can man reform himself, independently of divine principles. Without descending to particulars, I relapsed into conviviality and habitual dissipation. Strong drink ruined all my existing prospects. There were several religious men in the regiment, who expostulated with me on the folly of such conduct; but such were my ignorance and depravity, their words were as an idle tale. Nor, in fact, was I in other respects at home in the regiment. I missed the partners of my former dangers and hard service, men who not only talked of war, but had turned the tide of battle. We had also certain interests in which we seemed to be proprietors in common; and now I felt myself comparatively alone, and among strangers. New friends are like new wine: when it is old, it drinks better. We lay for some time at Newcastle, and from thence removed to Tynemouth Castle: while at the latter place, I was the means, under Providence, of saving the life of a fellow-creature. During a heavy gale of wind, a sloop was driven ashore near the barracks, and all hands on board were in danger of perishing. The waves broke frightfully over the deck, sweeping in their course every moveable, and threatening quick destruction to the ship. The crew clung to the rigging with trembling and uncertain grasp. Hundreds of spectators lined the shore; but though all felt deep concern, none knew how to assist. At last a rope was by some means conveyed from the vessel to the beach, and soon after hauled tight: a young sailor and myself then ventured on it, through the surf, and reached the vessel in safety. Among others, the Captain threw himself overboard, but missed his hold of the rope, and sank. He was under water some time, when I dived in search of him, and having fortunately grasped him by the hair, was able to raise his head above the surface of the water. The next moment we were both struck by a powerful wave, which sent us with rapidity on the shelving rocks, where we were picked up by several persons who came to assist. I was much exhausted for several hours, but in the evening was sufficiently recovered to walk to the inn, and inquire for the Captain's welfare. He had been carefully attended, and, though much bruised, was doing well. He knew me at the first glance, and exclaimed, "That's the man that saved my life. I hope the country will reward him." Several gentlemen, frequenting the Library and Reading-room, who saw the occurrence, were equally loud in their praises; and a Clergyman, I understood, moved that I be rewarded with ten pounds and a silver medal. For distinctions so flattering I ought perhaps to be grateful; for they are all the reward I ever had. Why the worthy Captain should expect the country to produce a premium for the saving of his life, I am at a loss to conjecture. One would have thought that the onus of doing that might have been laid upon a party much easier of access. Never from that time did I hear from these eloquently grateful parties.

CHAPTER VIII

In November, 1823, on another reduction in the army, I finally retired from the service. The leisure thus afforded induced me to look within, not with the superficial survey of former years, but with a desire and determination to discover my real condition as a moral and accountable creature: in other words, the facts and verities of the Christian religion were revealed to my mind with new and affecting power. To many this will appear strange, to some ridiculous; and there are a few who will ask, why a soldier of spirit, above all others, should trouble himself about the concerns of religion. I answer that question by asking another,—Why should he not? He has as deep an interest in Gospel truth as any other person; and if piety of life be deemed essential for any person in any station of society, it is not less so for him. I apprehend, that if there be any difference between civil and military life, in this respect, the soldier ought to be the *most* religious; for his life is usually in greater jeopardy than that of the man of peace. Death, it is true, comes to all men sooner or later; the soldier often anticipates its approach by the perils of active warfare. Others have objected, that for military men, who are proverbial for licentiousness, to set up for extraordinary sanctity, is not only uncalled for, but absurd and hypocritical. I again ask, Why so? If soldiers are actually so very bad, both in pretension and reality, they stand so much the more in need of religion to make them better. Salvation is a girdle which encompasses the world; and why a man is to be excluded from its benefits because he had defended his country's right at the sword's point, and hazard of his life and fame, I have yet to learn. But, say some, there is something so pitiful and gloomy in a soldier who professes to be religious. There we are again at issue; and I consent to try the question by this single test. I affirm the converse; and

aver, that pity must fall only on the irreligious, who are often
gloomy and sad from certain assaults of conscience, known only
to themselves; while some of the most intrepid and courageous
men who ever lived, were noted for obedience to divine law;
and, what is more to the present purpose, many of the ablest
warlike achievements ever effected, were planned and executed by
pious soldiers. What is more extraordinary still, we shall presently
discover that the success of many an expedition depended upon
that piety; and that the Almighty Ruler of the universe granted
or withheld the victory, to or from those whose hearts were right
with him. A distinguished Prelate of the Church of England has
observed, that "one murder makes a villain, millions a hero." The
line is forcible; and yet we must make a little abatement from
the innuendo it conveys, and on which the writer might not
have ventured, but for those licences of language to which poets
conceive themselves entitled. Between the two characters, here
placed side by side, there can be no possible analogy, upon any
fair and acknowledged principle. The first is a sneaking assassin,
who, under cover of night, cowers down in search of massacre.
Influenced either by satanic malevolence, or the basest avarice, he
steals to the bedside of slumbering innocence, and takes away life.
If by the term hero, we are to understand the Marshal or conductor
of an army, the affix 'murderer' is a little strained and misapplied.
That Commanders on important emergencies are compelled to
he prodigal of human life, is admitted. The very nature of the
profession renders the evil inevitable. But see the difference the
chief officer acts under heavy responsibilities for his country. If it
be invaded, he is to repel the intruders; or, if offensive measures are
deemed necessary by the State, he is to lead on, and carry them
into effect. Could all this be performed without the loss of a single
life, no doubt he would be happy: but the measure, though ever so
desirable, cannot be thus secured; for the enemy opposes force to
force: still his design is, not to destroy, but to conquer and the loss
of human life, the murders that ensue, are not the objects sought;
they are the unavoidable incidents which follow the prosecution of
certain designs, previously determined; of which, the execution is
laid upon the shoulders of the military chief. Besides, the murder

of millions is by no means an essential ingredient in the character of an hero. That term simply means, a man eminent for bravery, or the first of his class in any respect; so that the opprobrium created by my poetical quotation, when examined, seems to have slight foundation in justice and propriety. War is, indeed, a great evil, and can be justified only on principles of self-defence. When a nation is invaded, or attacked in relation to her undoubted rights and privileges, then she has a pretence for war. I will not assert that the attack ought to be awaited. While methods are adopted for security at home, it may be proper to meet the enemy half way, and, by timely resistance, avert those greater evils which would attend a system of pusillanimous neglect.

It is not a little singular that one of the first battles recorded in Scripture consisted of a well-conducted expedition formed and led on by one of the greatest saints that ever lived; and the circumstances, so far from being stated to his disparagement, evidently redound to his honour. Soon after the combat in the vale of Siddim, which was full of slime-pits, Lot, the nephew of Abram, was taken prisoner, and his property carried away by the four Kings commanding the victorious forces. When the disaster was made known to Abram, he armed and led forth his trained servants, three hundred and eighteen in number, and pursued the army unto Dan, He there made the needful dispositions for the approaching conflict; and, as his detachment was of far inferior numerical strength, when compared with the opposing force, he properly resolved upon a night attack. To use the emphatic language of holy writ, there "he smote them, and pursued them unto Hobah, which is on the left hand of Damascus;" and to show that the discomfiture was complete, it is added, "he brought back all the goods, and his brother Lot, the women also, and the people." This action is enhanced, when the principle is examined, which induced it. Abram fought, not for his own profit, but for the welfare and credit of his country! When rewards were tendered, he refused them. "I have," said he unto the King of Sodom, "lift up mine hand unto the Lord, the most high God, the possessor of heaven and earth, that I will not take from a thread even to a shoe-latchet, lest thou shouldest say, I have made Abram rich."

The valour and success of a religious Captain are also shown during the hostile advances of the Israelites through the wilderness, nearly five hundred years after the event just recited. Among other opponents, Sihon, the Amoritish King, endeavoured to dispute their passage. We do not discover that recourse was had to tedious and doubtful negotiations. It was probably shown to the Israelitish leader, by divine impulse, that, with enemies so treacherous, treaties were vain. At all events, an immediate battle took place; Israel smote the foe with the edge of the sword, after which the forces "turned and went up by the way of Bashan; and Og the King of Bashan went out against them, he and his people, to the battle at Edrei." That Monarch fell, and all his people; and it is remarkable that the Israelitish chieftain was no other than the meek and pious Moses, who had received the special command of the Almighty to extirpate the enemy, who, we have therefore reason to believe, had filled up the measure of his iniquity, and was no longer fit to live.—An instructive and highly curious circumstance is recorded in the Book of Joshua, which discovers that religion not only sits well upon the warrior, but that impiety is the bane of military life. In consequence of a certain trespass committed by Achan the son of Carmi, the Israelitish army became absolutely useless. They fled before the men of Ai, who "chased them from before the gate even unto Thebarim, and smote them in the going down, so that the hearts of the people melted, and became as water." Now, mark the difference when Joshua took the command. Five Kings, with their combined armies, advanced against the Gideonites, who, naturally alarmed, despatched a messenger to their allies, requesting help. Joshua, like all other good men, lost no time in doing a good action. He did not let the grass grow under his feet. He came on the enemy "suddenly, and went up from Gilgal all night, and slew them with a great slaughter at Gideon, and chased them along the way that goeth to Beth-horon, and smote them to Azekah, and unto Makkedah,"—What is, in some respects, more singular, the Israelites were subsequently delivered from a foreign yoke by the heroism of a religious woman. This was Deborah, a prophetess, the wife of Lapidoth. For twenty years her country had groaned beneath the iron hand of Jabin, the Canaanite, of whose numerous army Sisera was Captain. Under the direction of Deborah, the Israelites, amounting only to ten thousand, joined battle with their oppressors. The adversary was completely beaten, so that not a man survived to tell the tale of their defeat: and, lest the shadow of doubt should rest upon these active operations, conducted as they were by the wise and good, they were celebrated, and thus rendered immortal, by one of the noblest odes on record, written, without doubt, under plenary inspiration; while pointed maledictions are levelled against those lukewarm friends whose supineness kept them from the righteous fray. Let us listen a minute. "The inhabitants of the villages ceased, they ceased in Israel, until that I Deborah arose, that I arose a mother in Israel. They fought from heaven; the stars in their courses fought against Sisera. The river of Kishon swept them away, that ancient river, the river Kishon. O my soul, thou hast trodden down strength. Curse ye Meroz, said the angel of the Lord, curse ye bitterly the inhabitants thereof; because they came not to the help of the Lord, to the help of the Lord against the mighty. So let all thine enemies perish, O Lord: but let them that love him be as the sun when he goeth forth in his might." The result of these spirited demonstrations was of the roost substantial order; for it is particularly noted that the land had rest forty years. We find, also, that Gideon and Jephthah were of the same noble line of godly soldiery. The former rescued his country from Midianitish despotism; and the latter put down the children of Ammon. "He smote them from Aroer, even till thou come to Minnith, even twenty cities, and unto the plain of the vineyards, with very great slaughter." I scarcely need add, that the sympathy of succeeding generations has been excited by his rash and thoughtless vow connected with the virtuous and noble-minded conduct of his daughter. But his fame, as the brave and pious defender of his people, can never be tarnished.—About eleven centuries before the Christian era, another prodigy arose. This was a man of superhuman physical power; and, what is most remarkable, the feats resulting from his prodigious strength were performed chiefly, if not exclusively, when, as the Scriptures term it, "the Spirit of the Lord came mightily upon him; "and when that influence departed, he became weak as other men. In other words, while his heart was right with God, he prevailed; and when he forsook the Rock of his salvation, defeat and ruin were nigh. In the height of his glorious career, he slew a thousand men with the jaw-bone of an ass; and when in danger of perishing from thirst, a miracle was wrought in his favour. "God clave an hollow place that was in the jaw, and there came water thereout; and when he had drunk, his spirit came again, and he revived: wherefore he called the name of that place En-hakkore," or, the well of him that cried. It is true he lost his life at last, and, in the interim, had been sadly abused; but his end was triumphant; and he fell, buried beneath the bodies of the slain. This remarkable man judged Israel twenty years and if we survey the dreadful excesses in which the people indulged, as recorded in the latter part of the Book of Judges, the restraints of some such influential ruler as Samson appear to have been necessary. When there was no King in Israel, every man did that which was right in his own eyes; and that was, in most instances, uniformly wrong.—Another of the heroes of antiquity, whose biography illustrates our meaning, is Saul. The immediate cause of his first achievement arose from the conduct of Nahash, an Ammonit; who insulted the men of Jabesh-Gilead by epistolary insolence, and the threat of future out rage. Unable to defend themselves, they contrived to obtain seven days' respite for consultation. This they employed in sending messengers to Gibeah, specially empowered to obtain immediate help. When the tidings reached the ear of Saul, he was greatly moved: the Spirit of God came upon him measures were directly adopted to repress the raging of the Heathen, and the deputation were sent back, to assure their friends that, "to-morrow, by that time the sun be hot, ye shall have help." Faithful to the promise, Saul and his men were in sight by the morning watch; and the Ammonites, though three hundred thousand of them shone in arms, were utterly routed. Saul was a courageous man, and an approved soldier. Though at last slain in battle, and his countrymen were defeated, it should he remembered that he had offended and forsaken his God, by an improper invasion of the office of the priesthood; had been weak enough to consult a wizard at Endor; and, under a malignant influence, had several times attempted the life of his best earthly friend. The varied vicissitudes of his life, and his untimely end, are therefore to be viewed as proofs of the position now sought to be maintained. Pious soldiers fight best. When Saul served God, he beat the Philistines; when he ceased to serve God, the Philistines slew him. The occasion of his death was touching, and called forth from a hand of no common skill a lament not easily surpassed: "The beauty of Israel is slain upon the high places: how are the mighty fallen! Ye mountains of Gilboa, let there be no dew, neither let there be rain, upon you, nor fields of offerings: for there the shield of the mighty is vilely east away, the shield of Saul, as though he had not been anointed with oil. How are the mighty fallen, and the weapons of war perished!"—But of all the warriors whose history is recorded in Scripture, none is to be compared with David. Almost every step of his eventful life, from the period when he was taken from the sheep-cote to his complete establishment on the throne of Israel, was marked by a spirit of singular enterprise and valour, regulated and impelled by fervent piety. He is described even in youth as "a mighty valiant man, and a man of war, and prudent in matters, and a comely person, and the Lord was with him." His combat with Goliath exhibits an astonishing instance of cool and determined resolution, especially when the simplicity of his attire and weapons are contrasted with the panoply of the tall Egyptian. The Israelitish slingers it is said, could hurl stones with amazing force, and precision so wonderful as to strike within an hair's-breadth of the intended mark. David was, no doubt, a proficient in this art, of which the issue of the duel is sufficient proof. The Philistine came on, wrapt probably in steel, and in formidable array, preceded by his armour-bearer. He then commenced a speech, somewhat Homeric, but replete with invective, in which, like an overgrown coward, he impudently invoked the curses of his gods upon his antagonist, and ended by intimating that his shattered remains should soon be the vultures' meal. David's answer was finely conceived, and as well expressed. Without further delay, he addressed himself to the fight; "he put his band in his bag, and took thence a stone, and slang it, and smote the Philistine in his forehead, that the stone sank into his forehead, and he fell upon his face to the earth." The military prowess and

superior talents of David were afterwards shown, during a lengthened course of brilliant operations, in which he was generally
successful. Perhaps in nothing was his skill more observable than in
his retreat from Saul, who, for no assignable cause but the pressure
of an evil spirit, sought the life of his ablest officer. The superiority
of David's tactics, at this period, is the more conspicuous, when we
reflect upon the inferiority of his corps, both in number and
quality. When driven into the cave of Adullam, the whole of his
adherents amounted to only four hundred men, and from the
character given, queer ones too. "And every one that was in distress,
and every one that was in debt, and everyone that was discontented,
gathered themselves unto him, and he became a Captain over
them." Two things are here remarkable: one is, that the commander
was able, with his multiplied privations, to keep his men from
mutiny; and the other, that their physical strength, collectively
considered, though so contemptible in itself, was sufficient to
second, and carry out into practice, the evolutions of their leader.
The piety and valour of David were equally conspicuous, some six
years after, in the reprisals be made upon the Amalekites. Taking
advantage of his absence, these marauders had burnt Ziklag, and
carried away considerable property; what was worse they had taken
the women, including David's two wives. As usual, in heavy public
calamities, the populace, instead of striving to mitigate the trouble
of their leader, spake of stoning him; but David, who was never
easily cast down, surmounted existing difficulty, and "encouraged
himself in the Lord his God;"—not that he rested merely in passive
wishfulness for better days, as some foolish people have done;—he
instantly pursued the enemy, and, having providentially over taken
a young Egyptian, who had fallen out of time ranks through
sickness, he induced him, on promise of protection, to act as the
guide of David's party. Thus directed, the pursuers overtook the
foe, who, like a clan of straggling freebooters, and totally unaware
of danger, were "spread abroad upon all the earth, eating, and
drinking, and dancing. And David Smote them from the twilight
even unto the evening of the next day; and there escaped not a
man of them, save four hundred young men, who rode upon
camels, and fled." The defeat of the Philistines at Rephaim may also

be quoted in confirmation of the principle sought to be established. David had confidence in his own resources; and few warriors had greater right, for they were generally well based, and worthy of trust. But the goodness of his own theory never diminished his Sense of dependence upon God, or the desire to consult his will. David inquired of the Lord, Shall I go up to the Philistines? The answer was in the affirmative, with the promise of success. David then advanced to Baal-perazim, and defeated the enemy. He then observed, "The Lord hath broken forth upon mine enemies before me, as the breach of waters. Therefore he called the name of that place Baal-perazim." Defeated, but not destroyed, the Philistines again rallied, and Spread themselves in the same spacious vale. David the second time asked counsel of God; and having received permission, he moved on to the attack. The directions David received on this occasion were remarkable. The Signal for the onset was a preternatural noise, resembling the trampling of feet on the ground upon which certain fruit-trees grew. "When thou hearest the sound of a going in the tops of the mulberry-trees, then bestir thyself." All this took place; obedience followed, and the Philistines were smitten. That these principles of active piety were diffused through the whole of David's future career, must be evident on the slightest survey of his history. He feared God, and very little else. Religion and valour marched abreast, and his enemies melted like wax. His confession, at the close of life, moreover, shows the excellence and superiority of his plan. "God is my strength and power; and be maketh my way perfect. He maketh my feet like hinds' feet, and setteth me upon my high places. He teacheth my hands to war, so that a bow of steel is broken by mine arms. The Lord liveth, and blessed be my rock, and exalted be the God of the rock of my salvation." As collateral evidence of the possible existence and moral worth of a pious soldiery, it is worth notice, that in the New Testament, which divulges the religion of peace and love, the writer of the Epistle to the Hebrews in exhibiting "a great cloud of witnesses," whom he sets forth to defend and exemplify the truth, takes care to include therein, with special commendation, several of the heroes to whom allusion has been made. Were it not that the time failed, as we are expressly told, he had a desire to expatiate largely on their respective merits and services. He is, therefore, obliged to content himself with an extract, as it were, from the army-list, adding only a brief summary of a few of the more splendid excellencies of each. There are delightful notices of Gideon, and Barak, and Samson, and Jephthah, and David, and Samuel; who through faith subdued kingdoms, wrought righteousness, obtained promises, stopped the mouths of lions, quenched the violence of fire, escaped the edge of the sword; out of weakness were made strong; waxed valiant in fight; turned to flight the armies of the aliens; and of whom, waving all other encomium, we are told in one comprehensive sentence, that "the world was not worthy."

Evidence, in some respects, of a higher class than this, may be gathered by a little attention. We are told by Matthew, that when Jesus was entered into Capernaum, there came unto him a Centurion who had a palsied servant, and was, consequently, much distressed. In the exercise of faith, (for nothing else or less could inspire the language,) the Centurion pleaded most conclusively, "Lord, I am not worthy that thou shouldest come under my roof; but speak the word only, and my servant shall be healed." The sequel may be anticipated. The servant was healed in the self-same hour; and when Jesus heard of the steadfastness of the Centurion's confidence, he added, "Verily I say unto you, I have not found so great faith, no, not in Israel." We see, also, on another occasion, among numerous suitors who pressed around John for counsel, previously to his imprisonment by Herod, certain soldiers demanded of him, "And what shall we do? And he said unto them, Do violence to no man, neither accuse any falsely, and be content with your wages." Now, if the military profession had been absolutely unlawful, this great forerunner of our Lord, without doubt, would have said so. Nothing of the sort is glanced at. Indeed, the recommendation of contentment, with reference to the amount of their pay, supposes, not only the lawfulness of the occupation, but a right on their part to compensation for services rendered. Had a thief or a drunkard asked, What shall we do? the answer would have been, in substance, to the first, "Steal no more;" and to the second, "Flee from thy crime." Indeed the cautionary remarks just named are enough to show that the existence of the military character was contemplated without censure; and that, therefore, it is essential to society in its present state. That a rapacious body of soldiery is a nuisance, must be admitted; but that may be said of a rapacious body of men in general. One thing is clear: a man may be a soldier, and yet religious; and it is not a little singular, that it is of a military man, and he a Roman officer, that Jesus affirmed, "Verily, I say unto you, I have not found so great faith, no, not in Israel." This I account no common triumph for the soldier. In fact, we are distinctly told that our Saviour himself, humanly speaking, felt surprised at the man's faith: "when Jesus heard it, he marvelled." And it has been observed by a good critic, that throughout the whole Gospel, Jesus is never said to wonder at anything but faith, which wonder in Christ is to be interpreted as a high expression of esteem.

Independently of the instances cited from sacred record, the page of profane history furnishes numerous instances of sound and practical piety among the professors in thorough and repulsive art of war; and had we leisure for copious extract, there would be no difficulty in arranging a formidable staff, composed of such persons,—of men, too, who had been eminently successful in the strategy and science of hostility. One of the earliest and most extraordinary manifestations of Christian zeal is recorded to have happened to the Theban legion, in the reign of Diocletian, the Roman Emperor; who, it is said, rather than conform to the rites of Paganism, suffered martyrdom by the order of Maximian, to the number of six thousand. Another instance of ancient military piety is recorded in the ease of the Thundering Legion, a name given to those Christians who served in the Roman army of Marcus Antoninus, in the second century. It seems that when that Emperor was at war with the Marcomanni, his army was enclosed by the enemy, and reduced to the most deplorable condition, by the thirst under which they languished, in a parched desert. Just at this time they were singularly relieved by a sudden and unexpected rain. This event was attributed to the Christians, who were supposed to have effected this by their prayers; and the name of the "Thundering Legion" was given to them, on account of the thunder and lightning that destroyed the enemy, while the shower revived the fainting Romans. Our own Alfred the Great combined in his own person that union of piety and courage which, when associated, are so truly noble. He was born at Wantage, in Berkshire, in 849: Those were dark ages; and the Prince, we are told, was twelve years of age before a master could be procured in the western kingdom to teach him the alphabet. He felt the misery of ignorance; he saw the oppression of his country; and determined, if possible, to remove both. His improvement in letters was astonishing. He ultimately acquired great erudition: had he not been illustrious as a King, he would have had fame as an author; and an old history of Ely has asserted, that he translated the Old and New Testaments. On ascending the throne, he found that the Danes had penetrated into the heart of his kingdom; and before he had reigned a month, he was obliged to take the field against these formidable enemies. After numerous battles, fought with varied success, he finally expelled them from the kingdom. Alfred reigned twenty-eight years; during the last three of which he enjoyed profound peace. He died A. D. 900, and was buried at Winchester. All historians agree that he was one of the most valiant, wise, and excellent Kings that ever reigned in England. There is great reason to believe, that we are indebted to this Prince for trial by jury; and the Doomsday-book, which is preserved in the Exchequer, is thought to be no more than another edition of Alfred's Book of Winchester, which contained a survey of the kingdom. In private life, Alfred was one of the most amiable men in his dominions; and of so equal a temper, that he never suffered either sadness or levity to enter his mind. He was a remarkable economist of his time; and an explanation has been given of the method he took for dividing and keeping an account of it. He caused six wax-candles to be made: on the candles the inches were regularly marked; and having found that one of them burned just four hours, he committed them to the care of the keepers of his chapel, who from time to time gave him notice how the hours went: but, as in windy weather the candles were wasted by the impression of the air on the flame, to remedy this inconvenience he invented lanterns, there being then no glass in his dominions. Of the piety of this consummate General there can be no doubt. Just before his death he was visited by his son, to whom he gave the following admirable advice:—"My dear son, sit thee down beside me, and I will deliver thee true instruction. I feel that my hour is coming: my countenance is wan. My days are almost done. I shall go to another world, and thou shalt be left alone in all my wealth. I pray thee, strive to be a father and a lord to thy people. Be thou a father to the children, and a friend to the widow. Comfort thou the poor, shelter the weak, and with all thy might right that which is wrong. Govern thyself by law: then shall the Lord love thee, and God above all things shall be thy reward. Call upon him to advise thee in all thy need, and he shall help thee in all thou undertakest."

Godliness is profitable also for the private soldier, and contributes to the confirmation of his courage. One of the directions given by Oliver Cromwell to the soldiers of his army was, that every man should carry a Bible in his pocket: the edition distributed was that since known by the name of Field's. This arrangement, so much in accordance with the spirit of the times, was carried into effect when the Protector assumed the command of the Parliamentary army against Charles the First. Among the rest, there was a wild young fellow, who ran away from his apprenticeship in London, for the sake of plunder and dissipation. This fellow was obliged to be in the fashion. Being one day ordered out on a skirmishing party, or to attack some fortress, he returned back to his quarters in the evening without hurt. When he was going to bed, pulling the Bible out of his pocket, he observed a hole in it: his curiosity led him to trace the depth of this hole into his Bible, when he found that a bullet had gone as far as Ecclesiastes XI. 9. He read the verse, "Rejoice, O young man, in thy youth; and let thy heart cheer thee in the days of thy youth, and walk in the ways of thy heart, and in the sight of thine eyes: but know thou, that for all these things God will bring thee into judgment." The words were set home upon his heart, by the divine Spirit, so that he became a sound believer in the Lord Jesus Christ, and lived in London many years after the civil wars were over. Not that it is intended to impute any extraordinary sanctity to the aspiring person then at the head of affairs in this country. Capable of the deepest dissimulation, an apparent concern for the honour of religion was the pretext on which he endeavoured to compass, and actually secured, the conquest of the realm. Pretended messages from heaven were every-day occurrences. His speeches, correspondence, and conversation, were conducted in the phraseology of Scripture; and the names even of his soldiers and adherents were bartered for others selected from holy writ, and mingled together in grotesque profusion. "Cromwell," says Cleveland, "hath beat up his drums clean through the Old Testament. You may learn the genealogy of our Saviour by the names in his regiment. The Muster-Master has no other list than the first chapter of St. Matthew. Independently of Praise-God-bare-bones, and his surly party, a specimen of newly-engrafted names may be taken from a jury, enclosed in the county of Sussex, about that time. There were Messieurs Kill-sin, Weep-not, Fly-debate, Be-faithful, Standfast-on-high, Graceful, More-fruit, Fight-the-good-fight-of-faith, with several others equally modest; among all of whom the same determination to emblazon their assumed excellencies might be seen."

Religion, and its saving effects, are the same at every period; and, descending the stream of time, we may strengthen our case by relating an account of late, but genuine, piety in the last hours of a brave and accomplished officer. After the battle of Bergen, in Germany; among the many wounded who were brought into Frankfort-on-the-Maine, was the Right Honourable George C. Dykern, Baron, Lieutenant-General of the Saxon troops, in the service of the King of France. He was born of an ancient and noble family in Silesia, on April 10, 1710; so that it was on an anniversary of his birth-day that he received his wound. He was of equal abilities as a Minister in the closet, and a General in the field. In his younger years he had gone through a regular course of study in the University, and had made great proficiency in philosophy, especially in mathematics. He afterwards studied polemic divinity, till he reasoned himself into an infidel. During his illness, he showed not the least desire for pious company or serious discourse, till the surgeon let his valet-de-chambre know that he could not live long. The man then asked his master whether he did not choose to be visited by a Clergyman. He answered, with warmth, "I shall not trouble those gentlemen: I know well myself what to believe and do." His man, not discouraged, continued thus: "My Lord, have you ever found me wanting in my duty, all the time I have been in your service?" He answered, "No." "Then," replied he, "I will not be wanting now: the surgeons count you past hopes of recovery, but every one is afraid to tell you so. You stand upon the brink of eternity. Pray, Sir, order a Clergyman to be called." He paused a little, but soon gave his hand to his servant, thanked him for his honesty, and ordered him to send for me.[1] When I came, the man told me plainly the General was a professed infidel. I went in, and, after a short compliment, said, "I am told, my Lord, your life is near an end; therefore I presume, without any ceremony, to ask you one plain question is the state of your soul such that you can entertain a solid hope of salvation?" He answered, "Yes." "On what do you ground this hope!" He replied, "I never committed any wilful sin. I have been liable to frailties; but I trust in God's mercy, and the merits of his Son, that he will have mercy upon me." These words he uttered very slowly, especially "the merits of his Son." I made the following reply:—"I am apt to believe you are not tainted with the grosser vices, but I fear you a little too presumptuously boast of never having committed wilful sin. If you would be saved, you must acknowledge your being utterly corrupted by sin, and consequently deserving the curse of God, and eternal damnation. As for your hoping for God's mercy, through the merits of his Son, I beg leave to ask, do you believe God has a Son; that his Son assumed our nature, in order to be our Saviour; that in the execution of his office he was humbled unto death, even the death upon the cross; and that hereby he has given an ample satisfaction for us, and recovered our title to heaven?" He answered, "I cannot now avoid a more minute description of the state of my soul. Let me tell you, Doctor, I have some knowledge of philosophy, by which I have chosen for myself a way of salvation. I have always endeavoured to live a sober life to the uttermost of my power, not doubting but that the Being of all beings would graciously accept me. In this way I stood in no need of Christ, and therefore did not believe on him. But if I take the Scriptures to be a divine revelation, this way of mine, I perceive, is not the right one: I must believe in Christ, and through him come to God." I replied, "You say, if you take the Scriptures to be a divine revelation," He fetched a deep sigh, and said, "O God, thou wilt make me say, Because I take the Scriptures to be thy word," I said, "There are grounds and reasons enough to demonstrate the divine origin of Christianity, as I could show from its most essential principles, were not the period of your life so short: but we need not now that diffusive method, faith being the gift of God. A poor sinner, tottering on the brink of eternity, has not time to inquire about grounds and reasons rather betake yourself to earnest prayer for faith; which if you do, I doubt not but God will give it you." I had no sooner spoken these words, than, pulling off his cap, and lifting up his eyes and hands, he cried out, "O Almighty God, I am a poor cursed sinner, worthy of damnation; but, Lord Jesus, eternal Son of God, thou diedst for my sins also! It is through thee alone I can be saved! O give me faith, and strengthen that faith !" Being extremely weak, he was obliged to stop here. A little after, he asked, "Is faith enough for salvation!" "Yes, Sir," said I, "if it be living faith." "Methinks," said he, "it is so already; and it will be more so by and by: let us pray for it." Perceiving he was very weak, to give him some rest, I retired into the next room; but he soon sent to call me. I found him praying; and Jesus was all he prayed for. I reminded him of some scriptures, treating of faith in Christ; and he delighted with them, indeed he was quite swallowed up with the grace of Jesus, and would bear of nothing but "Jesus Christ, and him crucified." He cried out, "I do not know how it is with me: I never in my life felt such a change. I have power to love Jesus, and to believe in him whom I so long rejected. O my Jesus, how merciful thou art to me!" About noon I stepped home; but he sent for mc directly, so that I could scarcely eat my dinner. We were both filled with joy, as partakers of the same grace which is in Jesus Christ; and that in such a manner as if we had been acquainted for many years. Many officers of the army came to see him continually, to all of whom he talked freely of Jesus, of the grace of the Father in him, and of the power of the Holy Ghost through him; wondering without ceasing at his having found Jesus, and at the happy change, by which all things on this side eternity were become indifferent to him.

In the afternoon he desired to partake of the Lord's supper, which he received with a melting, praising, and rejoicing heart. All the rest of the day he continued in the same state of soul. Towards evening he desired, that if his end should approach, I would come to him, which I promised; but he did not send for me till next morning. I was told by his valet, that he slept well for some hours, and then awaking, prayed for a considerable time, continually mentioning the name of our Lord, and his precious blood; and that he had desired several of the officers to make known his conversion to his Court, which was that of Poland. After some discourse, I asked, "Has your view of Christ and his redemption been either altered or obscured since yesterday?" He answered, "Neither altered nor obscured. I have no doubt, not even a remote one. It is just the same with me, as if I had always thus believed and never doubted: so gracious is the Lord Jesus to me a sinner." This second day he was unwearied in exercises of faith and prayer. Towards evening he sent for me in haste. When I came I found him dying, and in a kind of delirium: so I could do no more than give him now and then a word of comfort. I afterwards prayed for him, and those that were present, some of whom were of high birth and rank. I then, by imposition of hands, as usual, gave him a blessing; which being done, he expired immediately. Prince Xavier, who was there, could not forbear weeping. The rest of the officers bewailed the loss of their General; yet praised God for having shown such mercy towards him. I wrote an account of it with out delay to his mother, and had an immediate answer. She was a lady of seventy-two, of exemplary piety: she praised God for his mercy, adding, that He had now answered the prayers which she had never ceased to offer on her son's behalf for eleven years.

Churchill, Duke of Marlborough, one of the greatest Generals this country ever produced, is also, in many valuable respects, to be considered as an example of Christian valour. No indecent expression, says his biographer, ever dropped from his lips; and herein he was imitated by the genteel part of the army. His camps were like a quiet, well-governed city; and, perhaps, much more mannerly. Cursing, swearing, and blustering were never heard among those who were reckoned good officers; and his army was, beyond all contradiction, the best academy in the world to teach a young gentleman wit and breeding; a sot and a drunkard being what they scorned. The poor soldiers who were, too many of them, the refuse and dregs of the nation, became, after one or two campaigns, by the care of their officers, and by good order and discipline, tractable, civil, orderly, sensible, and clean; and had an air and a spirit above the vulgar. The service of God, according to the order of the established Church, was strictly enjoined by the Duke's special care. In all fixed camps every morning and evening were prayers. He was so great a discourager of vice, as to give particular directions to the Provost Marshal to chase away all lewd women from about his quarters; and before a battle, the Chaplains of the several regiments, by his special order, performed divine service; as also, after a victory obtained, solemn thanksgiving was observed throughout the army. There is nothing extravagant in concluding, that the capabilities of the brave men who won the fields of Ramilies and Blenheim were matured and rendered available by the salutary restraints and impulses of Christian faith and practice.

Prince Eugene must also be added to our honourable association. Descended from the ancient house of Savoy, he was called to sustain an important part in the affairs of Europe during the early portion of the seventeenth century, and acquitted himself with singular bravery and talent. He had offered his services to the Imperial army, and in the war between the Emperor and the Turks, evinced uncommon military talents, so that every campaign proved a new step to his advancement in the service. He gave the Turks a memorable defeat at Zante; commanded the German forces in Italy, where he foiled Marshal Villeroy in every engagement, and at length took him prisoner. He afterwards distinguished himself greatly, when the Emperor and Queen Anne united against the exorbitant power of Louis the Fourteenth. In depicting his character it has been said, that "he was valiant without pride; victorious without cruelty; indefatigable without avarice; a friend without guile; a foe without revenge; a soldier without vice; a Christian without bigotry; whose universal fame will bury churches, outlive time, and stand up with eternity!" He composed, and was in the habit of using, the following remarkable prayer:—"O my God! I believe in thee: do thou strengthen my belief. I hope in thee: do thou confirm my hope. I love thee: vouchsafe to redouble my love. I am sorry for my sins: O increase my repentance! I adore thee as my first principle; I desire thee as my last end; I thank thee as my perpetual benefactor; I call upon thee as my supreme defender. My God! be pleased to guide me by thy wisdom, rule me by thy justice, comfort me by thy mercy, and keep me by thy power. To thee I dedicate all my thoughts, words, and actions; that henceforth I may think of thee, speak of thee, act according to thy will, and suffer for thy sake. Lord, my will is subject to thine in whatsoever thou wiliest, because it is thy will. I beseech thee to enlighten my understanding, to give bounds to my will, to purify my body, to sanctify my soul. Enable me, O my God, to expiate my past offences, to conquer my future temptations, to reduce the passions that are too strong for me, and to practise the virtues that become me. O fill my heart with a tender remembrance of thy favours, an aversion for my infirmities, a love for my neighbour, and a contempt for the world. Let me also remember to be submissive to my superiors, charitable to my enemies, faithful to my friends, and indulgent to my inferiors. O God! help me to overcome pleasure by mortification, covetousness by alms, anger by meekness, and lukewarmness by devotion. O my God! make me prudent in undertakings, courageous in dangers, patient under disappointments, and humble in success. Let me never forget, O Lord, to be fervent in prayer, temperate in food, exact in my employs, and constant in my resolutions. Inspire me, O Lord, with a desire always to have a quiet conscience; an outward modesty, as well as inward; an edifying conversation, and a regular conduct. Let me always apply myself to resist nature, to assist grace, to keep thy commands, and deserve to be saved. My God I do thou convince me of the meanness of the earth, the greatness of heaven, the shortness of time, and the length of eternity. Grant that I may be prepared for death; that I may fear thy judgment, avoid hell, and obtain paradise: for the sake and merits of my Lord and Saviour, Jesus Christ. Amen."

The man who could give expression to his desires in words so suitable, comprehensive, and devout, must have had his mind deeply imbued with a sense of the divine goodness, and his own sinfulness. The dependence on Almighty aid, in the spirit of which the petitions are generally offered, evinces no slight acquaintance with sacred truth. One or two phrases are however, unguarded. "Enable me, O God, to expiate my past offences." That is anti-scriptural. To expiate is to atone for, or annul the guilt of a crime by subsequent acts of piety, as if present obedience could obliterate past iniquity. The thing is impossible. Sin is an infinite evil, and can be atoned for only by a sacrifice of infinite value. Besides, the work of human redemption is complete, and admits no rude and ignorant addenda on the part of man. The blood of Christ is infinitely, efficacious and meritorious. No other help is found; no other name is given by which we can salvation have. "Wherefore he is able to save them to the uttermost that come unto God by him, seeing he ever liveth to make intercession for them." The other mistake of the Prince consists in a seeming approach to the Almighty, on the ground of Popish dogma. He prays for grace "to keep thy commands and deserve to be saved." To deserve, implies worthiness and merit; but man is without both. It cannot be, that in a spiritual sense, he should be possessed of either. We are to be saved through the merits of the Saviour; our own must not be mentioned. So with regard to the other quality, "worthy is the Lamb that was slain;" but in that attribute no human being has any share. With these abatements, we may safely exhibit the prayer as one which neither soldier, sailor, nor citizen need disown; and the writer must be classed among those heroes who, though liable to an occasional theological inaccuracy, are not ashamed, while they serve their country, to fear God, and render to him the homage of their lives.

And how finely was the Christian character exemplified in the life of Colonel Gardiner! This gentleman, when a mere youth, was engaged in active service. He signalized himself by uncommon exertions at the battle of Blenheim. At that time, destitute of religion, he sought "the bubble reputation, e'en in the cannon's mouth;" and while in the act of leading on his men to a desperate assault upon the enemy's intrenchments, swearing most profanely, a musket shot struck him in the month, and came out at the back of his neck. The infliction of the wound was so instantaneous, that in the rage of the moment, though conscious of being struck, he thought he had swallowed the bullet. In almost the next moment he was undeceived, and fell senseless. There he lay, weltering in blood, for some time; but being of a hale and vigorous constitution, he was observed, when the fury of the fight had diminished, among a heap of the dying and dead, to be yet alive. Surgical help was directly obtained, and he was mercifully given back from the very gate of death. It is well known that he afterwards became an eminent Christian. His conversion to the faith, like that of Paul, was sudden, decisive, and glorious; and late in life he fell by the blow of a Lochaber axe, nobly fighting, when nearly all others fled, at the battle of Preston field,—a capital instance of bravery, refined and exalted by the purity of religious principle.

The goodly fellowship of our devout and enterprising heroes must also include another associate this is no less a person than Frederick the Great, of Prussia,—a man who, when almost the whole of continental Europe had combined to dismember his kingdom, arose with gigantic prowess, and defended himself with such singular ability and courage, that, while his numerous and powerful enemies were repelled, his influence as a Monarch was firmly established. That the mind of Frederick was deeply imbued with scriptural truth, is confirmed by his celebrated confession of faith; which, for clearness of conception, and the forcibleness of the terms in which his sentiments are expressed, shows that he knew the truth. He was unhappily led away in old age by the subtleties of Voltaire, who had contrived to insinuate himself into the presence of Prussian. royalty; but that apostasy on the part of His Majesty may be viewed in part as an error of feeble senility, nor does it destroy, or even derogate from, the value of the testimony yielded to religion by the mastermind of Frederick, when the suffrage of his credence was worth having, in the prime and vigour of his days, and the more leisurely exercise of his masculine intellect.

Old Colonel Berdeleben belongs undoubtedly to our corps. He was a favourite of the great Frederick of Prussia, who lavished several honours upon the worthy veteran. Deeply grateful for the distinction thus conferred, but more entirely overcome with a sense of divine goodness, he observed, "Should I die this moment, I die in the favour of God and My King. I truly rejoice that my Sovereign has assured me of his favour; but of what avail would the King's favour be towards the consolation of my conscience, and what would it help me in my present situation, did I not possess the favour of God!" Reasonings like this may be scorned, but they cannot be confuted.

The late French Emperor may perhaps be quoted as an exception to our rule; for he had no religion, and yet was successful. But this wants looking at. To be sure, Napoleon was a mighty hunter of the human race; he drove furiously, and often astonished his compeers by boldness of enterprise, and rapidity of movement. He was, no doubt, an instrument in the hands of Providence for the accomplishment of certain designs; the eventual tendency of which, the world has, it may be, yet to learn. His warmest admirers must not, however, claim for him the homage due to an universal conqueror. He was foiled twice, at any rate; once at the opening of his career, and once at the close. Sir Sydney Smith repulsed him at Acre, and his Grace of Wellington at Waterloo. So that religion has the best of it, after all.

1. Dr. Fresenius, senior of the Clergy at Frankfort.

CHAPTER IX

INSTANCES of genuine conversion to the faith of the Gospel, attended by the fruits of the Spirit, are also to be met with among what are generally termed "common soldiers," by which are understood the private men composing the main body of an army, by whom, as making up the physical force employed, the brunt of actual fighting is chiefly sustained; and it has pleased the great Head of the church so to magnify his grace, that many of these men, when exposed to the most imminent peril, were enabled not only to perform their duty with coolness and intrepidity, but to rejoice in the midst of privation and suffering. No serious and intelligent man can forget that about a century ago, a most remarkable revival of religion took place in these lands; and the influence, it appears from authentic records, extended to the British army. Ninety years since, a pious soldier, engaged in one of the German campaigns then in operation, has observed, "The day we marched to Maestricht, I found the love of God shed abroad in my heart, that I thought my very soul was dissolved in tears. The day we engaged the French at Dettingen, as the battle began, I said, 'Lord, in thee have I trusted, let me never be confounded.' Joy overflowed my soul, and I told my comrades, 'If I fall this day, I shall rest in the everlasting arms of Christ.'" He did not fall; and about ten months afterwards, in another written communication, directed to his Pastor, he seems more happy than ever, though in circumstances which, in ordinary cases, would have been destructive of mental calm ness. At the close of a severe action, he states, "As to my own part, I stood the fire of the enemy above seven hours; then my horse was shot under me, and I was exposed both to the enemy and our own horse. But that did not discourage me at all; for I knew the God of Israel was with me. I had a long way to go, the balls flying on every side, and thousands lay dying and dead on either hand. Surely I was as in the fiery furnace; but it never singed one hair of my head." Providentially, the veteran was not left to stand alone; for true godliness is essentially communicative. He adds, "Going on, I met one of our brethren with a little dish in his hand, seeking for water. He smiled and said he had got a sore wound in his leg. I asked him, 'Have you gotten Christ in your heart?' He answered, "I have, and have had him all day." Now, it is not possible that there can be any mistake here. Persons reposing on the lap of ease, and without an earthly desire unfulfilled, may contrive, with but moderate devotion of heart, to keep up, least, the semblance of contentedness; for the profession of faith is not costly when trials are all away: but when a man, just in the jaws of destruction, and with scarcely the hope of relief, can express and exemplify such confidence in Almighty goodness, we may rest assured he possesses some power beyond, and superior to, that which nature yields. The name of the soldier whose remarks I have quoted was John Haime; and he lived to be a useful member of the church He was favoured, while in active military service, with the correspondence of one of the most venerable and learned Ministers of that age. A copy of one of the letters thus received from him has been preserved, and is worthy of all acceptation, not only on account of the wisdom of the advices it contains, but of the affectionate regard shown, in the midst, probably, of multiplied engagements, to an absent member of the flock. "It is a great blessing," observes the writer, "whereof God has already made you a partaker: but if you continue waiting upon him, you shall see greater things than these. This is only the beginning of the kingdom of heaven, which he will set up in your heart. There is yet behind, the fullness of the mind that was in Christ; 'righteousness, peace, and joy in the Holy Ghost.' It is but a little thing that men should be against you, while they know that God is on your side. If he gives you any companion in the narrow way, it is well; and it is well, if he do not. So much the more will he teach and strengthen you by himself; he will strengthen you in the secret of your heart, and, by and by, he will raise up, as it were out of the dust, those who shall say, 'Come, and let us magnify his name together.' But, by all means, miss no opportunity; speak, and spare not. Declare what God has done for your soul; regard not worldly prudence; be not ashamed of Christ, or of his word, or of his servants; speak the truth in love, even to a crooked generation; and all things shall work together for good, until the work of God is perfect in your soul."

We learn from the above account, first, that a truly devout soldier is a truly valiant one; secondly, that so far from having occasion to rest, as it were, on the threshold of Christian experience, he is to press to the mark in common with the faithful, "until the word of God is perfected;" and, thirdly, that this view of the matter is taken by a profound and enlightened judge of human nature,— for the letter now recited was composed and forwarded by the Founder of Methodism. But, although grateful remembrance is made that the Almighty has preserved my life, and though convinced that he is able to keep his faithful people in the most trying situations, let it not be supposed that I consider war as an immaterial occurrence, and a light evil: on the contrary, experience has shown me that it is one of the worst and most destructive calamities by which humanity can be visited. Saved, as we have been in this country, from the tempests which have so repeatedly swept the European continent, and knowing nothing of "the horrid alarum of war," save through the medium of Gazettes and hear-say evidence, we are apt to overlook the mischief inflicted on those, upon whose peaceful residences the unwelcome avalanche has broken. The despatches of naval and military Commanders, being written in an official and rather glossy style, tend naturally to maintain the deception, and inflame vanity, that longs to catch the igniting spark. With the superiority and immense importance of our naval force, every one is familiar; and nothing was more common during the late bitter and protracted war, than accounts in the daily journals, of actions fought on the high seas, or at the entrance of hostile harbours, in which might be perceived the same ingenious rejection of unpleasant allusions, while victory and conquest, as though they cost nothing, rejoiced in every sentence. Some variation was, of course, observable in these spirit-stirring epistles; but the main points of communication were generally similar: "Discovered a suspicious sail on the weather beam; gave chase immediately, and cleared

for action. She proved to be a fine vessel, almost new, of superior force, and full of men. Got within range at two p m., and gave her a broadside, which did prodigious execution. Having disabled her rigging, we ran her on board; and, though the resistance was desperate, in ten minutes the capture was complete. We had only ten killed and thirteen wounded; while the enemy, in consequence of his peculiar obstinacy, lost more than three times that number."
Certain officers are then recommended for promotion; the gallant crew are presented to the notice of the Lords of the Admiralty and the affair, emblazoned by thousands of impressions, is conveyed by the obsequious press from Berwick-upon-Tweed to the Scilly Isles. It is true, souls have been hurried, by mortal strife, into the eternal world; the widow's tear will flow; orphans will be left to sigh in sadness and destitution: but their grief will expend itself in silence and secrecy for in the exultation of victory and triumph, who can find time to turn aside and weep?

As for several years I literally fought my way through the world, it is natural to suppose that the reasons and results of war have frequently attracted my notice. The alleged and ostensible objects for which one monarch or ruler has engaged in war with another, are to punish some slight or injury, which the nation, or its dependencies, or some one of its allies, may have sustained; or to prevent or repel the assaults and invasions of its neighbours. In modern times, those who think of war, enlarge eloquently upon the law of nations, the rights of civil society, and especially the balance of power. This latter phrase has been exceedingly in fashion through the range of diplomatic lore; and the conflict, maintained through a long and dreadful struggle, to give equilibrium to the balance in question, has cost an expenditure of blood and treasure previously un known in the history of this hemisphere. The truth is, that where war is determined, pretences are easily invented or discovered; as those who are for ever in search of a hook on which to hang a fault, seldom fail of success. Such then are the feigned or genuine motives for war; but every man who looks beneath the surface of political expediency, is convinced that other and more really efficacious reasons are to be detected. Avarice, ambition, religious bigotry, the absence of all religion, desire of dominion, thirst for fame, private pique and animosity, with other dispositions equally censurable, have been the actual though unmentioned causes of many of those sanguinary contests by which the face of nature is marred and spoiled.

Another remarkable circumstance is, that not the most distant reference is made to the motives just named in the manifestos of belligerent powers. Hostile papers of that sort are commonly made up of lengthened and lachrymose details of grievances and injuries, altogether insufferable by a great and independent nation. On these accounts, which, for any thing the public know, may be true or false, mistaken or absurd, the world is to rise in arms, battle and murder are to begin, and the children of one common Parent, whose nature and essence is love, are to commence and prosecute the work of mutual destruction. Other reasons are, however, assigned for war. Political writers have gone so far as to assert that war, though its miseries are admitted, is a necessary evil, and tends to purify the community, by affording an outlet to the scum and refuse of the population. "No body," says Bacon, "can be healthful without exercise, neither natural body nor politic;" concludes, therefore, that "to a kingdom or state, a just and honourable war is the true exercise." The pass to which we arrive on such an hypothesis is clearly this: Every war is just and honourable if we are to believe the asseverations of those who wage it; therefore, all wars and commotions involving the loss of life are tributary to health and "true exercise." According to another speculatist, whose ingenious lucubrations have excited great remark, redundant population is one of the primary causes of war. "One of its first causes," says Malthus, "and most powerful impulses, was an insufficiency of room and food; and greatly as the circumstances of mankind have changed since it first began, the same cause still continues to operate, and to produce, though in a smaller degree, the same effect. The ambition of Princes would want instrument of destruction, if the distresses of the lower classes did not drive them under their standards. A recruiting Sergeant always prays for a bad harvest and a want of employment, or, in other words, a redundant population." This redundance he proposes to obviate, and thus counter act one of the principal causes of war, by creating obstacles in the way of marriage. This advice may be very sincerely given; but I, for one, see differently, and believe that the authority of good government maybe sustained by plans, not only different from, but directly opposed to, this antichristian theory. Let other methods be adopted. Repress intemperance, encourage industry, patronize religion, suppress frivolity, extend agriculture, afford increased facilities to manufacture and commerce, and if there be a disposition and fairness of opportunity for emigration, encourage and help forward the outward-bound parties. When these duties, in their interminable ramifications, are performed, the pressure of an indolent and worthless population will be materially relieved. At all events, we may wait till they are tried, before measures are adopted likely to tear in pieces the morals and mechanism of society. It remains, after all, to be proved that a nation gains in going to war. If the experience of the last half century is to decide the question, I incline to think that the advantages realized on either side will lie in a small compass. It is true, the honour of Britain is unsullied: the fame of her arms has resounded through the globe; it has been the favourite theme both of historians and poets. "Her march is on the mountain wave, her home is on the deep." Nor can it be forgotten, say her eulogists, that the last contest with France was terminated with great glory. This I shall not dispute; but in estimating the value of glory, whether national or private, there is, perhaps, no better method than to survey the results, especially with regard to their permanency and principles of endurance. What these are, with respect to the unprecedented expenditure of the late war, no Englishman, with a house over his head; need be told. Never, surely, was there any thing half so glorious as the conflict with republican France, for, unless public credit be forfeited, which cannot be permitted, no one need fear that the results will cease. Every quarter reminds us of their immutability; of their passing away no apprehensions need be entertained; and future generations will inspect them as we do an Egyptian pyramid,—they will meditate upon the vastness of ancient expenditure, and wonder why it took place.

The moral evil of war is yet to be named; and this is the greatest of all. It commences even before a blow is struck. The constitution and mere assemblage of a large army, containing, as it does, numbers of young men in the vigour of life, and without sufficient occupation, enervates the mind, begets an injurious love of ease, and diverts the faculties from those steady and useful pursuits to be found in the arts of peace. We accordingly find that the immediate encampment of an army of friends is, for divers weighty reasons not long concealed, a visit by no means desirable; and many an otherwise happy family has had occasion to remember the day when such acquaintances approached. As to actual contest, and the aggressive move of a hostile army, they are so destructive that whoever commences war without necessity is guilty of an atrocious offence against the human race, and is accountable for all the consequences that may follow. The Christian regards it with detestation and horror, as one of the greatest evils with which it has pleased Providence to arm the hands of its ministers to punish and afflict mankind. Without additional research for the reasons of war, they may at once be traced to human depravity. Sin is the cause of all. Where the Spirit of Christ is manifest, there can be no war; for the principles which excite it are destroyed. True religion is essentially pacific. It teaches every man to his brother; and one petition in the prayers of David is, "Scatter thou the people that delight in war." Quarrelsome piety, like harmless vice, is a contradiction in terms. Love is said to be the fulfilling of the law. This is the grace that modulates and perfects all the rest. "Whether there be prophecies, they shall fail; whether there be tongues, they shall cease; whether there be knowledge, it shall vanish away;" but the Spirit of love shall never fail. The purpose for which the Redeemer came into the world was, to proclaim peace and good-will to man; and one of the signs of his universal reign will be, that "he shall judge among the nations, and shall rebuke many people; and they shall beat their swords into ploughshares and their spears into pruning-hooks: nation shall not lift up sword against nation, neither shall they learn war any more."

One advantage, in the opinion of some persons, seems to lie with the system of modern warfare. It does not, they say, appear to be conducted at so great an expense of human life. This they think is evident if we advert to the prodigious slaughter between conflicting armies in early ages. Abijah, King of Judah, we find, appeared in the field with four hundred thousand men. This astonishing multitude was opposed by another, twice as numerous; for we read that Jeroboam, King of Israel, confronted his opponent with eight hundred thousand. The fight must have been attended with dreadful animosity, as it is added, (2 Chron. XIII. 3–17,) there were five hundred thousand slain in one battle. We are also told of Pekab, son of Remaliah, King of Israel, who in one day killed one hundred and twenty thousand men of the troops of Judah. (2 Chron. XXVIII. 6.) Another ruinous battle is also recorded. Asa, King of Judah, having an army of five hundred and eighty thousand men was attacked by Zerah, King of Cush, who had an army of a million of men. Zerah was entirely routed by the troops of Asa. (2 Chron. XIV. 9–13.) The immense slaughter which attended some of the battles in the Greek and Roman wars, is familiar to most readers; where the greater part of the vanquished army was frequently put to the sword. In modern warfare., it has been urged, even of the large armies that have appeared in the field on the continent of Europe, we seldom find so many as thirty thousand killed and wounded on both sides,—a number greatly inferior to that which fell of the Romans at Cannæ, and by no means equal to the loss of the Carthaginians at the battle of Zama. This diminished slaughter is attributed, and perhaps with justice, to the use of fire-arms; for it used to be computed that in this mode of fighting, not more- than one musket-ball in forty takes effect, and not more than one in four hundred proves fatal. Recent events have, however, gone far to show, that in the hands of finely disciplined soldiers, the weapons of the present period are exceedingly formidable. During the later actions of the war, almost every one was eventually decided by the bayonet and sabre; and with regard even to musketry, so unerring is the aim of regular firing, especially when practised with the rifle, that the effect, though at a considerable distance, is appalling. At the disastrous engagement near New-Orleans, the American force, under General Jackson, were posted behind a well-constructed entrenchment, composed of cotton-bales five feet high. Behind this impervious breastwork, the men were placed, each with a rifle gun, which was loaded by others, as fast as the front men could fire. Every shot took effect; and the. British, placed, no doubt, in a false position, were struck down by an enemy who durst not advance, and whom they could not so much as see. To say nothing, therefore, of the losses experienced by Napoleon, in his memorable Russian campaign, where the climate was his most deadly foe, it would be easy to show from actual returns, that the loss of life and limb, at several engagements long after that period, in proportion to the total number of men on the ground, that the weapons now in use, when actively handled, are, in the fatality of their effect, little less murderous than those of the olden time. Political writers have affirmed, that the wars consequent on the French revolution of 1791 cost the lives of five millions of human beings. The number of broken hearts, and ruined fortunes, has not, I believe, been computed.

The evils entailed by war are perpetuated to the close of open contest, and even beyond it. The disbanding of an army naturally throws into society a numerous body of men, little used to manual labour, without sufficient visible means of subsistence, and not much inclined to settle down on the quiet avocations of domestic life. Hence it has been observed, that the conclusion of hostilities abroad is usually succeeded by disorder and tumult at home; and not unfrequently, that robbery, and other crimes, destructive of international comfort and peace, were of alarming prevalence. Such are the instruments and munitions, and so seriously injurious are the results, of an art, the express and ultimate object of which is, to destroy life. Roll rapidly, ye intervening years, which are yet to interpose between the present and a better state of things! May the time hasten, when the ingenuity of man shall be no longer misapplied in inventions so hateful; when earth-born malice and resentment, by which it is called into action, are subdued; and in place thereof shall arise the spirit of peace and amity, as a mild and holy dove, to hover over the world, ruling in the hearts of all, and bringing into willing bonds every power of the soul to the obedience of Christ.

But this is a digression. With regard to myself, a powerful conviction rested at this season on my mind, that I was not in the right path; but being shackled with the trammels of Popery,

which I surveyed with increasing suspicion, I scarcely knew how
to proceed. During the time I was in Ireland, my besetments on
this account were painfully distressing. "If the blind lead the blind,
shall they not both fall into the ditch!" and for some time my
spiritual guides con ducted me into many a miserable quagmire
of superstition and absurdity. On complaining of uneasiness of
mind, I was directed to proceed forthwith to the Priest, in order
to confess and receive, absolution. My misgivings, as to the value
of these services, grew stronger; but the importunity of friends
prevailed, and away I went. On arriving at the chapel, which,
in fact, was a barn, I found a crowd of persons, all waiting to be
relieved of their respective moral burdens. His Reverence at length
appeared; and a haughtier figure I do not remember to have seen.
On commencing the service, which to me was an intolerable
jargon, a fierce rush was made by those without for admission. The
reason for such haste did not consist in any specially devout desire
first to catch the benedictions of the reverend gentleman. We had
been informed that it was a deadly sin to eat before confession; so
that hunger had nearly driven us to extremities; and an open door,
leading to what it might, was hailed with delight, as the promise
of relief of some sort. On pressing forward, I unfortunately broke
my watch-glass, which by no means tended either to sweeten or
equalise my feelings and after a tremendous row, which had nearly
ended in a fight, I was ushered into the presence of the Priest.
"Tell out your sins," said he. This was a terrific commencement;
but there was no escape. I therefore related several particulars of my
past life, not forgetting several occurrences that took place during
my campaigns abroad. He then advised a course of penance, and
ordered me to see him again, stating that on a future occasion he
should administer the Eucharist, after which all would be well.
I hope he obtained a forgiveness better than that he pretended
to bestow. I was then compelled to apply to Father K—, a deep
old file, at the parish chapel. On advancing to him, he sung out
for money due, as he said, to the Church. After such an opening,
I had no relish, either for his advice or pardon. I was induced,
however, to give him an other trial a few weeks afterwards; but,
if possible, I fared worse. In this instance the Priest had chosen a

public ale-house for his station. Some of the audience were adding to existing sin, by excessive drinking; others were confessing sins already committed; and a few were receiving absolution. I left this scene with unmingled disgust; and, as might have been expected, felt my mind depressed, as before. Just at this season I was taken seriously ill; and having been given over by the physician, spiritual consolation was judged needful. The old Priest was accordingly introduced; but finding on his arrival that I had declined subscribing to the Church, a solitary question was all he asked, and he retired. This Priest soon after died. The Almighty was pleased, however, to restore me to health; but no peace of mind could I procure. Having met with another Catholic counsellor, he stated that about seven miles from my residence were six holy wells; and that, if after twelve months penance, I went round those wells on my bare knees, devoutly saying an Ave Maria and a Pater Noster, I should find relief. To increase the number of pilgrimages to the spot, booths were erected in the vicinity, under which provisions of various sorts were sold, not forgetting a copious store of whisky. This intolerable abuse has, I understand, been suppressed; and the only wonder with me is, that it ever obtained, even among the most credulous.

After a careful inspection of Popish doctrine, conducted with all the care and perseverance I possessed, the conclusion to which I arrived was, that the precepts and practices of Catholicism are utterly at variance with the revealed will of God, and subversive of sound morality. In no part of the creed is this more evident, than in those directions which allow the sale of indulgences. This scandalous impiety first aroused the attention of Luther, and the early Reformers. The following is the form of an indulgence, as held forth in the sixteenth century:—"May our Lord Jesus Christ have mercy on and absolve thee, by the merits of his most holy passion. And I, by his authority, and that of his blessed Apostles, St. Paul and St. Peter, and of the most holy Pope Leo X., granted unto me in these parts, do absolve thee; first, from all ecclesiastical censures, and then from all thy sins, transgressions, and excesses, how enormous soever they may be, even such as are cognisable by the Holy See alone; and, as far as the keys of the holy Church extend,

I remit to you all punishments which you deserve in purgatory on their account, and I restore you to the unity of the faithful, and to that innocence and purity which you possessed at baptism; so that when you die, the gates of punishment shall be shut, and the gates of paradise and delight opened; and, if you shall not die at present, this grace shall remain in full force when you shall be at the point of death. In the name of the Father, and of the Son, and of the Holy Ghost." By way of comment on the preceding article, the Catholic Clergy have observed that, "if any man shall purchase letters of indulgence, his soul may rest secure with regard to its salvation. The souls confined in purgatory, so soon as the money tinkles in the chest, instantly escape from that place of torment, and ascend into heaven. The efficacy of indulgences is such, that the most heinous sins would be remitted and expiated by them, and the persons be freed from punishment and guilt. This is the unspeakable gift of God, to reconcile men to himself. Lo! the heavens are open: if ye enter not in now, when will ye enter? For a little money ye may redeem the soul of your father out of purgatory from torments. If you had but one coat, you ought to strip yourself immediately, and sell it, in order to purchase such benefits." Thus, with feigned words, these Jesuitical gentlemen make merchandise of the people. The principal design is evident; and that is, to secure the money. Archbishop Tillotson has observed, speaking of the superiority of the Reformed religion, "We make no money of the mistakes of the people; nor do we fill their heads with fears of new places of torment, to make them empty their purses in a vainer hope to be de livered out of them: we do not pretend to have a mighty bank and treasure of merits in the Church, which they sell for ready m giving them bills of exchange from the Pope on purgatory; when they who grant them have no reason to believe they will avail them, or be accepted in the other world." Bad as is the plan of purchasing heaven by money, as these deceivers teach, it is not the worst feature in the disposal of indulgences; for among other methods resorted to by the heads of Papacy to support a rotten fabric, indulgences for future convenience in this world, and an exemption from punishment hereafter, were given to those who would fight for the Church, or, in plain terms, persecute all others.

Bishop Burnet states, that a jubilee was granted after the massacre at Paris, to all who had been in that butchery; and they were commanded to go and bless God for the success of that action. The Pope sent Cardinal Urson, his Legate, to France, to thank the King for so great a service done to the Church, and to desire him to go on, and extirpate heresy, root and branch, that it might never grow again. And as the Legate passed through on his journey to Paris, he gave a plenary indulgence to all who had been actors in the massacre." It may not be amiss, if we state, that by a plenary indulgence a man returns to the state he was in after baptism; and, did he die that instant, his soul would go at once to paradises without passing through purgatory. On this principle, the furies who shed the blood of the saints in France were so folly meet for the inheritance of the saints in light, that the alembic of purgatory, through which persons less saintly must pass, might in their happy case be omitted. The depravity connected with the sale of this filthy article has extended itself in other modes. In a book printed in Rome, in the year 1514, by the authority of the Pope, entitled, "The Tax of the Sacred Roman Chancery," is to be found a table containing a list of prices for which certain sins may with safety be committed. The book was afterwards reprinted at Paris, Cologne, and Venice; and has since been translated into English, under the title of "Rome, a great Custom-House of Sin." It informs the world for what price the pardon of heaven, and absolution, might, for particular crimes, be obtained. For instance, pardon—

	£	s	d
For stealing holy things out of a consecrated place	0	10	0
For a layman murdering a layman.	0	7	6
For murdering father, mother, wife, or sister	0	10	6
For a Priest keeping a concubine	0	10	6
For burning a house maliciously	0	12	0
For forging the Pope's hand	1	7	0

Besides absolutions for crimes too shocking to be mentioned, from 9s. to £2 10s.[1] The preceding statement requires no comment. To enlarge upon its tendency, would be to blacken the chimney. Its design, on the part of the monkish brotherhood who invented and maintain it, is to make a penny, by means at which a modest devil would blush; and proves, by demonstration strong as holy writ, that the abettors of such crimes are the true descendants of that scoundrel hierarchy, at whose decline and fall the truly great and good will rejoice and be exceeding glad.

Before now, instances have been known in which the fraternity were foiled with their own weapons. A certain nobleman once told Tetzelius, a mighty preacher of indulgences, that he had a mind to commit a very heinous sin, and desired an indulgence or present pardon for it. This was granted for a considerable sum; and when the money was paid, the bull was given. Some time after, this nobleman took occasion to meet Tetzelius in a certain wood, and, breaking open his chest, robbed him of his entire stock of indulgences. When Tetzelius threatened him with all manner of curses, the nobleman showed him the bull he had paid so dear for; and, laughing at him, observed, that this was the very sin he had a longing to commit, when he was so fully absolved.

Equally absurd, though not so malignant in its immediate result, is the doctrine of purgatory, of which the Scriptures know nothing. The hypothesis on which this notion is founded seems to he an opinion that some are not quite good enough to go to heaven, and yet too good to be sent to hell; an idea evidently borrowed from the fabled invisible domains of heathen writers. In errors of this sort, and indeed of any description, our resort must be "to the law and to the testimony;" and if the truths therein contained are contradicted by an angel of light, we are not to believe him. The holy Scriptures leave no ground for the doctrine of purgatory. "There are twelve hours in the day, wherein men ought to work: work while ye have the day; for the night cometh, when no man can work." When death are probation ceases; the die is cast, the destiny is fixed, and cannot be revoked or amended. St. Paul asserts, that, "if the earthly house of our tabernacle were dissolved, we have a building of God, a house not made with hands, eternal in the heavens." He also affirms, that when "we are absent from the body, we are present with the Lord;" which is impossible, unless we are to conclude that our Lord is in purgatory. We are told, moreover, in the Gospel, that "the beggar died, and was carried by angels into Abraham's bosom;" not into purgatory, or the Popish limbo, but into paradise, whither the thief upon the cross also went. We find also that Moses and Elias appeared on the mount, in glory, with our Lord and his Apostles. So that they could not have been confined in purgatory, even before the death of Christ. The inference is, there is no such place. "Blessed are the dead who die in the Lord, for they rest from their labours:" but purgatory is not rest; it is a species of future ordeal; and God cannot deny himself, or contradict his promises. Papists affect that Augustine taught the doctrine of purgatory; but this pretext will avail little: for if it could be proved, the weight is nothing against Scripture. There was, indeed, a time when he had some debate in his mind upon the subject, and observed, "that such a matter as a middle state for purgation might be inquired of:" but after more diligent investigation and thought, he says, "We read of heaven and of hell, but the third place we are utterly ignorant of; yea, we find it is not in the Scriptures. Nor will any thing help thee, but what is done while thou art here. As the last day of man's life finds him, so the last day of the world shall hold him. Nor is there for any body any third place that he can possibly be in, but with the devil, who is not with Christ." The scheme of purgatory, like the other legends of Papacy, was doubtless invented with a special view to the "main chance," that is, the cash. When a Roman Catholic talks of securing bliss, he means, making money and it is clear that, in this view the doctrine now exploded is intimately connected with indulgences, and that they stand or fall together. This invisible trial was never heard of till the year 600; and the first who directed prayers for the dead to be used, in the Church of Rome, was Odillo, Abbot of Cluny, in the year 1000.

Transubstantiation is another of the absurdities of Papacy; which no man of sane mind can comprehend, much less receive. "Since Christ, our Redeemer," observes the Council of Trent, "has said that it was truly his own body which he offered under the appearance of bread, it has always therefore been believed in the church of God, and is now again declared by this holy Council,— That, by the consecration of the bread and wine, there is effected a conversion of the whole substance of the bread into the substance of the body of Christ our Lord, and of the whole substance of the wine into the substance of his blood; which conversion is fitly and properly termed by the holy Church, Transubstantiation." To this proposition is annexed, in the usual spirit of that persecuting Church, "If any one shall deny these statements, he is accursed." This is advancing upon us with a vengeance. I see only one alternative here for a reasonable being. We are compelled either to take leave of our senses, or expose ourselves to eternal ruin. We are to receive a positive, palpable contradiction, as confirmed truth; that a consecrated wafer, made of flour and water, is the real body of Christ; that the wine, compressed from fruit, is his real blood; and, what is more, though we are sure that the bread and wine have been thus prepared, we are nevertheless called upon to believe that they were not. We are to believe that He who fills heaven and earth, and is immutable, is as small as a crumb of bread or a drop of wine, and can be eaten and drunk. In fact, we are expected to give implicit credit to impossibilities; as if religion, instead of being a reasonable service, was a tissue of absurdities, and a cunningly devised fable. The conclusion is inevitable. Transubstantiation, like most other items of Popish belief, is opposed to reason and Scripture. It can have no other than an ideal existence; and is compounded of such stuff as dreams are made of. Hence it has been asserted, that, even a century ago, several discerning persons in the Church of Rome were grown so sensible of the weakness of the doctrine, that they would be glad quietly to dispose of it; but the Council of Trent, with the purblind zeal which has ever characterized this fallen Church, have riveted it so fast to their religion, and made it so necessary and essential a part of their belief, that they cannot now disengage it. It is a millstone hung about the neck of Popery, that will some day sink it; and, in the opinion of many well-informed men, it is a weight that will make the pillars of Saint Peter's crack, and requires more volumes to make it good than would fill the Vatican.

Nor is the matter mended if we contemplate the worship of the Host, and homage paid to images and pictures. Like many other of the antics of Popery, these are novelties, and were not known till 1216. Pope Adrian the Sixth, it is said, had so much doubt of their value, that in his own practice he used the precautionary form, "I adore thee if thou art Christ;" and judged the people should say the same. His suspicions were well founded. As no power whatever can work a self-contradiction, so no being can make that which is already made; but Christ was many years before the Eucharist; therefore no power could make the Eucharistic bread to be the man Christ Jesus. Of course it ever remained a creature, and adoration offered to it is idolatry. So of images. Referring to these, an old writer remarks, "Now would any one be pleased to consider the pains taken in the formation of images, he would be ashamed to stand in such fear of a thing that the hand of the artist had been so long playing upon, to make a god. For this wooden god, taken perhaps out of some old faggot or pile, or a piece of some forlorn stump, is hung up, hewn, planed, and chiselled into shape; or if it he a deity of brass or silver, it is ten to one but the pedigree is derived from a dirty kettle, or worse than that. But if it happen to be a god of stone, then the mallets are set to work upon him; but as he is not sensible of any hardships endured in the preparation, it is to him of inferior moment. Well, the image is cast, fashioned, and filed; hut, pray, when does it become divine?" It may be soldered, put together, and set upon its legs; but, after all, the article is of no value. Then comes the Catholic Priest, with his consecrating potentialities; and now, behold your god! ye deluded worshippers. The truly enlightened Christian sees through the folly of such practices. He knows that all divine or religious worship is wholly due to Jehovah. If not wholly, not at all; for any reason that would take away a part, must take away the whole. If, therefore, wholly due to him, then can no part thereof, however small, be given away from him, without injustice and impiety. Luther was the man, raised up by an Almighty Providence, to curtail the influence of the 'man' of sin." His vast intellectual powers were devoted to the revival of letters; he watched their progress, and rejoiced at the victory of ancient languages over the Inquisitor. Supported by an indefatigable zeal and wonderful industry, Luther acquired the most perfect acquaintance with the sacred Scriptures, the Fathers, and other

ecclesiastical antiquities. In every encounter he over whelmed the
scholastics with his arguments and wit, and covered their science
with confusion. His individual character was uprightness. Ardent
and calm, high-spirited and humble at the same time; his language,
when provoked by injurious treatment, was irritable and warm;
mild, and inimical to every species of violence in action; cheerful,
open, and of a ready wit; a pleasant companion; studious, sober,
and a stoic in himself; courageous and disinterested. He exposed
himself with tranquillity to every risk in support of what he
believed to be the truth. Commanded to appear at the Diet of
Worms, he presented himself there, notwithstanding the terrible
and very recent example of John Huss, with dignity, simplicity, and
firmness. Far from setting Rome at defiance at the first, he wrote
submissively to the Pope, and exhibited no other appearance of
superiority but that of his immense knowledge over Cardinal
Cajetan, and the other theologians deputed by the Court of
Rome to convert him. Being an Augustinian Monk and Doctor,
he had been sent to Rome on the business of his order; and there,
every thing that struck his eye filled his heart with indignation.
After having refused the offers of the Court, after having been the
friend, the adviser, and the spiritual father of so many great men
and Princes, he might have acquired vast wealth; but that he did
not want. Luther lived for nobler purposes, and died in a state
bordering on poverty, leaving to his wife and children only the
esteem due to his name. The German nation acknowledges Luther
for the reformer of its literature and of its idiom. One of his first
cares was to publish a faithful translation of the Bible in the vulgar
tongue, from the original. It may easily be conceived with what
avidity this glorious work was received, and what a general
sensation it excited. "No writer, for many ages," says an admirable
scholar, "had seen writings bought with such avidity, and so read,
from the throne to the cottage; the popularity, the natural ease, the
energy of expression which prevailed in them, and a doctrine
which cheered and elevated the soul, gained him the good-will of
the most upright and judicious of all classes." Luther has been
accused of violence; but then, we should consider the insufferable
provocation he had to endure. Had he not been ardent and

vehement, how could he have become the leader of such a revolution? Let us listen to one of the Papal invectives launched against him by Clement the Fifth: "May God strike him with imbecility and madness; may heaven over whelm him with its thunders ; may the anger of God, with that of St. Peter and St. Paul, fall upon him in this world and in the next; may the whole universe revolt against him; may the earth swallow him up alive; may his name perish from the earliest generation, and may his memory disappear; may all the elements be adverse to him; may his children, delivered into the hands of his enemies, be crushed before his eyes." Such were the maledictions of the modern Shimei; keeping in remembrance also that the Pope, according to the creed of every good Catholic, is a person of perfect and impeccable infallibility. And what a bungling attempt is the usage of penance to purchase heaven! Papists tell us, that confession to a Priest is of infinite value, and amounts to an exchange which God allows, of the temporal punishments we have deserved by sin, into these small penitential works. Yet, it is to be feared, say they, that the penance enjoined is seldom sufficient to take away all the punishment due to God's justice on account of our sins, the balance of the account remains unpaid, and must be settled in purgatory. After confession, the penitent is ordered to say, "I beg pardon of God, and penance and absolution from you, my ghostly father." The Priest then gives the absolution, and adds, "May the passion of the Lord Jesus Christ, the merits of the blessed Virgin Mary, and of all the saints, and whatsoever good thou shalt do, and whatsoever evil thou shalt suffer, be to thee unto the remission of thy sins, and the increase of grace." In conformity with this piece of priestly fraud, many poor creature have submitted to miserable hardships; some have worn hair shirts, having, given themselves a certain number of stripes; others have taken long and painful pilgrimages; and in Spain and Italy these woeful travellers are frequently observed, almost naked, loaded with chains, and groaning at every step. But of all the proofs which may be adduced to discover the true character of this base and fallen Church, her persecuting spirit is the most conclusive. This has always been seen. The friends to the Reformation were anathematized and excommunicated; and the life of Luther was often in danger, though at last he died on the bed of peace. Innumerable schemes were resorted to for the purpose of overthrowing the Reformed Church, and wars were waged with that view. The invincible Spanish Armada, as it was vainly called, had this end in view. The Inquisition, which was established in the twelfth century, was a dreadful weapon. Terrible persecutions were carried on in various parts of Germany, and even in Bohemia, which continued thirty years; and the blood of the saints was said to flow like the waters of a river. Poland, Lithuania, and Hungary were similarly visited. In Holland and the Low Countries the most amazing cruelties were exercised under the merciless and unrelenting hands of the Spaniards, to whom the inhabitants of that part of the world were then in subjection. Father Paul states, that the Belgian martyrs amounted to 50,000; but Orotius observes, that at least twice that number suffered by the hand of the executioner. In France the same diabolical spirit prevailed. After a succession of cruelties, practised in various forms, a most violent persecution broke out in the year 1572, in the reign of Charles the Ninth. Many of the principal Protestants were invited to Paris, under a solemn oath of safety, upon occasion of the marriage of the King of Navarre with the sister of the French Monarch. The Queen dowager of Navarre, a zealous Protestant, was, however, poisoned by a pair of gloves before the marriage was solemnized. Coligni, Admiral of France, a brave and virtuous man, was basely murdered in his own house, and then thrown out of the window, to gratify the malice of the Popish Duke of Guise. The Admiral's head was afterwards cut off, and sent to the Queen-mother; and his body, after having been submitted to a thousand indignities, was hung up by the feet on a gibbet. After this, the murderers ravaged the whole city of Paris, and, in the course of three days, butchered above ten thousand persons, among whom were several of the nobility and gentry, and others of high moral reputation. The streets and passages resounded with the noise of those who met together for murder and plunder; and a prodigious multitude of men, women with child, maidens, and children, were involved in one common destruction. From the city of Paris, the massacre spread through the whole kingdom.

In the city of Meaux two hundred Protestants were thrown into prison, and, after the persecutors had ravished and killed a great number of women, and secured piles of plunder, they executed their upon those in confinement. Calling them out one by one, they were killed, like sheep appointed for the slaughter. In Orleans they murdered above five hundred men, women and children, and enriched themselves with their spoil. Similar cruelties were practised at Angers, Troyes, Bourges, La Chanité, and especially at Lyons, where above eight hundred Protestants were inhumanly destroyed. Children were killed while hanging on their parents' necks: parents were torn from the embraces of their offspring, and put to death: ropes were put about some, who were dragged inhumanly about the streets, and thrown half dead into the rivers. What aggravated the cruelty of these scenes, and is demonstrative of the sanguinary spirit of Papacy, is, that the news of these excesses was received at Rome with boundless satisfaction. When the letters of the Pope's Legate were read in the assembly of the Cardinals, by which he assured the Pope that all was transacted by the express will and command of the King, it was immediately decreed that the Pope should march with his Cardinals to the church of St. Mark, and in the most solemn manner give thanks to God for so great a blessing conferred on the see of Rome and the Christian world; and that on the Monday after, solemn mass should be celebrated in the church of Minerva, at which the Pope, Gregory the Thirteenth, and Cardinals were present; and that a jubilee should be published throughout the whole Christian world, to return thanks to God for the extirpation of the enemies of the truth, and of the Church in France. In the evening the cannon of the castle of St. Angelo were fired, to testify the public joy; the whole city was illuminated with bonfires; and no one sign of joy was omitted that was usually made for the greatest victories obtained in favour of the Romish Church.

But these persecutions, though black as Erebus, were far exceeded in cruelty by those which took place in the time of Louis the Fourteenth. The troopers and dragoons, hired for the purpose, went into the houses of Protestants, where they destroyed the furniture, broke the looking-glasses, wasted their corn and wine, and sold what they could not destroy; so that in four or five days the Protestants had been plundered of property worth a million of money. But this was only the beginning of sorrows. They turned the dining-rooms of gentlemen into stables for horses, and treated the owners of the houses where they quartered with the greatest insolence and cruelty, lashing them about, and depriving them of food. When they saw the sweat and blood run down their faces, they sluiced them with water; and putting over their heads kettle-drums, turned upside down, they made a continual din upon them, till the un happy creatures, thus abused, lost their senses. At Negropelisse, a town near Montauban, they hung up Isaac Favin, a Protestant citizen of that place, by his arm-pits, and tormented him a whole night by tearing his flesh with pincers. They made a great fire around a boy, twelve years of age, who, with hand and eyes lifted up to heaven, cried out, "My God, help me!" and when they found the youth resolved to die, rather than renounce his religion, they snatched him from the fire just as he was on the point of being burnt. In several places the soldiers applied red-hot irons to the hands and feet of men, and to the breasts of women. Mothers that gave suck they bound to posts, and let their perishing infants lie languishing in their sight, crying, and gasping for life. Some they bound before a great fire, and, when half dead, let them go. Amidst a thousand other till then unheard-of cruelties, they hung up men and women by the hair, and some by their feet, on hooks in chimneys, and smoked them with wisps of wet hay till they were suffocated. Others they plunged repeatedly into wells; and many they bound, and then with a funnel forced them to drink wine till the fumes destroyed their reason, when they made them say they were Catholics. If any, to escape these barbarities, endeavoured to save themselves by flight, they were pursued into the fields and woods, where they were shot like wild beasts. On these scenes the Popish Clergy feasted their eyes, and derived astonishing amusement from them.

Nor did England escape. Though Wickliffe, the first Reformer, died peaceably in his bed, yet such was the malice of persecuting Rome, that his bones were ordered to be dug up, and cast on a dunghill. The remains of that excellent man, which had rested undisturbed four-and-forty years, were accordingly disinterred; his bones were burnt, and the ashes cast into an adjacent brook. In the reign of Henry the Eighth, Bilney and many Reformers were burnt; and when Queen Mary came to the throne, persecution was let loose with ten-fold terror. Hooper and Rogers were burned in a slow fire. Saunders was cruelly tormented at the stake a long time before he expired. Taylor was put into a barrel of pitch, and fire was set to it. Ferrar, Bishop of St. David's, with seven other illustrious persons, were sought out and burnt by the infamous Bonner, in a few days. Sixty-seven persons were burnt in the year 1555, among whom were the famous Protestants, Bradford, Ridley, Latimer, and Philpot. In the following year, eighty-five persons were burnt.—Ireland has also been drenched with the blood of Protestants, nearly fifty thousand of whom were murdered in a few days in different parts of the kingdom, in the reign of Charles the First. The persecution began in October, 1641. Having secured the principal gentlemen, and seized their effects, the common people were murdered in cold blood: thousands were forced to fly from their houses and settlements, naked and destitute, into the bogs and woods, where they perished through cold and hunger. Some were tortured to death; many hundreds were drowned in rivers; some had their throats cut; and, among a few of the villains concerned, it was deemed sport to try who could make the deepest wound in the body of an Englishman. Young women were abused in the presence of their nearest relations: nay, the children of the furies thus engaged were taught to kill the children of the English, and dash out their brains against the stones.—What shall we say, also, of South America? It is computed that, of the natives residing in the extensive Spanish territory, fifteen millions were sacrificed in forty years to the genius of Popery; and it is supposed that, at different times, not fewer than fifty millions of Protestants have been the victims of the persecutions of the Papists, and put to death for their religious profession. Such is mystic Babylon! "And I saw under the altar the souls of them that were slain for the word of God, and for the testimony which they held: and they cried with a loud voice, saying, How long, O Lord, holy and true, dost thou not judge and avenge our blood on them that dwell on the earth? And in her was found the blood of prophets, and of saints, and of all them that were slain upon the earth."

1. Rev. Jacob Stanley's Dialogues on Popery.

CHAPTER X

No one, I apprehend, will wonder, that at the close of the preceding view, my mind was at rest as to the course most advisable. A voice seemed to sound in my ears, "Come out of her, my people, that ye be not partaker in her sins." Infallibility is attached, to the Pope, though it is known that for a hundred and fifty years together the Popes were apostates rather than Apostles, and were frequently thrust into the Papal chair by the intrigues and trickery of harlots. Besides, some of these infallible personages occasionally quarrelled, not only with all the world beside, but with each other, and sometimes with themselves. The Council of Nice, A.D. 325, decreed with an anathema, as usual, that no new article whatever should be added to the creed. Twelve hundred years after, the Council of Trent added twelve new articles, coupled with another anathema, on all who would not embrace them. Here then are two sets of gentlemen, all equally infallible, and all equally opposed to each other. Neither can I find any passage in the word of God that justifies the invocation of angels and saints. I think it better to draw nigh to God by Christ, through the influence of the Holy Spirit, to the exclusion of all other agencies, whether in heaven or earth. Equally senseless is the practice of resorting to relics, of what ever kind they be. Beads, salt, boxes, scapulars, and such like trumpery, appear to me as vile deceptions. Neither do I approve of the doctrine of penances: it smacks of human merit, and works of supererogation, which are not only contrary to scriptural truth, but impossible in themselves. We are taught to love God with all our heart, and mind, and soul, and strength, and our neighbour as ourself. Can man do more than this? And yet something more must be done, before we talk of merit. But if all were fair and smooth, and nothing contradictory or absurd could be found in

the general tenets of the Romish Church, her persecuting spirit
alone would decide my judgment. Here there can be no mistake;
and if the Bible be true, Papacy must, from that circumstance
alone, be a delusion. With gratitude unfeigned, I thank God, who
has delivered me from such antichristian articles of faith. I entirely
reject them, persuaded that the are the mere invention of crafty
men, who, under the pretence of superior sanctity, are among the
most consummate hypocrites on earth ; and heartily rejoice that
though such articles were once the terror, they are now the sport
of en lightened society. Glorious and important inroads have been
made in the empire of superstition; and the intercessions of the
saints will continue to arise for the extension of genuine truth;
to be accompanied, we trust, with the speedy and final fall of
those who for ages have plagued the human race. The prayer is
universally offered:

> Avenge, O Lord, thy slaughter'd saints, whose bones
> Lie scatter'd on the Alpine mountains cold;
> Even them who kept thy truth so pure of old,
> When all our fathers worshipp'd stocks and stones,
> Forget not: in thy book record their groans,
> Who were thy sheep; and in their ancient fold
> Slain by the bloody Piemontese, that roll'd
> Mother with infant down the rocks. Their moans
> The vales redoubled to the hills, and they
> To heaven. Their martyr'd blood and ashes sow
> O'er all the' Italian fields, where still doth sway
> The triple tyrant; that from these may grow
> A hundred fold, who, having learn'd thy way,
> Early may fly the Babylonian woe.

Nothing yields more substantial support to a well regulated and
enlightened mind than a conviction of the divine unchangea-
bleness. On earth all is mutable, and nothing more so than man
himself. He cometh forth like a shadow, and continueth not. The
circumstances in which he is placed undergo a successive, though
perhaps unperceived, alteration. That which yesterday seemed

worthy of all dependence, is today suspected, and to-morrow is not. We fancy some people to be our friends; the trial comes, and they turn out mere acquaintances. At last we discover a real friend; he is one of a thousand, and mutual attachment is sworn,—when sickness intervenes, and just when intimacy begins to ripen, he is carried to the grave. Hope of temporal prosperity puts forth her bud and blossoms, and imagination is ready to gather the clustering fruit,—when disappointment, that cold and bitter blast, at once arises, and all our fond anticipations are blighted and gone. But there is a Friend that sticketh closer than a brother; and there are consolations placed by the Gospel within the reach of humanity, so suited to that nature, so permanent in themselves, and so far beyond the reach of this world's influence, that it is the highest point of wisdom to secure them at any price. Not that religion precludes the real and temperate enjoyment of earthly advantages: it rather improves and refines our faculties, rightly to estimate and relish them. But it loosens the affections from worldly good, and transfers them to our future inheritance. It discovers to man that this is not his home, and that the day is coming when he must arise and depart. By the communications of divine and saving grace, it confers the preparation of heart, without which no man can safely enter upon that state of existence, in reference to which this life is merely the vestibule and preparatory step. Honour and wealth may conspire to produce present enjoyment, especially if the mind be inert, and incapable of looking at futurity but what is the condition of such when the summons shall arrive, "This week," or perhaps, "this night shall thy soul be required of thee?" "for what can it profit a man, if he gain the whole world, and lose his soul?" That these sentiments are unpalatable to the gay and thoughtless, I am aware; but, since they are founded in eternal truth, that cannot be helped. Their importance is evident at every season of life; and if, even in youth, they merit notice, and ought to be cherished, what excuse can he plead, who in the meridian of his diurnal span, or when evening casts its shadow, forgets the flight of time, and stands negligently on the verge and precipice of life's peninsula, apparently unconscious of his condition, though eternity's dread gulf gathers visibly around? An affecting question is asked by the Prophet

Zechariah, "Is not this a brand plucked out of the fire?" and it is with no small propriety that the inquiry is made concerning myself. I have wandered over sea and land; have been in perils both of flood and field; in "hair-breadth 'scapes" I have rivalled Othello's self; for several years I was dangerously familiar with the bayonet-point and whistling bullet; and have followed a profession whose element is strife and bloodshed. While thousands have fallen, I am preserved in the land and light of the living; and, what is perhaps an equal mercy, am placed in a situation in which I have become conscious of these obligations, and where the privileges of church-fellowship exist in rich abundance. It would be ungrateful, also, were I not to acknowledge the uncommon kindness with which several of the officers under whom I served furnished me, on application, with testimonials relative to my previous conduct in the army. It would be mere affectation were I to profess myself indifferent to opinions so generously expressed; and as military reputation, founded on faithful services, is frequently the only riches of which an old soldier can boast, I shall be pardoned for introducing some extracts from letters received about this time from several gentlemen well known in superior military circles. I ought to premise, that I had applied to Lieut. Col. Williamson, Commandant at the Royal Military Asylum, Chelsea, for admission into that institution as one of the superintendents of the children; to secure which, I found it necessary to obtain respectable references as to previous character. Colonel (now General) Pearson observed concerning me, "I have much pleasure in stating, that his conduct on every occasion merited my most perfect approbation, and that I consider him highly qualified for any situation which requires activity, sobriety, and integrity; and as such I beg leave to recommend him." Major Page, under whose notice I had acted at Tynemouth, certified that he had known me for several years, during which period he was pleased to say, that my conduct as a soldier gave great satisfaction; and, With reference to an event in my life already alluded to, adds, "he particularly distinguished himself, and was the means of rescuing from a watery grave three or four sailors. I recollect his plunging through the surf and bringing a sailor on shore, at the time no boat would quit the beach. I cannot say too much in this soldier's praise; and nothing gives me greater pleasure than to recommend him." To make assurance doubly sure, Colonel Napier added, that I had served in the 43d regiment nearly eleven years; had been at the reduction of Copenhagen in 1807; at General Moore's retreat to Corunna in 1808, and the following year; and at the battles of Almeida, Busaco, Pomhal, Condeixa, Sabugal, Fuentes d'Onore, Ciudad Rodrigo, and Badajos, at which latter place he was severely wounded in the head and thigh." These nails, driven so forcibly, to fasten my respect ability, were clenched by Lieutenant-Colonel Puffy, who also spoke of me in very handsome and obliging terms. Captain Patteson then advanced, by stating concerning me, "I had every reason to be satisfied with his steady, sober, honest, and soldier-like conduct, and had frequent opportunities of observing his brave and valiant behaviour in the field." Besides these, which told heavily on the Board, I had a letter of similar import from Lieutenant-Colonel Booth, who was condescending enough to bring up the reserve, and inclose his recommendatory note in another written and directed to myself, in which he remarks, "I have great pleasure in stating what I remember of your character in the 43d regiment, for I have a perfect remembrance of you; and it is gratifying to myself that you remember your old corps with so great affection. You are entitled to our best wishes, as one of those good and gallant soldiers who contributed to support the reputation of the regiment during the Peninsular war." I have been induced to quote these flattering notices, not for the purpose of self-esteem, and finding food for vanity;—for, after all, I only did my duty; and for that, no one that I know of, whether in the army or elsewhere, is entitled to any extraordinary gratulations;—but I am anxious to show, that alertness and vigilance are neither unnoticed nor unrewarded in the British army; and that the superior officers are not unwilling to recollect an old and wounded soldier, when the recognition can assist him. Supported by such respectable rank and influence, my efforts to gain admission into the Asylum were successful, and in the month of December, 1823, I was received as a Company Sergeant.

After having been in this situation about four years, I became acquainted with several members of the congregation assembling at Sloane-terrace chapel, Chelsea; and my views of human depravity, of moral obligation, and "the exceeding sinfulness of sin," together with the necessity of a change of heart and life, were rendered much clearer than formerly. I perceived that in religion there is not only something to be professed, but a great deal to be experienced. The more I inquired and reflected upon myself, so much the more I was dissatisfied. At first I resolved to mend my morals, and live more scrupulously. But a brief trial showed me that my theory was good for nothing, nor would hang together. There was no relish of salvation in it; and in escaping from one evil, I ran headlong into a greater. My mind was afterwards led, by degrees almost imperceptible, to reflect deeply upon that infinite goodness by which I had thus far been brought through the great and terrible wilderness of this world. I began more clearly to perceive, that religion consisted in a divine change and desires to share in its blessings, till then unknown, created, no doubt, by the Spirit's influence, were continually present with me. But how to escape from the trammels of sin was the great and apparently unconquerable difficulty: "bound down by twice ten thousand ties," I began to fear that deliverance was impossible. I became sensible of my degraded condition, but had no power of escape. But my condition is described in holy writ with infinite accuracy; to add, therefore, to that which is perfect in itself, would be to darken counsel with needless verbiage: "For the good that I would, I do not; but the evil that I would not, that I do. I find then a law, that when I would do good, evil is present with me." The more I strove, the deeper I sank; until, wearied with the vain task of conquering sin by efforts founded on the strength merely of reason and propriety, I gave up the contest, and endeavoured to conclude that it would be time enough to enter on religious courses when I became old and good for little. The illusion was incomplete. It was not sufficiently specious to deceive even my own mind. Perhaps I ought rather to conclude, that the mercy of God would not permit me thus to wander into the congregation of the dead. I had no rest. My sins be came increasingly alarming; and I felt afraid of going to sleep, lest I should awake in perdition. Among several other places of public resort in the vicinity of my residence, and much frequented by military men, was "The Snowshoes," a public house of entertainment, of great convivial celebrity, where many pounds of my money had unfortunately gone astray. In spite of some vivid convictions to the contrary, I made an engagement to meet an old brother Sergeant, and "spend the evening," which, in gay language, generally includes the luxury of cigars and libations of strong liquor. It happened, providentially, that my friend was not ready by the appointed time, so that on my arrival I was seated alone, and had time for reflection. A few minutes before I entered the house, a prayer rose in my mind, that the Almighty would preserve me from the pending excesses, the ruinous effects of which, I knew, must fall both on myself and family. The check was so powerful that I halted at the threshold of the passage. In that instant, Satan suggested "Take a little, and get home in time." I accordingly went into the house and called for some liquor, but had not remained long before I felt myself suddenly struck by some powerful though unseen hand. My whole frame trembled, so that I was fain to lean against the table for support. Meantime I thought a voice repeated in my ear, "Go home!" My agitation was so great as to excite the attention of several persons in the room, who asked me what was the matter. Unable to reply, and determined to obey my invisible but friendly monitor, whom I considered as a gracious signal of Almighty direction, I hurried out of the place, went home immediately, and related the occurrence to my wondering family. This was only the beginning of miracles; and from that time I can trace the operations of the Spirit as they were graciously afforded, every link of which, as part of a golden chain, let down from on high, contributed to draw me from the miry clay of nature's dismal dungeon, to the light and liberty of Gospel day.

It so happened, or rather, was so ordered, that my daughter was placed in a school conducted by a worthy member of the Wesleyan society. One day the governess made some inquiries relative to the state of religion in our family. How she was answered by her pupil, I know not; but most likely the good instructress had reason to conclude that our devotions were not of the most exalted kind. Be that as it may, she kindly selected a tract, entitled "James Covey," and gave it to the child, with directions to read it at home. My daughter, aware of the prejudice

I had entertained against Methodism, was afraid to show me the tract. It was, at length, so contrived that the "Covey" should attract my notice. After a cursory glance, it struck me there was some Methodist contrivance about the matter; I therefore threw the tract upon the fire, and desired that my daughter might be removed from those fanatical folks. Satisfied with the exploit, I left the house, and resumed my employment; but on taking off my hat, for the purpose of hanging it up, I observed what appeared to be a sheet of paper, folded up inside the crown, beneath the lining. On taking it out, to my surprise, there was " James Covey" again. The truth is, that this tract, though thrown upon the fire by my ungodly rashness, was taken off with equal haste, and superior wisdom, and had been placed in my hat, by the hands of my excellent wife. Wondering, at first, how it came there, and impressed with the oddness of the circumstance, I thought, that as pains had evidently been taken by some one to draw my attention, it would be ungrateful were I entirely negligent; and that, at all events, a slight inspection could not poison my mind, especially if confined to the first page or so. I accordingly began to read, but soon passed the bounds I had assigned. As I went on, the tale was so charming that I felt anxious to ascertain the catastrophe in fact, I became so riveted to the performance, and saw, as if I had looked in a mirror, my own case so completely shown forth in the description of the sailor, that my almost impenetrable heart was melted, nor could I help exclaiming, "Lord, if I should turn to thee, like him, wilt thou have mercy on me?" I was much impressed with the similarity that, in some respects, existed between the sailor's life and my own. He had fought by sea, and I by land. He, in the days of his ignorance, had profaned the mysteries of the cross by disbelief and vanity I had done the same. He found mercy; and now, through the same medium, even by the new and living way, the desire, though late, was found in my heart to follow in the same course. Great searchings of heart followed the inquiries arising from the above tract. The more I looked into my own condition, the greater was the dissatisfaction felt. I found, not only that some things were wrong, but that little or nothing was right. I felt convinced, also, that the change required was of a spiritual kind; that old things were to pass away, and all things become new; and that if any man have not the Spirit of Christ, he is none of his.

In this condition of hope, mingled with sad uncertainty, I continued a wearisome time. One Sunday forenoon I attended the chapel already mentioned, with the hope of receiving instruction and encouragement; and, with respect to the former, I succeeded. I had been told that the Minister appointed to preach on that day, had been useful to others; which begat a hope respecting myself. Prayers having been read, be ascended the pulpit. The simplicity with which the services were so far conducted, especially when contrasted with the multiplied ceremonies of the Romish Church, powerfully affected my mind. It appeared to me, that the difference between the two lay precisely here; Papists cultivate the forms of religion, with little of the power; while here the power was present, with as much only of the form as served to give seriousness to the worship. In the Catholic chapel, one is apt to be taken up with circumstantials, while spirituality of mind, so essential to true devotion, is well-nigh destroyed. There is the gaudy attire of the Priest, who performs his part by reading certain lessons in a language which not one in twenty understands. Then an elegant picture, or image, is exhibited, before which the Priest, as if smitten with some sudden emotion, pretends—for it is merely a studied piece of acting previously rehearsed—to be melted into humility. He accordingly commences a series of genuflexions and homage, on which, from the formality observed, the principal value of the service seems to depend. Lads dressed in white surplices then enter, bearing large wax-candles. Anon is heard the tinkling of a small bell, while an ignited perfume of some sort, contained in a silver chafing-dish, and suspended by a chain, is waved by one of these juvenile clericals for general gratification. Laying aside these extraneous matters, the use of which is above my comprehension, the Preacher in the Protestant chapel now alluded to adopted a widely different plan. He was in person of good figure, rather tall and slender, with marked benevolence of countenance; I think something under forty years of age; and was dressed in a plain

black suit of clothes, which, though sufficiently neat and
respectable to denote the sacred profession of the wearer, evinced
a noble carelessness of outward show or self-consequence. In
truth, he had much better ground of dependence. The service
began with singing a hymn. I should think that religion improved
the voice, as well as re formed the life; for every one appeared
able to sing, and the effect was beautiful. The Minister then
proposed prayer, to which all assented by kneeling in silence. The
petitions offered were singularly appropriate, and, although
evidently not a pre-composed form of words, were fluent and
comprehensive; and what rendered them remarkably seasonable
and well timed, they were so framed, as to apply to the apparent
rank, condition, and circumstances of the assembled congregation.
Another verse or two of a hymn was sung with equal effect,
immediately after which the Preacher selected a text and began
the sermon. Having nothing before him but the Bible, and as the
passage selected for discussion consisted only of a few words, I
concluded the homily would be rather brief. The result showed
that I knew little, either of it, or the Preacher. In Cathedral
service, one is used, when the reverend Dean ascends the pulpit,
to observe a handsome quarto manuscript, enveloped in a cover
of clerical jet, nicely squared, and paged to prevent mistake,
which is safely pressed upon the cushion, and containing, in
characters so legible as to defy mistake, the approaching lesson of
instruction. On the occasion to which I now refer, these
preparations were dispensed with. The good Pastor began his
discourse without the least hesitation; and being a man of pleasing
address, and of distinct, though not very powerful, voice, the
attention of an overflowing audience was immediately arrested.
After several introductory observations, of somewhat discursive
tendency, he applied himself to the explication of the passage
chosen for the occasion; and never in my life was I more
surprised. The remarks made seemed as if directly levelled at
myself, not recollecting that, as all have sinned alike, so all are to
be saved through one Mediator. I had imagined that the workings
of my mind were necessarily secret, and was sure the Preacher
knew nothing either of my life or creed. I therefore strove to

elude the unexpected application of unwelcome truth; but the thing was impossible; there was no getting away from the searching pursuit of the speaker. He traced the half-awakened sinner through all the lanes and by paths of subterfuge to which the pride of human nature is so prone, and having concentrated his energy, at once assaulted the conscience and convicted the heart. He then entered, with such minuteness, into my condition; gave such an account of the causes and cure of my uneasiness; hit upon my general train of thought and reasoning with nicety so miraculous; anticipated, and then overthrew, my doubts with such force; guarded the moral law with penalties so terrific; and depicted the wide waste of human transgression with a pencil so true, that all my resources vanished. What was also wonderful, he entered into and conducted the discussion with such earnestness, as clearly proved the deep interest he took in the matter. No legal pleader, however magnificent the expected fee, ever took more pains to prove his point. The observation contained in the body of the discourse were acute, and to me original: from some of them, native corruption naturally recoiled; hut before the mind had time to gather up itself, and put on the show of defence, he advanced some powerful scriptural quotation, so perfectly apposite and conclusive, that all resistance was vain. Nor was I less delighted with the trouble he took to make himself understood : not that his enunciation was defective, or his style obscure or far-fetched, but, afraid lest the least portion of his meaning should be misapprehended, he placed himself, as it were, in different positions, from which he took varied and delightful views of several cardinal points of Gospel truth; so that in the collected light, thus produced, it was next to impossible for the plainest understanding to misconceive his meaning. The general effect of this remarkable pulpit exercise was, to constrain, rather than compel, men to embrace brace religion; and this was effected by the presentation of motive, so judiciously selected, and so elegantly urged, that no human being, unless his heart were adamant, could hear without emotion and obedience. The sermon was closed by an energetic appeal to the congregation on the necessity of personal piety, and of taking an immediate step in order to secure it; and from the profound silence that prevailed, the appeal was, I doubt not, effective. Who, indeed, could sit for an hour unmoved, while an approved Minister of righteousness, not only, in formal phraseology, does his duty, by the cold and formal announcement of truth, but goes almost beyond himself, and strives, by every method zeal and ingenuity can devise, to render that truth attractive, and save the souls of men? Let me subjoin another observation. Deep and vivid as was the impression produced by the Preacher alluded to, I am not sure that he was to be numbered among those who are termed extremely popular. Not that I wish to speak lightly of those who are; and hope the day is not far distant, when not only the eloquent heralds of salvation, but the truth itself, shall triumph in the high places of the earth. But if the talents of our excellent friend were not splendid,—and I do not say they were not,—they were useful. He did not strew flowers, but dispensed wholesome nourishment. He cared not for words, but things. His aim was not to astonish, but to profit. He so preached, that while the instrument was concealed from notice, and made to appear of no importance, Christ and his salvation were put forward and exalted. Beside which—and here is the key to the cabinet, which contains the mysteries of an available ministry,—an unction from the Lord, as if at a renewal of the Pentecostal season, came down upon the word. The communings at Emmaus were revived, when Jesus himself drew nigh, and broke the bread of life; so that many were fain to say, "Did not our hearts burn within us, while he talked by the way, and opened unto us the Scriptures?" To my own mind, the entire service was very beneficial; that is, I acquired self-knowledge. The remembrance of my sins was grievous, and the burden, but for the mercy of God, intolerable. All my preconceived notions of bettering myself were exploded, nor could I offer any other prayer than that of the Publican, "God be merciful to me a sinner." I dare not mention the name of the Minister to whom these remarks refer; for he yet lives, and will, I trust, be pre served many years, a blessing to the church. For many subsequent months the ministry of the Rev. Philip C. Turner was rendered exceedingly serviceable to my mind.

People may think as they please, but religion is no fable; neither is the work of grace upon the soul of man a mere hypothesis, to be examined with suspicion, and embraced or rejected at humour. If there he a genuine and awful reality on this side eternity, this is one; nor would I suppress my belief in the fact, for the applause of millions. Truth is great, and, though it be surveyed with scorn, must finally prevail.

CHAPTER XI

My views of the way of life were by this time greatly enlightened: I had also thoroughly informed myself relative to the drift and tenor of Wesleyanism. Under a deep persuasion that the truth and power of scriptural piety prevailed among its professors, I joined their society, in January, 1828; and trust never to be found without its pale, till mortality is exchanged for life. Many persons are aware, and every one who intends becoming a member ought to know, that there are constantly held certain social weekly assemblies, entitled class-meetings, an entrance to one of which constitutes the beginning of membership. These are of first-rate importance. The conversations thus taking place under the direction of a Leader, who is so named on account of his supposed superior religious experience and stability, tend, beyond any other plan ever formed, to keep alive a sense of spiritual things during the busy sea sons of secular engagement; beside which, the general effect of these meetings, in reference to the society at large, operates as a bond of union, so strong and indissoluble, that wherever the members are found, and let the outward circumstances be what they may under which they meet, they have, in reference to spiritual things, and the mode of establishing their general worship, au immediate understanding. By the aid of this uniformity in opinion and belief, if a class were composed one half of London members, and the other half of Cherokee Indians, it would not, in a religious view, make the smallest difference. They would be sure to understand one another; for their pursuits are exactly the same. They walk by the same rule, they mind the same thing; and endeavour by one and the same simple process to keep the unity of the Spirit in the bond of peace. In support of these regular meetings, which are peculiar to this section of the church, many cogent and conclusive arguments are urged. It should he understood that they are intended to promote the purposes of experimental piety, and no thing else. Reasonings in their behalf are adduced from Scripture: "They that feared the Lord spake often one to another, and the Lord hearkened and heard, and a book of remembrance was written before him for them that feared the Lord, and that thought upon his name; and they shall be mine, saith he, when I make up my jewels." Proofs of their propriety are derived from analogy. In most worldly schemes, and in the circle of arts, the actual value of improvements and discoveries is estimated by experiment. The purity of metals is ascertained by tests too nice to admit of imposition. The power of mechanics is tried by the application of certain criteria. In scientific pursuits and lectures, the positions advanced are usually by experiment, exhibited for the mutual instruction of assembled professors. These plans are adopted to prevent mistake and error, and give to the art or Science those principles of perpetuity founded on demonstrated truth, that shall render them worthy of universal acceptance. Is religion, then, to be the only pursuit in the prosecution of which experience is superfluous? Shall a system of verities, involving eternal consequences, referrible to every human being, and, therefore, the most important the world ever saw, or can see, be suffered to float on the waters of contingency, when opportunities offer of coming at its nature and effect by actual experience? The reason, the happiness, the present well being, and the future condition of man, conspire in giving a decided negative, and to censure conduct so rash and ruinous. So, at least, the Wesleyans think,—and it will take some trouble to prove them wrong. I had not long met in one of these classes, which was conducted by a young man, the qualities of whose mind singularly fitted him for the office, when I discovered more clearly than ever my own moral deficiency and spiritual condemnation. I found, to my surprise, that several of the persons then present possessed a sense of their acceptance with God, through the merits of his, Son; and I was forcibly struck with the modest though decided manner in which this profession was made. The Leader, I observed, took the principal part in the conversation; and moderated, advised, or explained, on the passing topic, as occasion required. I had received the spirit of bondage again to fear, which confined me in the prison-house of condemnation, and the discovery of those high attainments, of which I had living proofs, sent me with all imaginable haste to the Scriptures and, sure enough, I found the Wesleyans knew what they were about. The confidence they spike of is expressly mentioned as the privilege of all true believers. In writing to "all that be in Rome, beloved of God, called to be saints," St. Paul exults in the thought that, "the Spirit itself beareth witness with our spirit, that we are the children of God." The same doctrine is enforced in his Epistle to the Galatians, " Because ye are sons, God hath sent forth the Spirit of his Son into your hearts, crying, Abba, Father." This delightful fruition of Christian experience was exemplified in the instance of the great Apostle himself. In addressing "all the saints in Christ Jesus which are at Philippi, with the Bishops and Deacons," he is so filled with holy exultation and hope, that he declares himself to be "in a strait betwixt two, having a desire to depart and to be with Christ, which is far better." And it is equally clear that this spiritual attainment was not an exclusive apostolical privilege; for in the epistle "to the saints and faithful brethren in Christ, which are at Colosse," he affirms concerning them, "And you, being dead in your sins, and the uncircumcision of your flesh, hath he quickened together with him, having forgiven you all trespasses." It is equally certain that those who live in the enjoyment of this distinguished mercy are conscious of it; for "He which establisheth us with you in Christ, and hath anointed us, is God; who hath also sealed us, and given the earnest of his Spirit in our hearts." No one, indeed, could possess a gift so estimable without knowing it, any more than a man could escape from dungeon-gloom into daylight without being sensible of deliverance. This doctrine is also held forth where some people never think of looking for it, that is, in the service of the Church of England. The worthy compilers of the book of Common Prayer seem in such haste to divulge the high attainment, that soon after the Morning Service has commenced, we are told that the Almighty "pardoneth and absolveth all them that truly repent, and unfeignedly believe his holy Gospel." In the collect for the Epiphany the assembled church is taught to pray, "that we, will know thee now by faith, may after this life have the fruition of thy

glorious Godhead through Jesus Christ our Lord." In the service for
Ash-Wednesday the same doctrine is finely held forth,— "Create
and make in us new and contrite hearts, that we, worthily lamenting
our sins, and acknowledging our wretched ness, may obtain of thee,
the God of all mercy, perfect remission and forgiveness, through
Jesus Christ our Lord." Verily, these are glorious truths and were
it not for their exceeding antiquity, I should conclude they were
composed by one of the Wesleyan Preachers.

With a cloud of witnesses so commanding and influential, I could
no longer question the truth of the doctrine of reconciliation by
faith in Jesus Christ; so far from that, I felt a desire to obtain the
blessing for myself. There was an impulse within me which seemed
to say, "Make the trial." This, I believe, was the call of mercy; and,
thank God, my heart was eventually inclined, to listen and obey.
But the anguish that succeeded was excessive. The more closely
I examined myself, the more aggravated and incurable my sins
appeared. In this state I went one evening to the class; but was so
cast down, and had fallen so deep into the Bunyanite slough of
despond, that I was nearly guilty of Pliable's error, who got out
on the wrong side. I had resolved to tell my Leader, that feeling
myself no better, I should come no more, and relinquish religious
profession. On entering the room and taking a seat, the thought
of my sinfulness almost drank up my spirit. It struck me, "Why do
you come here? You are a greater sinner than Mary Magdalene."
Nevertheless, I felt a desire, like the publican mentioned in the
Gospel, to look up, and adopt his penitential request. I asked the
Leader to pray, and he kindly consented. While we were jointly
engaged in this service, the Lord spake peace to my heart. The
change was indescribable, and inconceivable to all but the restored
sinner. My burden was gone, and I rejoiced in the God of my
salvation. I felt myself, as it were, elevated into a freer atmosphere,
surrounded by a new creation. The means of grace appeared of
more value than my daily food. I found special light and power
by reading the Scriptures on my knees, preceded or followed by
prayer. The retrospect of my past life fills me with amazement.

I am astonished at the infatuation under which I formerly
laboured, and at the forbearance of God who so long winked at

my waywardness and folly. I well remember, that some time since, on sitting down to dinner, which I used to do without the least acknowledgment to God, a religious friend, who happened to come in, civilly asked, if it was a custom to take my meals without asking the blessing of the Giver? He made another observation or two, no. doubt, with the best intention. Those were the days of soldierly hauteur and impatience. I was deeply offended with his interference, and felt half inclined to throw my adviser down stairs. My better sense, however, mastered the meditated revenge; and, thank the Lord, I was preserved from laying hostile hands upon a man whose good counsel was so sadly despised, and who was, no doubt, in many respects, a man far superior to myself. God forbid that I should cease to thank him for his restraining and enlightening grace.

But were I to retrace and collect all the causes, on account of which my gratitude arises, I know not where the end would be. One more I must mention, by reason of its magnitude. It is for delivering me from the errors and abominations of the Church of Rome. There was a time when I bowed down to an image; prayed to the queen of heaven; thought that the Pope had the keys of glory at his girdle, sat in a chair given to his predecessors by Peter himself, and that every one who died out of the pale of Catholicism was as sure of being lost, as those within were of being saved. Often have I joined in the showy but senseless ceremonies of that ceremonious Church, and wondered at the eccentric saturnine representations, which, like the shifting scenes of dramatic exhibition, beguiled the senses, but left the soul untaught. How long, O Lord, holy and true, wilt thou suffer the craft and subtlety of this delusive Church to exist? Arise, O God, and let thine enemies be scattered, while the implements of vanity shall be thrown aside and forgotten:

> "Cowls, hoods, and habits, with their wearers, tost
> And flutter'd into rags; then reliques, beads,
> Indulgences, dispenses, pardons, bulls,
> The sport of winds; all these upwhirl'd aloft,—
> Into a limbo, large and broad, since call'd
> The paradise of fools."

But if I rejoice, it must be mixed with trembling. I have greater cause for humility; and know, that ever since I had chosen the better part, had I been more faithful to the grace given, my spiritual progress would have been greater. Surrounded with a praying people, I felt anxious to adopt the Wesleyan method of offering up extemporaneous petitions. I saw many others had no difficulty in the exercise, whose addresses to the Almighty were remarkably copious and proper, though unaided by a printed form. "This," I thought, "is delightful; as the requests preferred arise from a sense of want, felt at the time; and I will join the company." I had miscalculated my gifts at that period; and accordingly, having uttered a few sentences, was unable to proceed. Somewhat disconcerted at this misadventure, I resolved to act with more caution, and applied to my Leader for a written prayer, which I proposed to commit to memory, before I attempted to deliver any thing more in public. His reply was, "Jesus will teach you how to pray." I felt at first rather discouraged at this answer, though I afterwards saw its propriety. My adversary, noticing the feebleness of my faith, immediately suggested, "There now, you see he cares nothing about you ; he neglects even your small request!" Thank God, I gradually surmounted the difficulty, and have ever since been enabled, by a few plain sentences, to give expression to my wants, and to join my fellow-Christians in their joint supplications to the throne of grace, the offering up of which has been so beneficial to the church of Christ.

Soon after this period I made another discovery, much more affecting and momentous than the deficiency of gifts,—it was deficiency of grace; and most seriously awful were the consequences. The scantiness of my knowledge, and very slender Christian experience, had so far warped my judgment, that I began to conclude that the work in my heart was complete; and as all enemies were destroyed, little more remained but to ascend quietly to heaven. Painful experience soon overthrew my air-built fabric, and taught the necessity of watchfulness and circumspection. It was about the season of Christmas, when being inveigled into company, by far too gay and mirthful for Christian gravity, I was unhappily seduced into the sinful practices then in the ascendant. I felt at first some checks of conscience, but unhappily disregarded them. The beginning of sin is like the letting out of water. Resistance must be immediate, or the mountain-torrent will defy opposition. The season of festive merriment, so called, continued for three days; and during the whole of that time, I was seduced by the indecent levities of thoughtless men, to whom I ought to have presented a better example. On the third night I awoke to a sense of my situation: my first sensations were like those of one who, having taken a wrong road, is suddenly smitten with the widening obliquity of his path, and knows not how to repair his error. My peace was gone. I felt that the Spirit of God was grieved, and had withdrawn his influence. Shorn of my strength, I had become weak as other men. I was afraid to be left alone, lest, impelled by satanic suggestion, I should rashly throw away my life. From this dread alternative I was, however, mercifully preserved. After some time, I so far rallied as to make an effort to pray; but I had no power to kneel before the Lord. Having betrayed my trust, I thought the divine anger had waxed hot against me, and that the weighty penal ties of the holy law would fall upon and grind me to powder; nor had I courage to open my Bible, as each of its denunciations seemed to stand in battle-array against me. I could neither eat nor sleep, so that my health visibly declined. My wife sent for medical help; but my case came not within the powers of the healing art indeed I was ashamed to see the good man who paid the professional visit. Nothing was fitted for my malady, save the balm of Gilead, and the heavenly Physician whose favour I had forfeited. Hope itself seemed to expire; the enemy of my soul whispered, "It will require at least twenty years to recover what you have lost; and where will you be by that time!" Such, indeed, was my deplorable condition, that I felt persuaded I should not survive many days. At last, when despair had almost devoured me, a gleam of encouragement, as the first dawn of light on the horizon's extremest verge, arose on my soul. Man's extremity, is God's opportunity. The relief was like life from the dead, and came just in time to save me from impending destruction. The resurrection of Lazarus was scarcely a greater miracle than this timely and critical deliverance; for in each instance there was an exertion of nothing less than Omnipotence.

Animated by this beginning of renewed confidence, I ventured again to approach the throne of grace. It was in the evening, at the family altar; and there the Lord, in his infinite mercy, was pleased to cancel my transgression, and write his pardon on my heart. With him who had fled to Tarshish, when overtaken in his folly, I was empowered to plead, "I am cast out of thy sight, yet will I look again toward thy holy temple." The Saviour looked on me as heretofore: the glance of him I had denied humbled me at his feet, and I felt ready to hide myself in the dust. The undeserved and extraordinary manifestation of divine clemency, I now experienced, was so overwhelming, that my faculties were hardly able to sustain it, and I had nearly fainted. That night, after a long and wearisome season, I retired to rest rejoicing; and from that period, all praise be to God, I have never been deprived of an abiding sense of his favour, and of my acceptance through the merit of his Son. I have great reason to be thankful that for several years last past, I have proved the all sufficiency of divine grace, and have been able, in some humble degree, I trust, to walk circumspectly, redeeming the time. I have long since discovered, and hope never to forget, that the work of God in the soul of man is to be progressively matured. In the journeyings of a Christian, no idle delays can exist with safety. He pulls against wind and tide; and if he cease to labour, the opposing current must waft him back. Philosophy teaches that nature abhors a vacuum. The same thing may be said of grace. Every portion of the space allotted as our earthly course, must be properly filled, so that our great Pattern and Example may be imitated, who was ever engaged in doing good, even to the unthankful. I must here crave permission to recite another instance of divine goodness to myself, the unworthiest of all the servants who wait upon the Lord. One evening I was invited to attend a band-meeting at Sloane-terrace chapel, at which one of the stated Ministers presided. I had for some time previously felt the necessity of more complete conformity to the will of God. I began to consider more deeply, that if religion had any importance at all, it was all-important, and demanded the undivided homage of my heart. Several passages of

Scripture bearing, as I thought, on the subject, were applied to my mind with great energy; especially the 25th verse of the 36th of Ezekiel: "Then will I sprinkle clean water upon you, and ye shall be clean; from all your filthiness, and from all your idols, will I cleanse you. A new heart also will I give unto you, and a new spirit will I put within you; and I will take away the stony heart out of your flesh, and I will give you an heart of flesh." Another passage in the New Testament, I thought had respect to the same subject, I JOHN I. 7: "But if we walk in the light, as he is in the light, we have fellowship one with another and the blood of Jesus Christ, his Son, cleanseth us from all sin." On the strength of these gracious declarations, the anticipation of some added and glorious spiritual blessing was present with me. As the time for holding the band-meeting drew nigh, unbelief arose, by whose evil agency I was greatly shaken. "What right have you to appear among the people of God? Why intrude yourself? You have been unfaithful already: do you mean to walk the same course again? Are you fitted for duty so sacred as that you approach, or to enter into the presence of God and his chosen people?" These were terrible siftings; but, sustained by the Almighty, I surmounted the assault, and kept to my determination. I pleaded the promises, and found them exceeding great and precious. My past unfaithfulness was, indeed, a source of deep repentance and regret; but I remembered it was written, "All manner of sin shall be forgiven unto men;" and, "Whosoever cometh unto me, I will in no wise cast them out."

According to my faith, so was it done unto me. My soul in confidence arose,— it rose and broke through all. The meeting was honoured with the Master's presence. Like the disciples at Emmaus, our hearts burned within us, while he opened our understandings, and applied his own merciful promises. God was pleased on this occasion to enlarge and renovate the hearts of his people. I was able with an unwavering hand to set to my seal that God is truth and love; and felt that from him alone proceeds the power to conquer inbred sin. The peace of God, which passeth all understanding, filled and satiated every power of my soul: while on earth, nor perhaps in heaven, shall I ever forget that season of holy exultation.

Wherefore to him my feet shall run,
My eyes on his perfections gaze;
My soul shall live for God alone,
And all within me shout his praise.

A few weeks after this memorable occasion, I had another visitation
of divine mercy. This was in my own house, and just at midnight.
I had indulged in wakeful meditations on the goodness of God,
when my faith became gloriously strong: I beheld the Saviour, high
on his mediatorial throne, dispensing the gifts of his grace, to fallen
and repentant man. I felt a powerful application of his merits to my
heart; was filled with an eager desire to be dissolved, and be with
Christ; and have reason to be thankful, that the healing influence
of this manifestation, though not always equally present, remains to
the present day. I love the Lord, because he hath heard the voice
of my supplication. Let my right hand forget her cunning, and my
tongue cleave to the roof of my mouth, if I prefer not Jerusalem
to my chief joy.

Conceiving it to be my duty to recommend religion to others,
I invited several of my friends and neighbours to hear the word
preached: of the effects produced upon them I am not perhaps
competent to judge. Some professed to differ with me in judgment.
Others, with the indifference of Gallio, put off my importunities to
a more convenient season. By a few my weakness was pitied; nor
was I altogether exempt from contempt and derision. But none of
these things move me. "All hail, reproach! and welcome, shame!"
Only bring me to heaven at last, and I will make no complaint,
though strait and thorny be the road. Instances, I think, remain, in
which my well-intended, though humble efforts, were not useless.
May the bread cast upon the waters be found after many days!
Anxious to do something more for the benefit of others, I have
been engaged for several years as a Visiter in the Stranger's Friend
Society, and a Missionary Collector; and I trust that He, in whose
hands are the hearts of all men, will favour me with his cheering
aid, in running the errands of his love.

In the course of the last year, it pleased God to try my faith by
taking away my eldest son, a promising youth of fourteen years

of age. This visitation was, however, rendered comparatively light, by a conviction, founded on satisfactory evidence, that he is gone to his eternal rest. As his long affliction and suffering were causes of no common grief both to his mother and myself, and were the means of bringing great glory to the grace of God, a brief sketch of his patient endurance, during the tedious hours of ill-health, together with his eventual triumph, and peaceful departure, may not be uninteresting. He was born at Dublin, on the 16th of February, 1820, and was named Thomas, after his father. From his birth, to the completion of the third year of his age, he was a child of delicate constitution, so that we had but faint hope of bringing him up; but in October, 1823, when on the route from Windsor to Chatham, his strength gradually increased. Change of air was probably serviceable; and from an infirm and sickly infant, he became a fine vigorous boy, remarkably active, and, humanly speaking, likely to live and do well. Our exultation was of short continuance. The Almighty saw fit to curtail the season of returning health. Thomas, by some unknown medium, caught cold; inflammation, affecting his sight, came rapidly on, and continued more or less for nearly three years: and although the best medical help was obtained, the sight of his right eye was irrecoverably lost. Almost immediately after, an abscess was formed near the hip-joint, which yielded to no remedy; and from that period the poor child gradually declined. But he was not forgotten, either by God or man: the hand of sympathizing, judicious friendship did all that was possible to diminish his sufferings. Sea-bathing having been recommended, he was removed to Herne-Bay, near Margate. After remaining there some time, he returned at the close of the summer, much improved in his general health. Cheered with the prospect of speedy recovery, he joined the family at home; and as he was our last surviving son, the only one left of three who had borne his name, and had followed two sisters to an early tomb, my anxiety for his recovery was painfully acute, perhaps sinfully so, bordering on impatience, and a disposition to arraign the wisdom of the Almighty's dispensations. On being visited by a reverend gentleman, to whom our family was much indebted for repeated acts of kindness, he asked, "Thomas, you are not permitted to take recreation and amusement as many of your age are: can you submit to your confined situation with contentment, knowing that the will of God is best?" This close question threw him into deep thought, but he gave no answer at the time. A little while after he burst into tears, lamenting that never had he been able to enjoy himself like other children. I availed myself of this moment of excited feeling, to speak to him on the nature of the soul, a future world, the happiness of heaven, the willingness and ability of God either to restore him to health, or to prepare and take him there; and reminded him that it was expressly said in Scripture, "Suffer little children to come unto me, and forbid them not." I also endeavoured to show him, that with regard to human events, whether pleasing or painful, joyous or adverse, "all things work together for good to them that love God." It is a singular fact, that after this conversation I never heard him repine: as the future months of his confinement moved silently on, he seemed to have a conviction that every thing was ordered for the best, and gave many pleasing proofs of intellectual and moral improvement. He read, wrote, and ciphered, with considerable propriety and correctness; and his chief recreation consisted in reading the Scriptures, especially the accounts of our Saviour's miracles, as recorded in the writings of the Evangelists.

Thomas had an excellent voice, and an aptness for retaining musical notes. He acquired a number of the hymn-tunes used in the worship at Wesleyan chapels, merely by hearing me sing them over two or three times: these were to him a source of never-failing solace, and the weary hours of affliction were often rendered easy and even pleasant, and became means of grace by these artless though fervent ascriptions of praise. The filial regard shown to his mother, who had watched by his side, and waited on him with unceasing solicitude, was also striking. Overpowered with gratitude for her kindness, he said, "God will repay you for the care and love shown to me."

The youth had now lain nearly in the same position, and in the same apartment, for several years, with but little alteration in his bodily ailments, excepting that his strength gradually decreased; but during the autumn of 1832 it was observed that he grew much worse. With the view of contributing to his comfort, he was then removed to a more quiet bed-room, less exposed to the bustle of secular affairs. This was to him not only an agreeable, but a highly profitable, change. He had better opportunity for meditation, and it proved to be the place of comfort and spiritual power. There the Lord was pleased to visit him by the communication of his grace, and to speak peace to his soul. We were not, at the time, acquainted with this cheering event; but soon afterwards, under a deep concern for his spiritual welfare, his mother said to him, "Thomas, I hope you are prepared to meet your Saviour." He instantly replied with tears of joy, "I am not afraid to die: God, for Christ's sake, in answer to prayer, has forgiven my sins. I should have mentioned this before, but feared you would not believe me." On returning home, I was informed that the Lord had been thus gracious to the lad; and soon after, with the view of ascertaining the genuineness of the work of grace on his heart, I entered into conversation with him, when I had the satisfaction of hearing from his own lips a clear and scriptural account of his conversion to God, so that it was impossible to entertain doubts of its reality. His subsequent conduct was also corroborative of the change thus wrought by divine power. The Bible became his constant companion. The sacred oracles therein contained, with devotional poetry, furnished the chief employment of his wakeful hours. He dutifully reminded his mother, when apparently immersed in worldly care, that "one thing is needful." Nor was he afraid to dwell upon the circumstances of his own approaching end. He was wont to say, "These withered limbs must be laid in the grave; but they will be again renewed, fashioned like the glorious body of our risen Saviour." On another occasion he said, "Father, I am ready to go. I know I am a child of God. His Spirit bears witness with mine that I am his. The blood of Jesus Christ has been sprinkled on my heart. I wonder how it was, that he looked on a poor boy like me. He must be a good Saviour, and I will praise him.

> Jesus, the name high over all,
> In hell or earth or sky;
> Angels and men before it fall,
> And devils fear and fly."

For several months before the death of my son, his disease became increasingly severe. To his former malady, dropsy was added, producing painful swellings in the lower extremities. The abscess in his hip was also enlarged, and became distressingly painful. These combined symptoms indicated speedy dissolution: of this he was sensible, and spake of its nearness with perfect composure. I was often astonished, considering his years, at the exertions which, even in this extremity, he made to assist him self, rather than give trouble to others: indeed, the love of cleanliness, and efforts to preserve it, shown throughout the whole of his long and afflictive confinement, and on which, in his peculiar case, so much of his comfort depended, had been noticed with surprise and commendation by all who had seen him. The Lord was pleased to wean his young mind from earth and earth-born attachments. On being told that the carriage of a royal Duke had just passed the door, he replied, "I should be sorry to exchange my condition for his. The sufferings of this life are not worthy to be compared with the glory that shall be revealed. O that it was the will of God to release me! but his time is best."

On the 4th of October, I observed an unusual and decided change in his countenance, and felt convinced that his earthly conflict would soon cease. Thomas knew it also, and rejoiced at the prospect. On the two following days, though unable to speak, he appeared, I thought, to have some internal conflict. There were indications of anguish, known probably in its full extent only to himself, which he had no power to divulge. The thought of this, and of my inability to help him, rent my heart, and excited feelings which will never be erased. In this emergency, I knelt down by the bed-side, and be sought the divine mercy in behalf of the suffering child. "Prayer ardent opens heaven;" and blessed be God, my supplications were heard: an alleviation of pain was soon apparent. The Lord would not lay, either upon the dying youth, or myself, more than we were able to bear. When a short time had elapsed, I stooped down, and putting my face close to his, asked him to tell us if he were happy. He had said nothing for several hours, but immediately replied, "I am happy; and I tell you of it now, because I may not be able to speak again." But he was able to speak again; and the power thus granted was well employed. A short time before he breathed his last, addressing himself to me, he said, "Father, I shall be looking out for you. Be faithful." The idea of meeting with his brothers and sisters, who were gone before, seemed to animate him greatly. He then observed, "What a mercy it is that God pardoned my sins before I became so ill as I am now! In such pain, how could I have sought his face? O death, where is thy sting? I am not afraid of you; for Jesus is mine." These were, I believe, the last words he was heard to titter: and on Tuesday morning, at seven o'clock, on the 8th of October, 1833, his happy spirit was released.

I should be guilty of great ingratitude, were I not to acknowledge my obligations to the gentleman who so effectively fills the office of Surgeon in the establishment to which my family is attached, for his kind and unremitted professional attentions shown to my late dear boy. The humanity of this friend was evinced, not by brief and occasional advices, in answer merely to personal application for help, but by constant and undeviating assistance, continued during the extended period of seven or eight years. I cannot requite him; for, of sympathy so seasonably shown, who can name the price? May the Lord remember him for good, and with the richer mercies of his providence and grace, repay the debt I owe, for the sacrifices of time and talent so benevolently afforded. I ought also to add, that several respectable friends from Sloane-terrace chapel, persons of sound Christian experience, were so good as to visit the youth repeatedly: with them he entered into free converse respecting the deep considerations of religion, and frequently adverted to his approaching change with the utmost calmness and serenity. Those considerate and condescending marks of esteem were continued even to the tomb. When the funeral took place, the Chaplain of the Asylum, who had with such oft-repeated care and generosity imparted his valuable instruction, performed the burial service, by reciting the emphatic and beautiful language of that noble form of devotion. Every mourner around the grave could join with heart-felt confidence, while the mortal remains were committed to their kindred dust, in sure and certain hope of the resurrection to eternal life.

After such an instance of early piety, exemplified, not when the sun of prosperity was at its meridian height, but when nature was failing,—and supported by energetic and powerful faith, which nothing less than the Spirit of Eternal Truth could inspire,—how should I escape were I to forget so great a salvation? So far as I am acquainted with my own heart, my desire is to glorify God while life shall last. Deeply sensible of its brevity, the nearness of eternity, and my accountability to Him from whom existence and all its advantages are derived, my desire is, to consider and consult the will of God, as my supreme and only law; to aim, by the influence of his grace, at an entire conquest over the corruptions of nature, and the implantation of those principles of purity, which the religion of the Gospel exhibits for acceptance and appropriation, and of which the true and only foundation is, "Christ in us, the hope of glory." My resolution, formed in dependence on divine aid, is to fight the good fight of faith, that I may lay hold on eternal life; and to follow the Captain of our salvation, "until he leads me forth to conquest, and a crown." The great and cardinal mistake, into which unenlightened man is prone to fall, consists in a notion of his own general goodness; that is, he is as good as most, better than many, and not half so bad as some that might he mentioned. He has no great objection to a little religion, provided it does not interfere with business, and never comes into collision with the main chance. He thinks religion means only an amendment of manners evinced by outward respectability of demeanour; whereas, its essence consists in a change of the principles which direct the life. "Out of the heart of man proceed evil thoughts," and all the sinful excesses that fill up the tremendous measure of moral evil. The heart therefore, as the spring of action, must be renovated and made holy. There is the arena in which the battle is to be fought and won. And why should any one doubt the reality of such visitations from on high? Jesus once said to the sick of the palsy, "Son, be of good cheer; thy sins be forgiven thee:" on another occasion, to a woman who had once greatly sinned, but was dissolved in repentant tears, "Thy sins are forgiven; thy faith has saved thee; go in peace." These facts are recorded for the instruction and encouragement of future generations. Nor, unless we pretend to limit the Holy One of Israel, can we call in question the continued exercise of the mighty power by which, wherever it pleaseth him, he redeems his people from all their iniquities.

In this state of mind and judgment I remain, and trust to continue while life lasts. That there is a God who ruleth over all, that there is one Mediator between God and man, who, with the Holy Spirit, ever reign three Persons in one God, I steadfastly believe. And that the Almighty directs the helm of universal nature, that he orders all things in heaven and earth after the counsel of his will, that his tender mercies are over all his works, that "Jesus Christ by the grace of God tasted death for every man," and that "he willeth that all men every where should be saved and come to the knowledge of the truth," are propositions, of whose soundness I cannot doubt. On all of my life that is past, I look back with humility and gratitude; on what is to come, with confidence. He that has thus far been my preserver and guide, will not forsake me in the end. "Being justified by faith, I have peace with God, through our Lord Jesus Christ." Nor can I reasonably doubt of the reality of the work; for "the Spirit itself beareth witness" to my adoption, that I am a child of God. I desire, therefore, tremblingly, but in the exercise of steadfast reliance on the promises, to exult in a consciousness of the divine presence; which, though invisible to mortal eye, is nigh to uphold and save. "Behold, I go forward, but he is not there; and backward, but I cannot perceive him ; on the left hand, where he doth work, hut I cannot behold him ; he hideth himself on the right hand, that I cannot see him; but he knoweth the way that I take: when he bath tried me, I shall come forth as gold."

The Almighty sustained me when foremost in the files of war, and no weapon was permitted to give the fatal blow. To repress vanity, and prove my dependence upon the shield of his protection, I was struck at the breach of Badajos. But mercy was mingled with judgment; and though I fell, it was to rise again. The injury was not mortal. Space was given for repentance; and now, such is the goodness of the Lord, he hath placed me among the living in Jerusalem. "For who hath despised the day of small things? For they shall rejoice, and shall see the plummet in the hands of

Zerubbabel, with those seven. His hands have laid the foundation, and his hands shall finish it. Not by might, not by power, but by my Spirit, said the Lord of Hosts."

> Contented now upon my thigh
> I halt, till life's short journey end;
> All helplessness, all weakness, I
> On thee alone for strength depend
> Nor have I power fro thee to move
> Thy nature and thy name is love.